Text and Photography copyright © Justin Bautista 2014
Mama Lotties Illustration by Amanda Breach - www.amandabreachillustrations.co.uk

Justin Bautista has asserted his right to be identified as the author of this Work in accordance with the Copyright, Design and Patents Act 1988 in the United Kingdom and in accordance with the Intellectual Property (Copyright and Related Rights) Act 2005 Sections 94 and 95 in Gibraltar

All rights reserved. No part of this book may be reproduced, stored in a retrieval system or transmitted in any form or by any means, electronic, mechanical, photocopying, recording or otherwise without the prior permission of the copyright owner.

THE GIBRALTARIAN CUISINE

Gibraltar may be small, but its unique and diverse culture has influenced more than just its people, architecture and history. Gibraltar's vast multifarious society can be experienced in the local cuisine.

Gibraltar's harmonious society has inspired an eclectic local cuisine frequently described as a cultural melting pot due to a mix of cultures integrated into its community over hundreds of years. In the late 1700s and 1800s merchants from Malta, Italy, North Africa and beyond serviced the stationed British Garrison. The population was bolstered further by migrants from Spain and Portugal. This is reflected in local customised dishes, many of which take their origins from the surrounding region.

Outside of the city centre on the eastern side of the Rock is Catalan Bay. The Bay evolved originally from a former Genoese fishing village whose original inhabitants were famed for their red hair. With the sea a strong part of its legacy, fish is a popular staple of Gibraltarian cuisine.

Every September a procession takes place and the Statue of Our Lady of Sorrows, the Patroness of Catalan Bay, is carried to the sea where the Bishop of Gibraltar blesses the water for a healthy year ahead.

As Gibraltar suffered through sieges, closed borders and lack of fresh produce during its history, many recipes were adapted to suit that which was available at the time. During these times, many families adjusted recipes to suit circumstances and without the ability to write, many of the recipes, just as it continues today, were not written down but passed down the generations. By doing so, many recipes may vary per family, but the essence of each remains the same.

"When I originally came up with the idea to create Mama Lotties, I envisaged it as a small website or book where I could keep the recipes I enjoyed. Little did I know that the idea would develop into what it has now become.

Mama Lotties was launched with the idea that I could share local Gibraltarian dishes. As a student in the UK, living away from Gibraltar on my own for the first time, I used to get homesick. One way I avoided this was by cooking the dishes I always enjoyed at home.

As the idea developed and interest grew, I became excited with the fact those recipes Gibraltarians have enjoyed for generations could be shared with all, particularly those living abroad.

I do hope everyone can enjoy those recipes I grew up with, which continue to remind me of home every time I smell and taste them. "

Justin Bautista

THANK YOU!

A huge thank you needs to be said to everyone who has participated in the creation of this book. Each and every person who has submitted a recipe, visited the website, commented and have been supportive throughout the development of Mama Lotties has played a part in the creation of this book.

In the following pages you will find a selection of recipes written, shared and enjoyed by the people of Gibraltar. They have been passed down through generations and with this book I hope they continue to be so, allowing everyone to enjoy the delicious recipes our small but rich culture has to offer.

Mama Lotties
— x x —

CONTENTS

STARTERS 08

MAINS
Poultry 36
Meat 54
Fish 82
Pasta 106
Vegetarian 116

DESSERTS
Cakes and Puddings 126
Gibraltarian Treats 150

INDEX 158

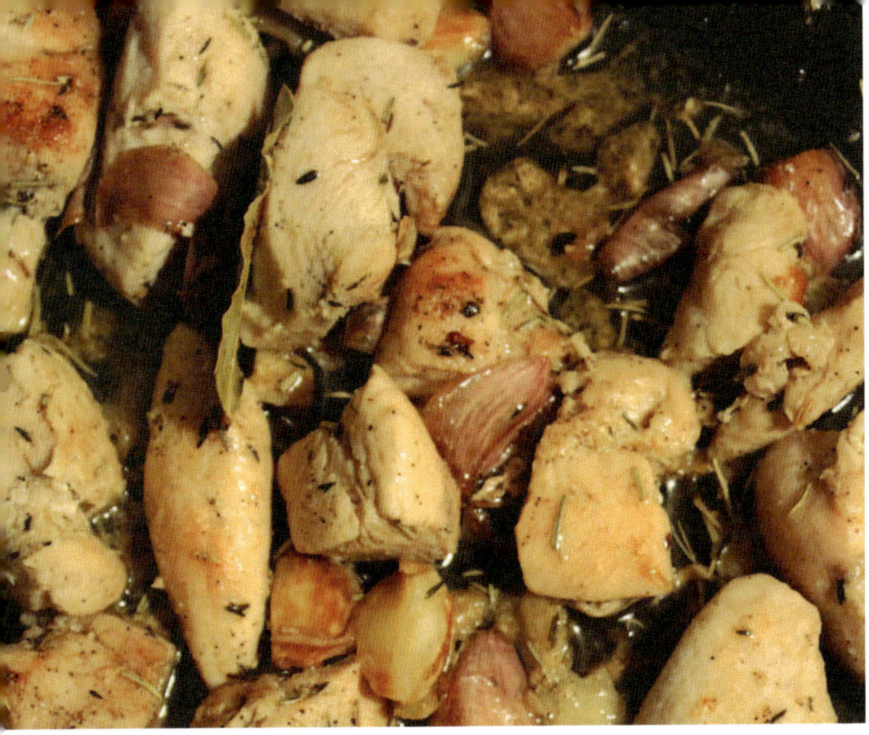
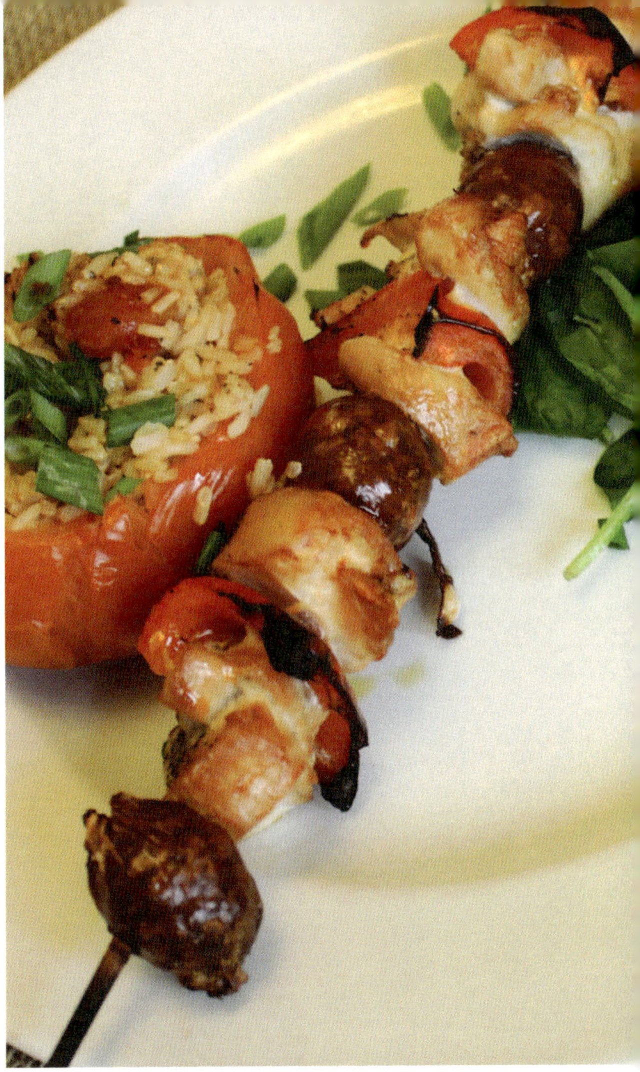
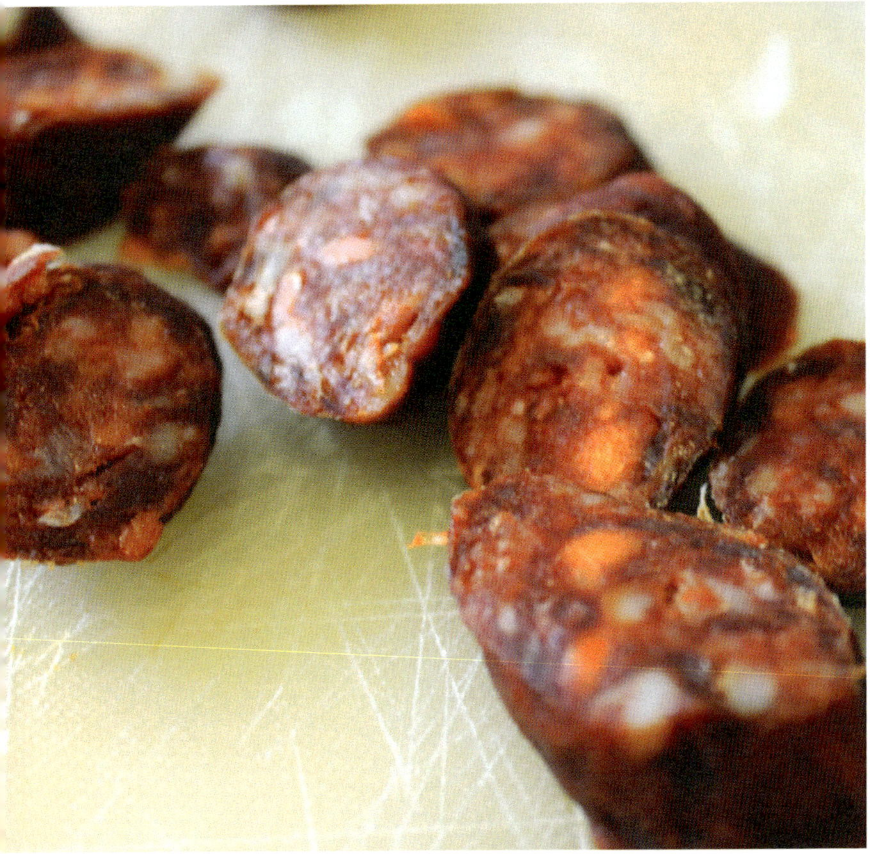
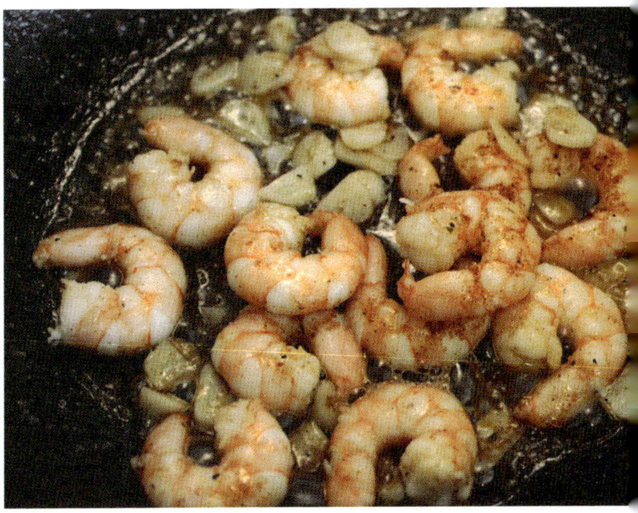
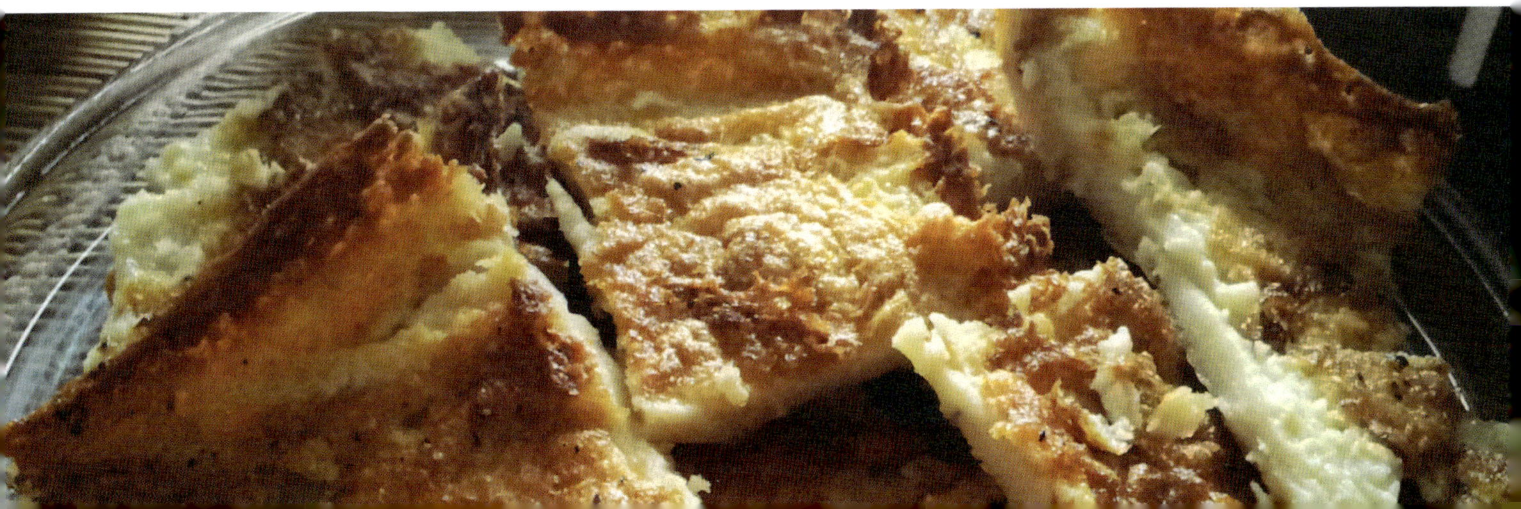

MAMA'S CALENTITA
THE QUINTESSENTIAL GIBRALTARIAN DISH

SERVES 4

INGREDIENTS

- 250 G CHICKPEA FLOUR
- 850 ML WATER
- 350 ML OLIVE OIL
- SALT
- PEPPER

Derived from the Spanish word meaning "hot" or "warm", the Calentita has become Gibraltar's national dish. The Calentita, inspired by and similar to the Italian "Farinata" and Genoese "Fainâ", was sold in the streets of Gibraltar, where vendors would shout out phrases in Spanish meaning "get it whilst it was hot." The name was then kept referring to the food rather than the temperature.

METHOD

1. In a bowl, mix together the chickpea flour, water, salt and pepper. Leave overnight or allow to settle for 2 - 3 hours before cooking.

2. Preheat oven to 225°C.

3. In your oven dish pour enough oil to cover the bottom.

4. Place your dish in the oven to heat up the oil. Once the oil is hot, carefully using a brush, spread along all the sides of your dish. Stir your mixture and pour immediately into your dish.

5. Place this back in oven for an hour.

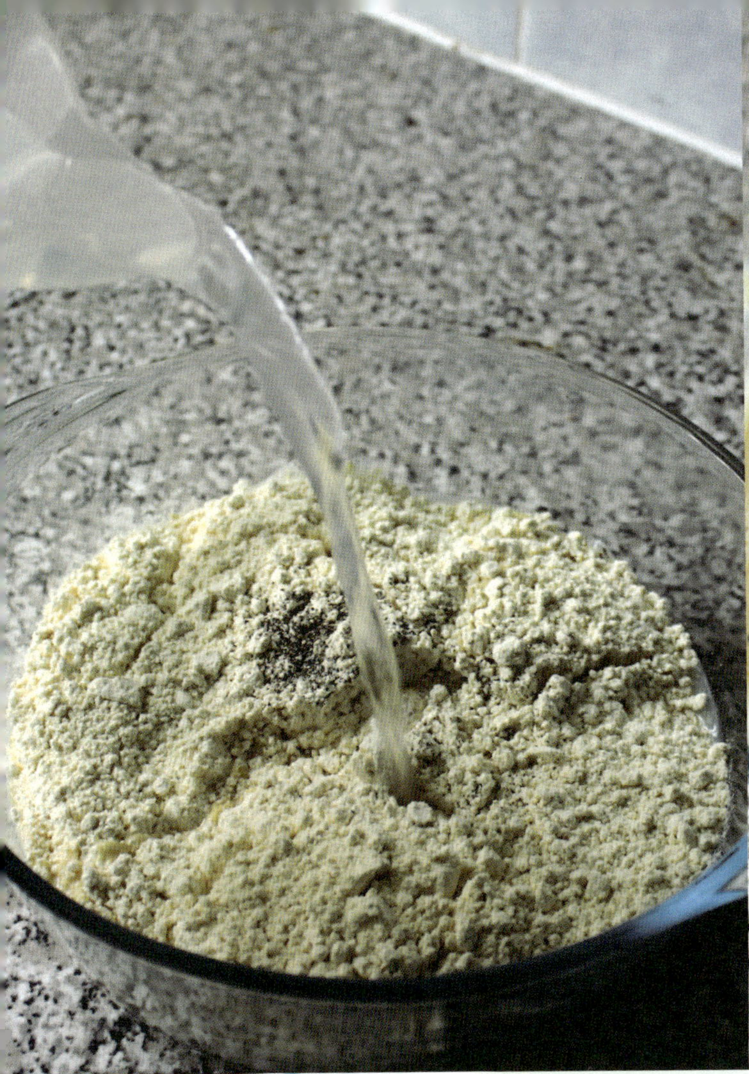
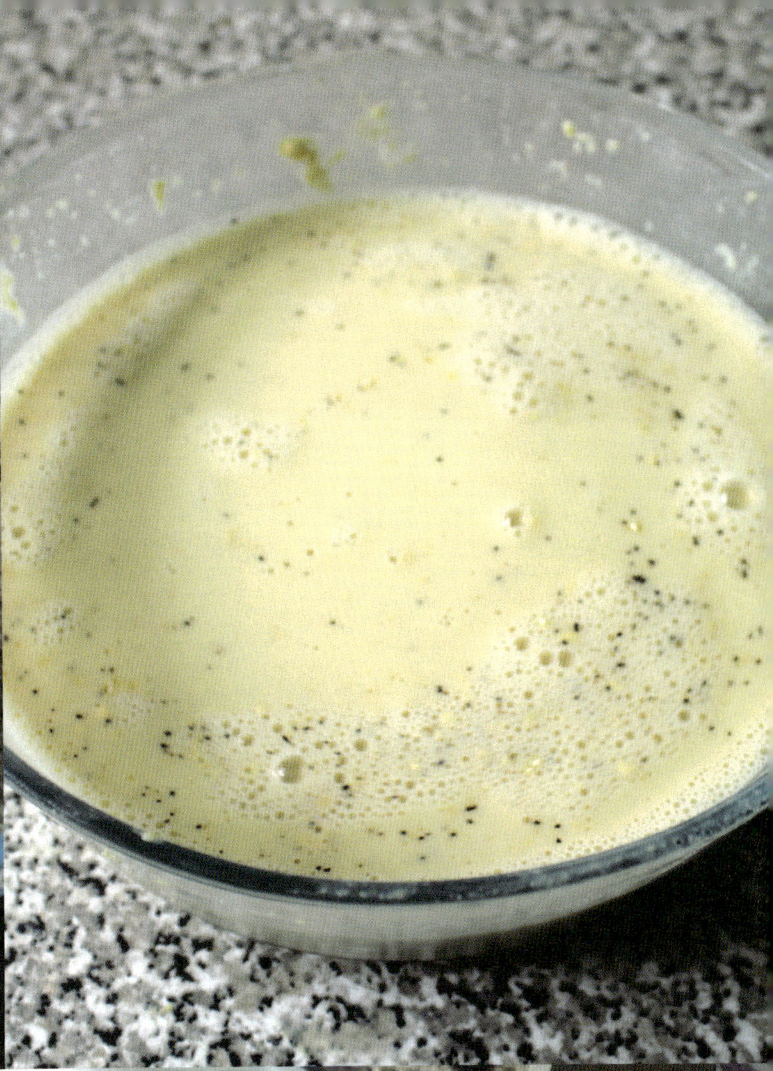
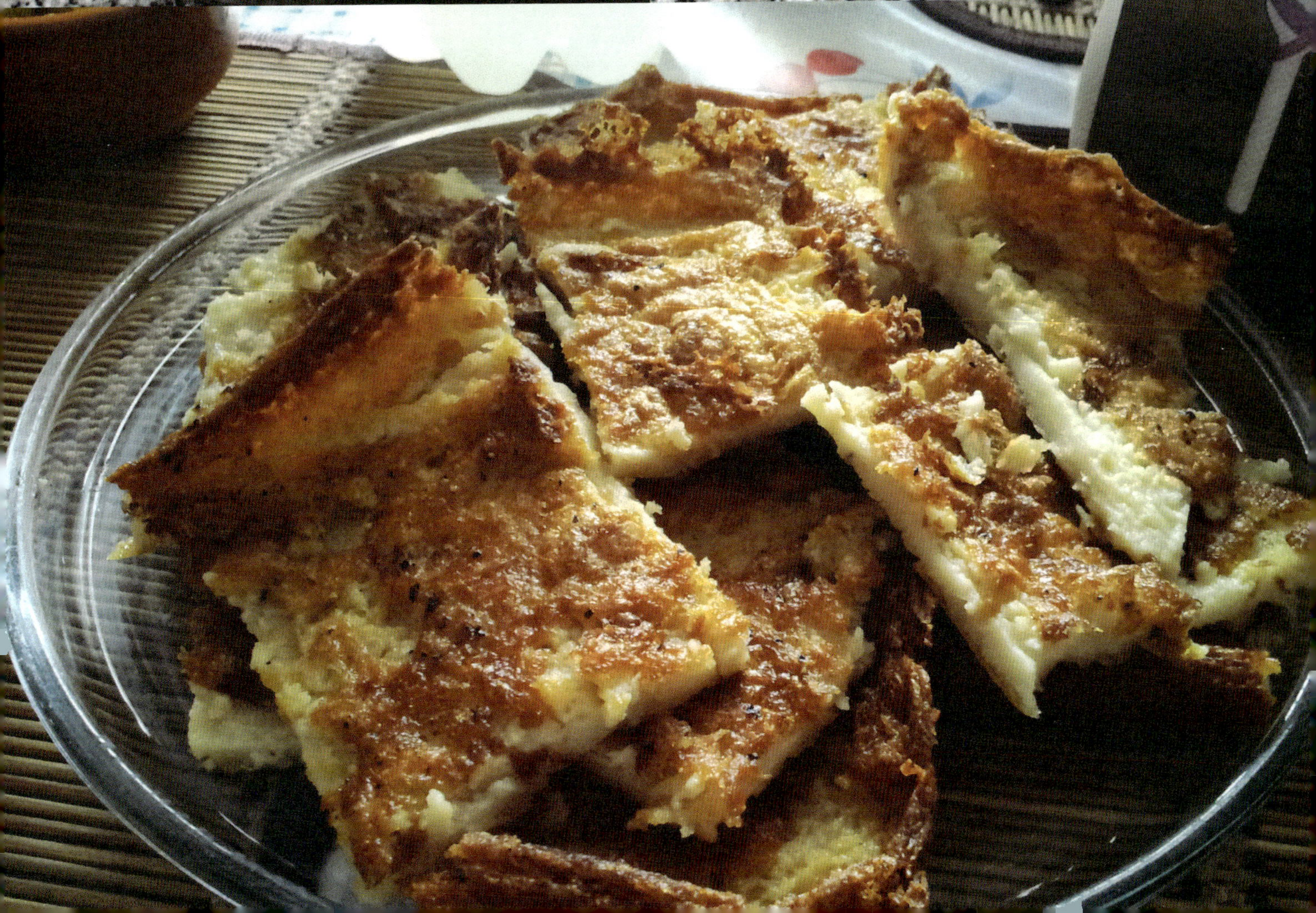

MAMA'S STICKY AND SWEET CHORIZO

SERVES 1

INGREDIENTS

- CHORIZO RING
- HONEY

This is something you can enjoy on your own or as a starter with friends.

METHOD

1. The amount of chorizo is entirely up to you, depending on the amount of people, but I used about a 1/4 of a 255g ring of chorizo.

2. Slice your Chorizo into smaller thick pieces and place them flat on a low heat, in a shallow pan. Allow to cook slowly and for the fat to melt; this will release the juices and flavour. After a minute or so turn the pieces over turn and fry them on the other side.

Now for the special ingredient…

3. Once your Chorizo has begun to cook and crisp grab a teaspoon of honey and pour it over everything. With a wooden spoon stir and mix everything together, continue stirring on a low heat for a few seconds so that the flavours and juices mix with the honey, but do not allow to burn.

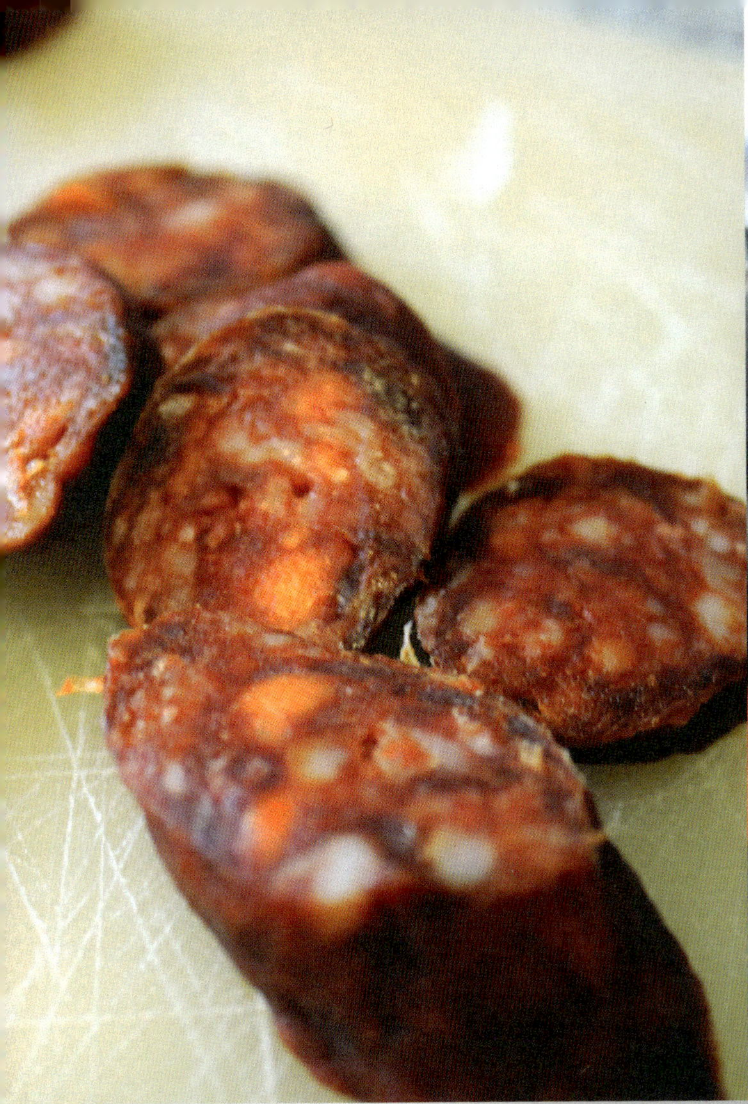
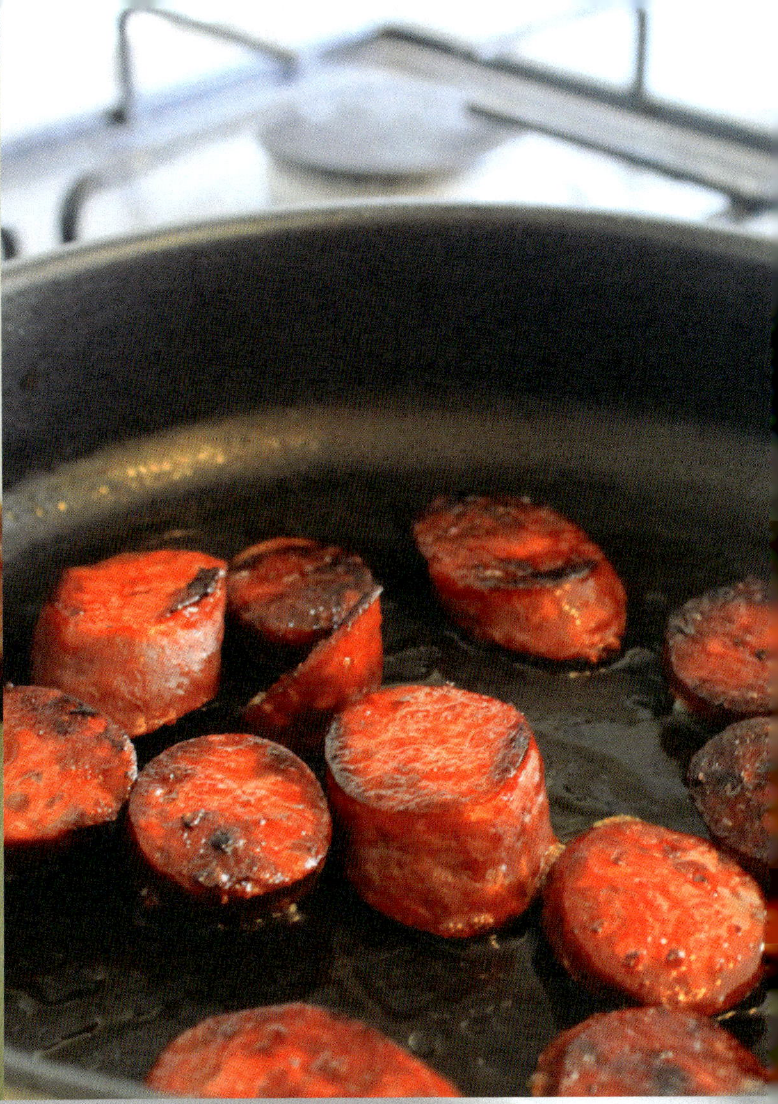
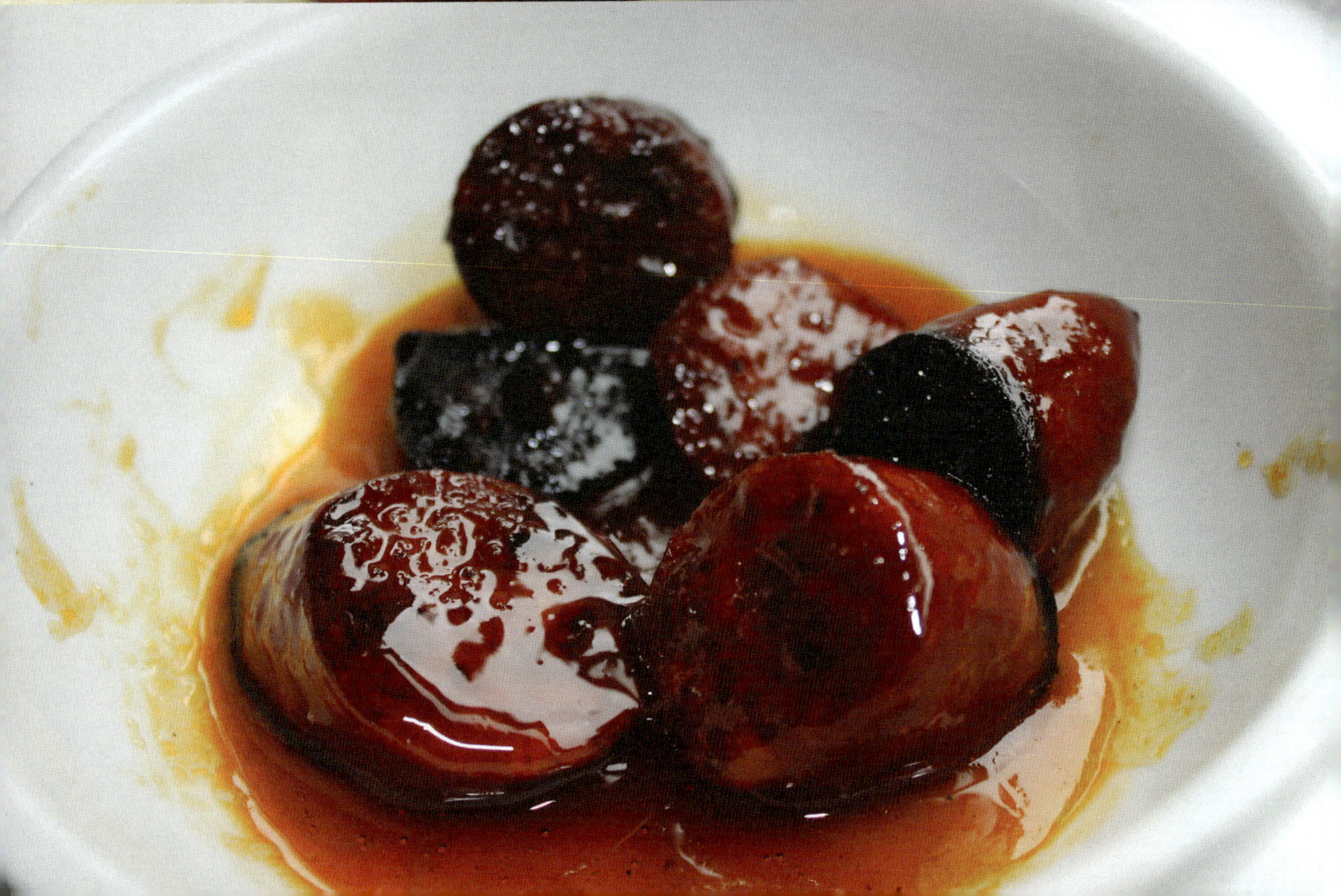

MAMA'S BOQUERONES RELLENOS
STUFFED ANCHOVIES

SERVES 5

INGREDIENTS

- 500 G OF ANCHOVIES (BOQUERONES)
- 4 TBS OF GRATED CHEESE
- 2 TBS BREADCRUMBS
- 1 GARLIC CLOVE
- PARSLEY
- SALT
- 2 EGGS
- FLOUR

A simply wonderful starter, the boquerones are fried with Mama's delicious stuffing. Great as a starter to share with the family on Fish days or as a snack...if any are left over.

METHOD

1. Clean, de-bone and butterfly the anchovies.

2. In a bowl, beat the 2 eggs and add salt, chopped garlic, parsley, the grated cheese and mix together.

3. Add the breadcrumbs and mix until everything is bound. *(if your mixture is still runny, add more breadcrumbs)*

4. Lay the fish skin side down and spread a little of the mixture on each fillet.

5. Once every anchovy is done, flour them and fry.

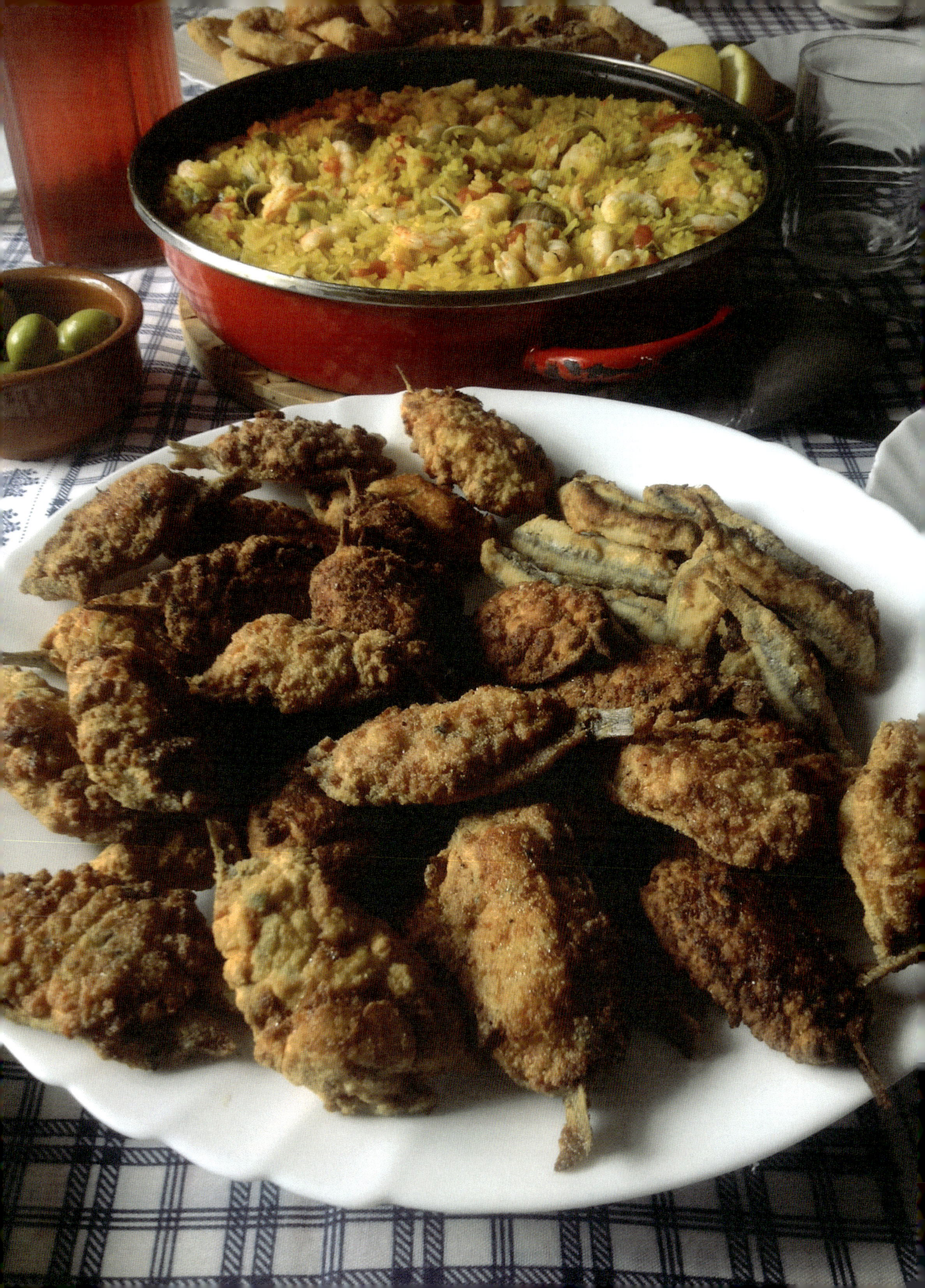

CHICKEN AND BACON BITES

SERVES 4

INGREDIENTS

- 4 CHICKEN BREASTS
- 4 RASHERS OF BACON
- COARSE MUSTARD
- HONEY
- LEMON
- SALT
- PEPPER

METHOD

1. Cut the 4 breasts into 3-inch slices and season with salt and pepper.

2. Wrap one rasher of bacon around each chicken slice.

3. Mix 2 teaspoons of coarse mustard and 3 tablespoons honey with the juice of half a lemon.

4. Place the chicken on a roasting tin and brush with the honey marinade.

5. Cook in the oven for about 20 minutes or until brown.

Make sure to check the chicken is thoroughly cooked throughout.

RECIPE BY ANA MARIA MORRO

MAMA'S FETA CHEESE, SPINACH AND SPICY TOMATO SALAD

SERVES 2

INGREDIENTS

- 1 RED BELL PEPPER
- 400 G TIN CHOPPED TOMATOES
- HALF AN ONION
- 4 WRAPS
- FETA CHEESE
- FRESH SPINACH LEAVES
- SALT AND PEPPER
- HOT SAUCE

METHOD

1. Chop your onion and bell pepper and lightly fry in a large pan until soft. Once soft, add your chopped tomatoes and season with a little salt and pepper. Add a few drops of hot sauce for that extra kick.

2. Cut your wraps into quarters and either toast or grill until nice and toasted.

3. Once ready, place everything on your plate, spinach first, tomato mix over and covered with feta cheese.
   (As much as you would like to enjoy)

4. Quick, easy and enjoyable both hot and cold.

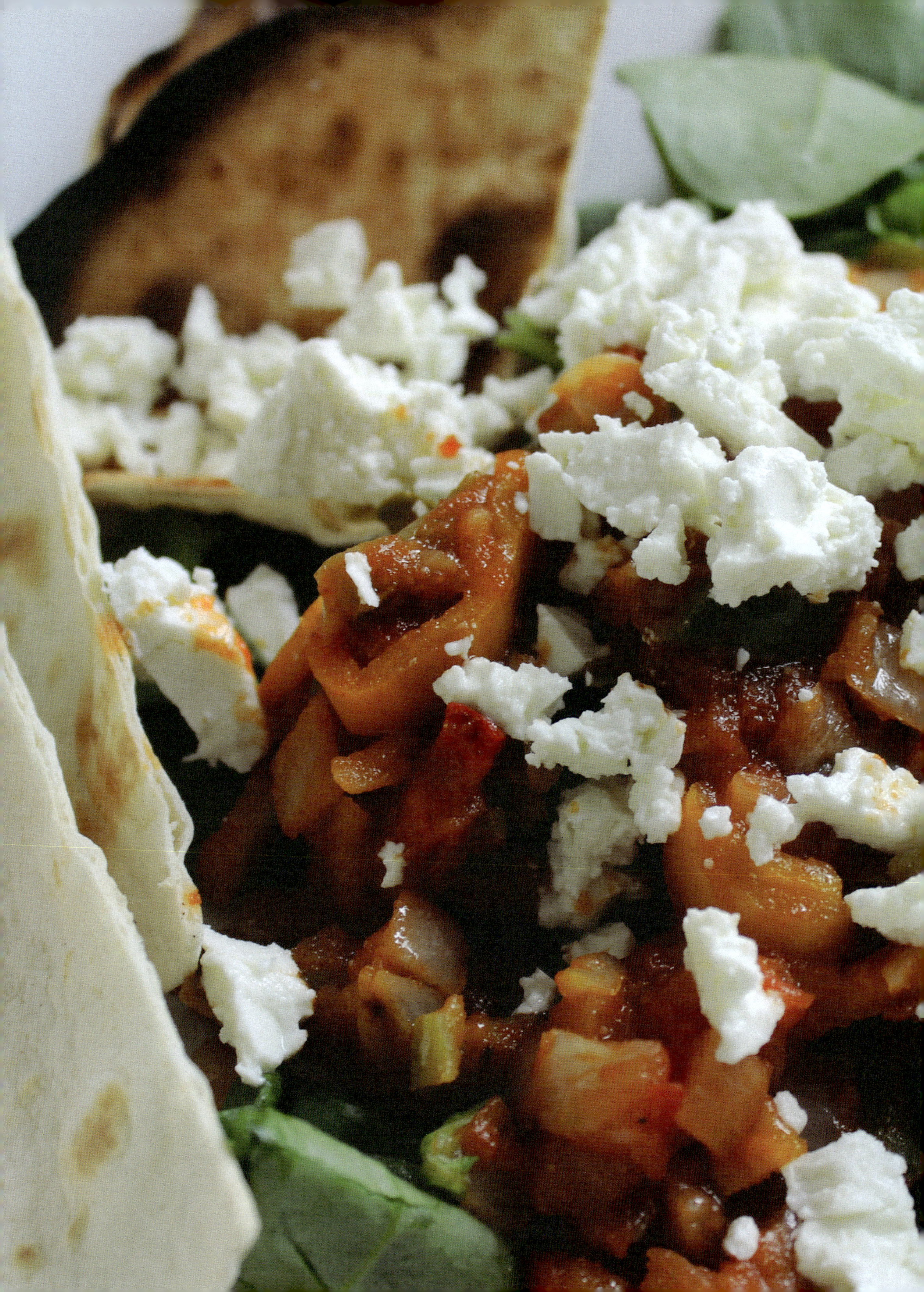

MAMA'S TORTA DE ACELGA*
SPINACH PIE

SERVES 4

INGREDIENTS

- 350 G SPINACH
- 300 G HARD EDAM CHEESE
- 30 G BREADCRUMBS
- 3 GARLIC CLOVES
- SALT
- PEPPER
- 4 EGGS
- 500 G PUFF PASTRY

One of my favourite Gibraltarian dishes and most definitely a filling one. I have always enjoyed it with puff pastry and continue to make it that way but many prefer to use short crust pastry. Although this can be served all year round, it is always available and seen throughout Christmas and Easter, served at room temperature for all to enjoy as a party snack.

METHOD

1. Preheat oven to 200°C
2. Wash and finely chop the spinach. Place the it in a bowl with salt and cover with boiling water. Leave this to one side.
3. Finely chop your garlic, drain your spinach completely, removing all the water, and mix in your garlic, breadcrumbs, 2 eggs and grated hard edam.
4. Line a small - medium oven dish with half of the dough.
5. Fill your pastry with the spinach mixture and crack an egg in the centre. Cover with the remaining dough, brush the top with a beaten egg and bake in the preheated oven at 200°C.

SUGGESTION

Although the traditional method is with hard edam, cheddar cheese can also be used, but keep in mind this will have a slightly different, yet still delicious flavour.

*INTERESTING FACT

Even though acelga translates into chard, the pie is referred to in Gibraltar as Spinach Pie and regularly made with Spinach. Either chard or spinach are acceptable, however taste could vary slightly.

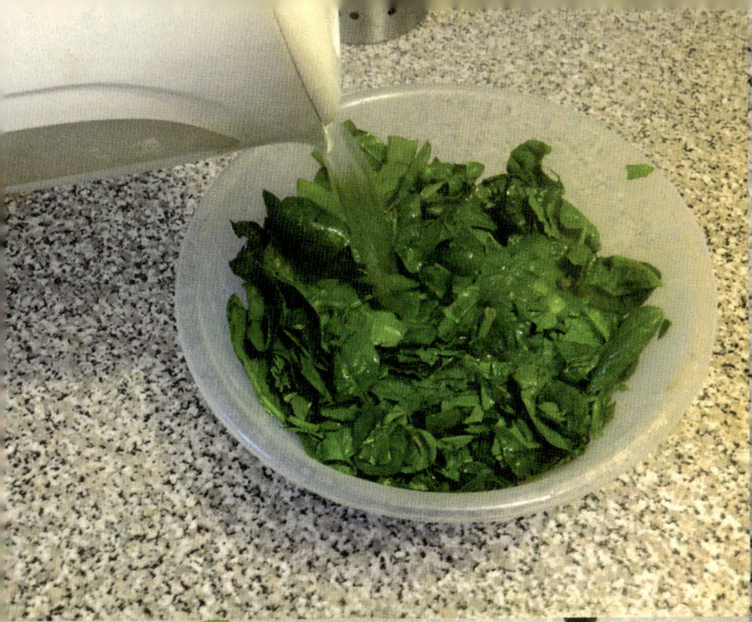
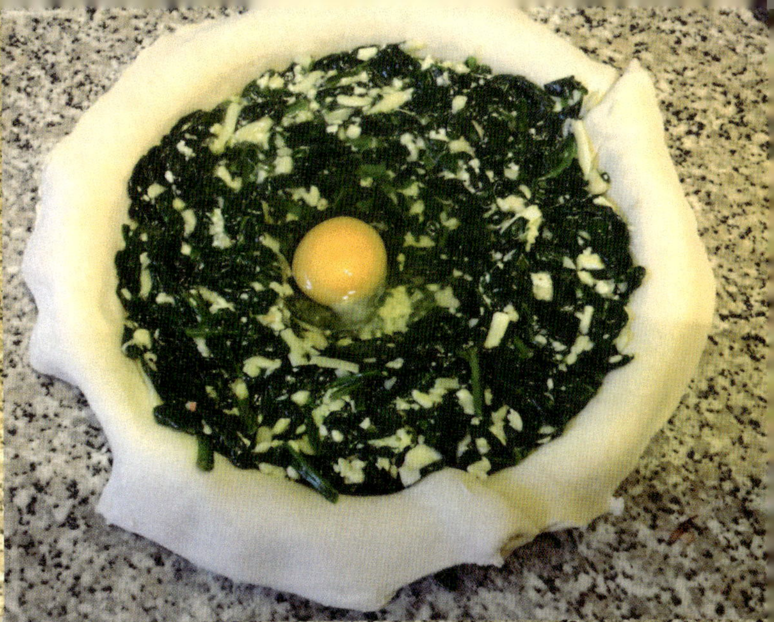
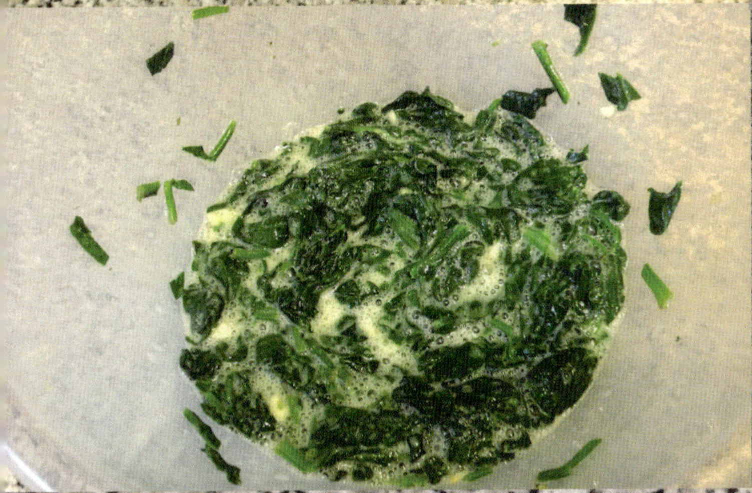
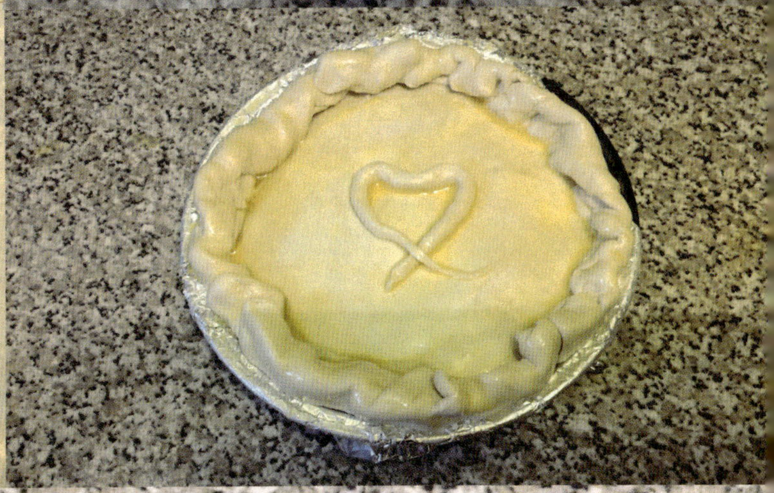
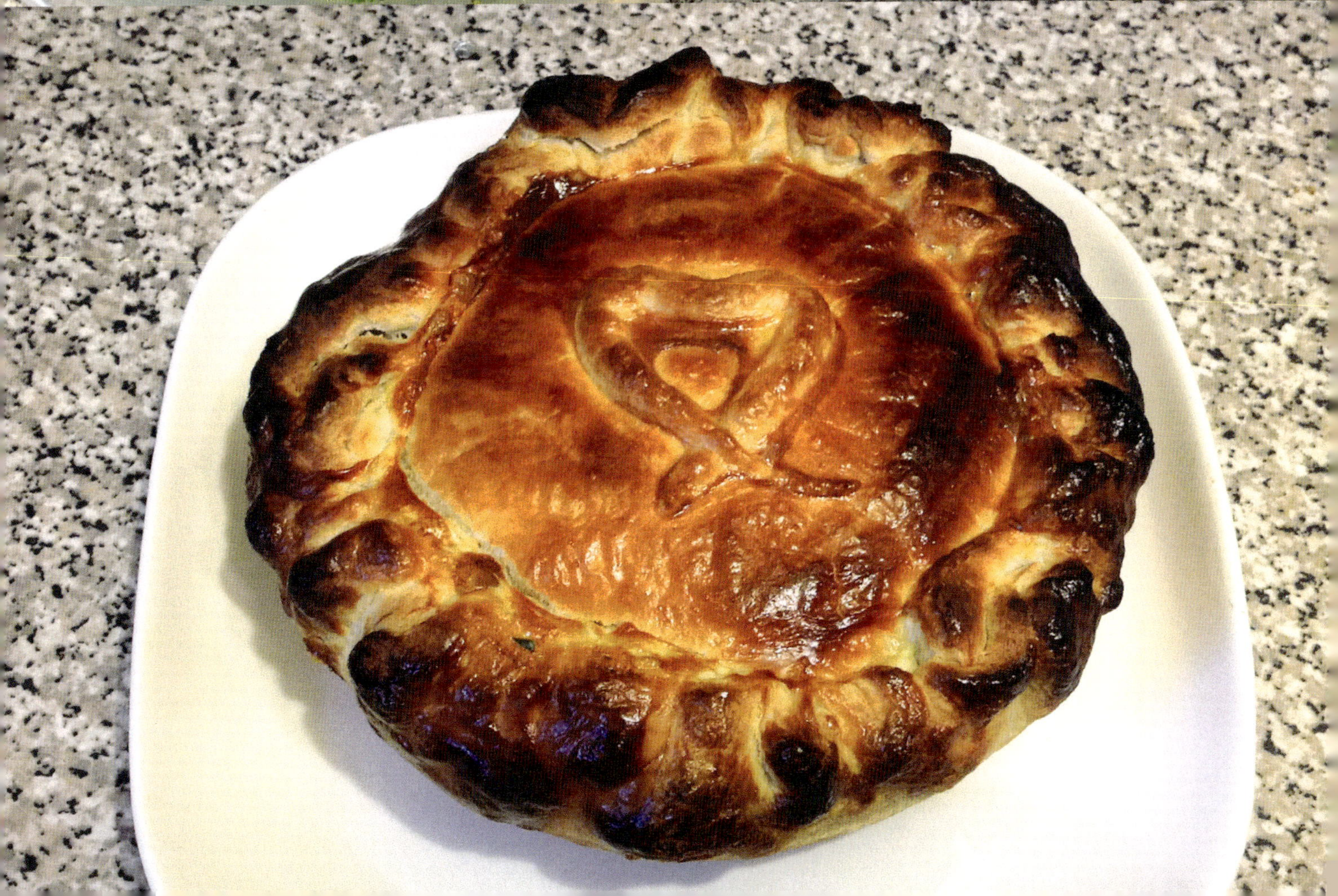

PASTRY-LESS TORTA DE ACELGA

SERVES 4

INGREDIENTS

- 400 G FROZEN SPINACH
- 30 G BREADCRUMBS
- 1 EGG
- 1 TBSP GRATED CHEESE
- 2 GARLIC CLOVES
- SALT

For those looking for a bit less pastry in their lives, there's always the pastry free option.

METHOD

1. Firstly defrost the spinach, then squeeze it to remove all excess water. Chop into smaller pieces and mix this together with the breadcrumbs, cheese, garlic, egg and salt.

2. Oil the sides of a small mould and spread the mixture. Heat oven to 175°C and cook until firm.

3. Cook for 10 minutes, then remove from the oven and cover the top with a plate. Flip your dish and plate over, and place the spinach pie back into the oven dish. Place this back in the oven for 10 minutes.

RECIPE BY ROSEMARIE MAÑASCO

MAMA'S CHICKEN REVUELTO
SCRAMBLED CHICKEN

SERVES 1

INGREDIENTS

- 1 CHICKEN BREAST
- 1/2 ONION
- 1 PEPPER
- HOT SAUCE
- SPINACH
- OIL
- 3 EGGS
- PARSLEY
- SALT

METHOD

1. Dice your chicken breast and fry with a bit of oil until seared.

2. Chop your onion and pepper into small pieces and mix in with your chicken and a handful of spinach. Stir in some hot sauce.

3. Whilst that is cooking, stirring occasionally, crack open 3 eggs into a bowl with some parsley and whisk with a fork. Season with salt and pepper.

4. When the chicken and mixture are ready pour in your eggs and stir until cooked.

MARUCHI'S ALMEJAS A LA MARINERA

SERVES 4

INGREDIENTS

- 1 KG FRESH CLAMS
- 1 ONION
- 4 GARLIC CLOVES
- HANDFUL OF PARSLEY
- 1 TBSP FLOUR
- 1 GLASS DRY WHITE WINE
- 3 TBSP OLIVE OIL
- SALT
- 2 TSP HOT OR SWEET PAPRIKA

METHOD

1. Prepare a pan with a tablespoon of olive oil and place over a low - medium heat. Add the chopped onions and fry until soft.

2. Chop your garlic cloves and add to the pan, stirring for a further minute.

3. Add the flour and the paprika and stir with a wooden spoon for thirty seconds.

4. Pour in your wine, season with salt and parsley and add in your clams. Cover and leave your pan for a few minutes, checking occasionally.

5. You will know the clams are ready when they are all open. Remove the pan from the heat and serve with crusty bread.

RECIPE BY MARUCHI GOLT

SUGGESTION

The clams should have been soaking in water for several hours prior to cooking, to get rid of any sand.

MAMA'S ALMEJAS AL AJILLO

GRANNY'S GARLIC AND WHITE WINE CLAMS

SERVES 4

INGREDIENTS

- OIL
- 500 G FRESH CLAMS
- 2 GARLIC CLOVES
- PARSLEY
- SPLASH OF WHITE WINE
- SALT

Simplicity at its best, this recipe is effortless but the results are most rewarding. A splash of white wine and the strong flavour of garlic bring together the great taste of the clams.

METHOD

(make sure the clams have been sitting in water for several hours before so they release any sand they have inside)

1. Pour a tablespoon of oil into your frying pan.
2. Slice the garlic and fry until it is just golden.
3. Add the clams and parsley and cover your pan.
4. Once clams are semi-opened, add a splash of white wine and stir.
5. Simmer for a couple of minutes longer.

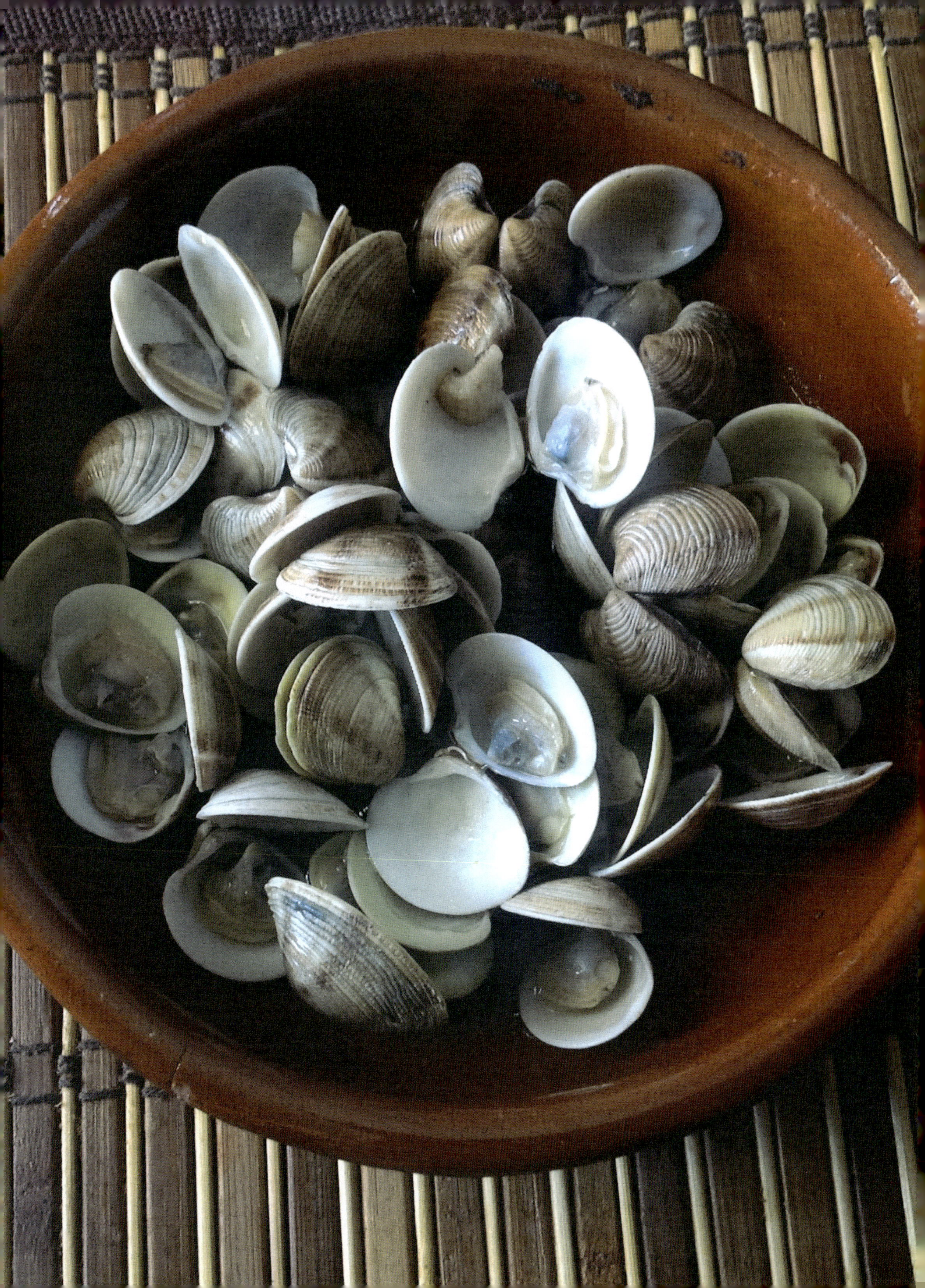

MAMA'S CALABACINES RELLENOS
STUFFED COURGETTES

SERVES 2

INGREDIENTS

- 3 MEDIUM COURGETTES
- 40 G GRATED CHEESE
- 2 EGGS
- 30 G BREADCRUMBS
- 1 TBSP OF CHOPPED PARSLEY
- 2 GARLIC CLOVES
- SALT
- PEPPER
- PLAIN FLOUR

Found on the menu of any Gibraltarian dinner party, these soft and delicate snacks are a great start to a meal or an addition to a party table.

METHOD

1. Cut the two ends of the courgettes and boil them in a pan with some salt and boiling water until tender. Once tender remove them from the boiling water and cut the courgettes in half *(lengthwise)*. When the courgettes are soft, scoop out the inside and place this in a sieve, pressing to remove any water.

2. Leave the skins to one side.

3. In a bowl, add the inside of the courgette and mix together with the cheese, egg, parsley, chopped garlic, salt and pepper, then add breadcrumbs until the mixture is slightly thickened.

4. Share out your stuffing mix evenly throughout the courgette skins and pass them through some plain flour, covering the whole courgette.

5. Fry in a little oil until lightly golden and place on a paper kitchen towel to remove any excess oil.

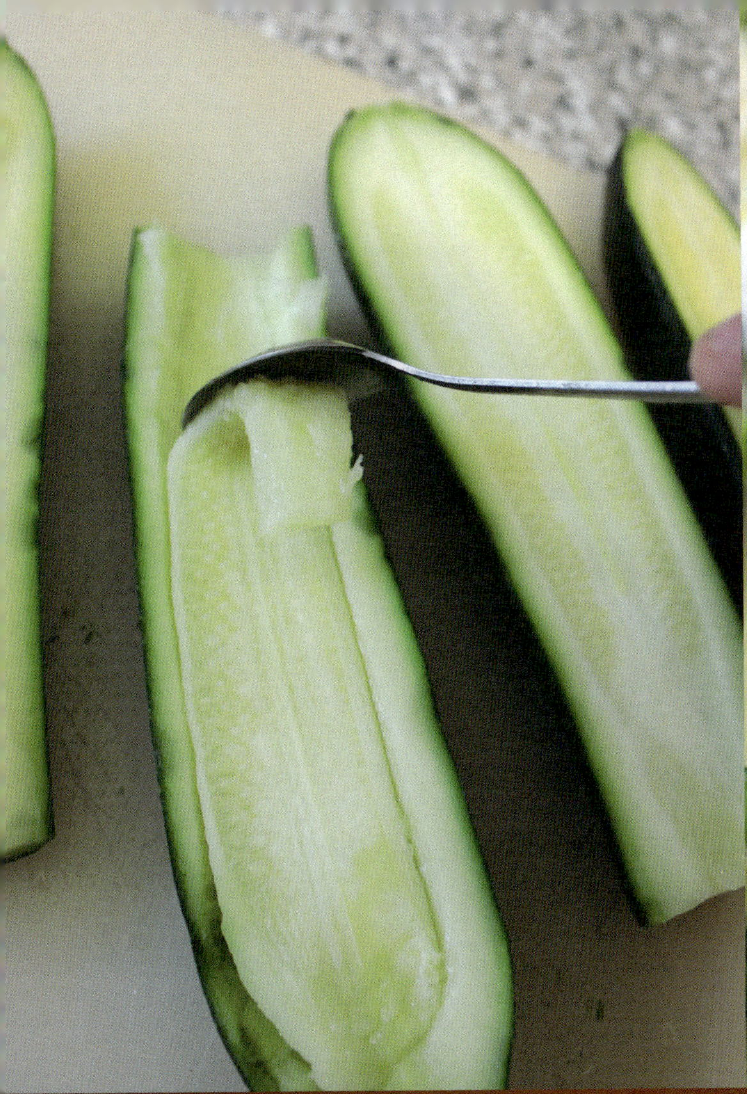
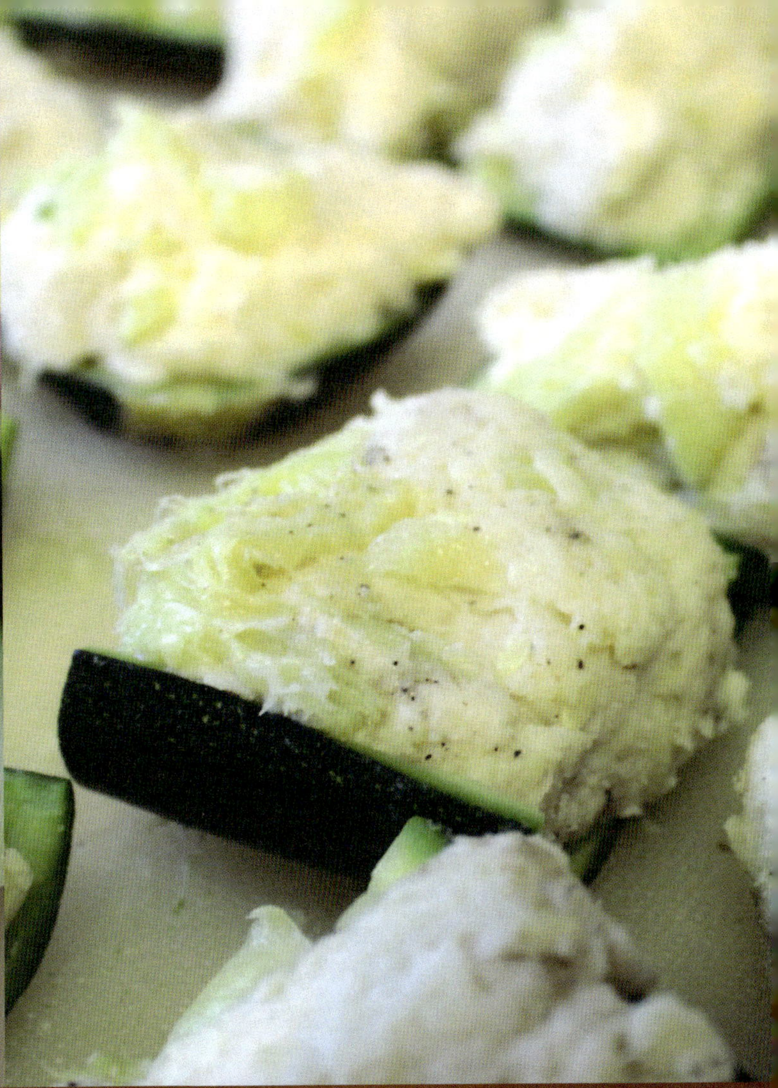
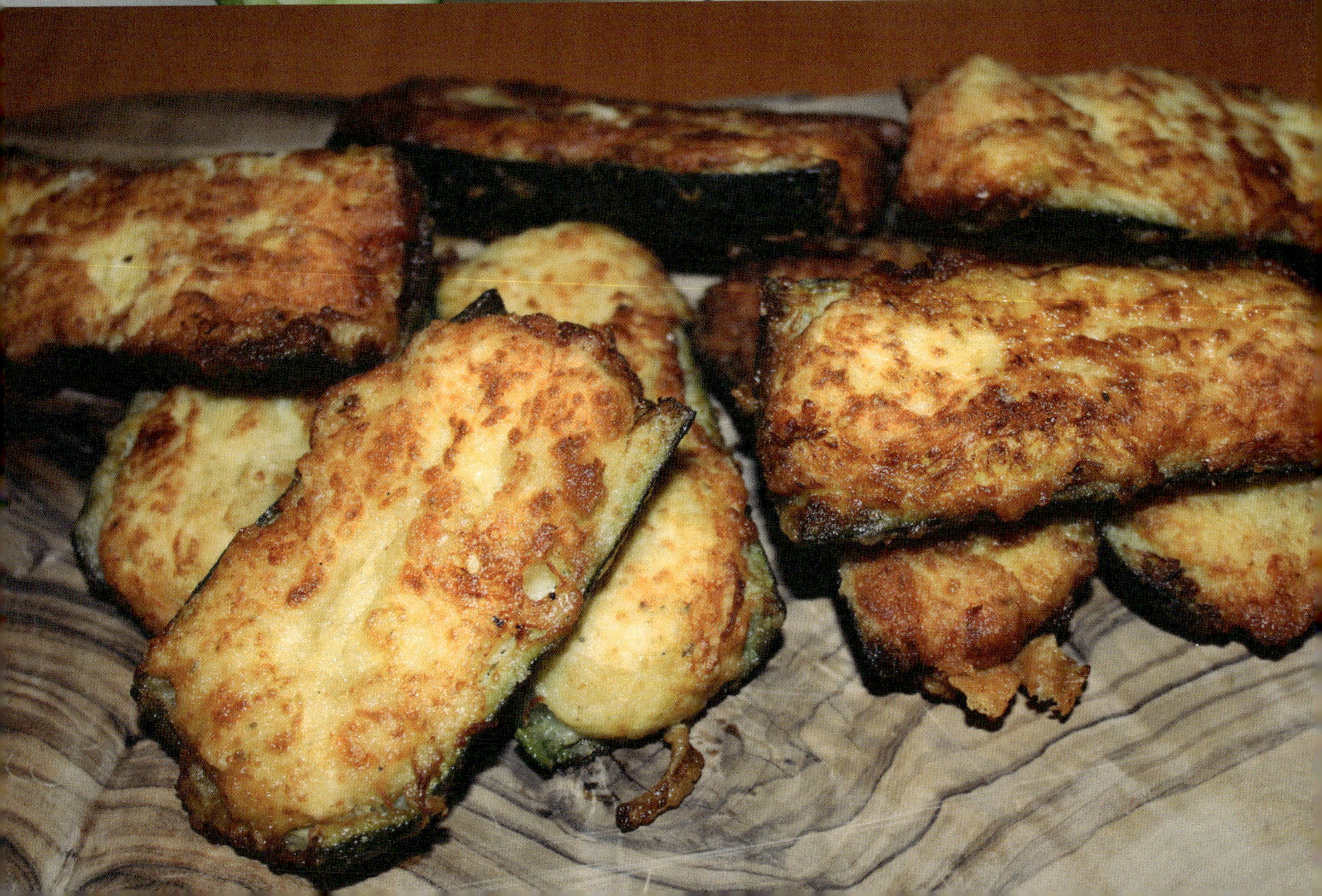

MAMA'S SOPA DE VERDURAS
GRANNY'S VEGETABLE SOUP

SERVES 3

INGREDIENTS

- 1 AUBERGINE
- 4 CARROTS
- 1 SMALL CABBAGE
- 1 SMALL CAULIFLOWER
- 2 CELERY STICKS
- SALT
- BLACK PEPPER

A gorgeous, smooth and heartwarming soup with a peppery kick. If you're feeling down and want a bit of home comfort, then make sure to give Mama's soup a go. You'll feel better in no time.

METHOD

1. Dice all your vegetables and cut your celery sticks in half.

2. Boil everything together in a large casserole dish and season with a bit of salt. Leave your casserole dish partially covered, stirring occasionally until the vegetables are soft. Top up with water when necessary.

3. Once everything is soft, remove the celery sticks and blend the rest of the vegetables together using a hand blender.

4. Place your boiled celery in the soup and serve.

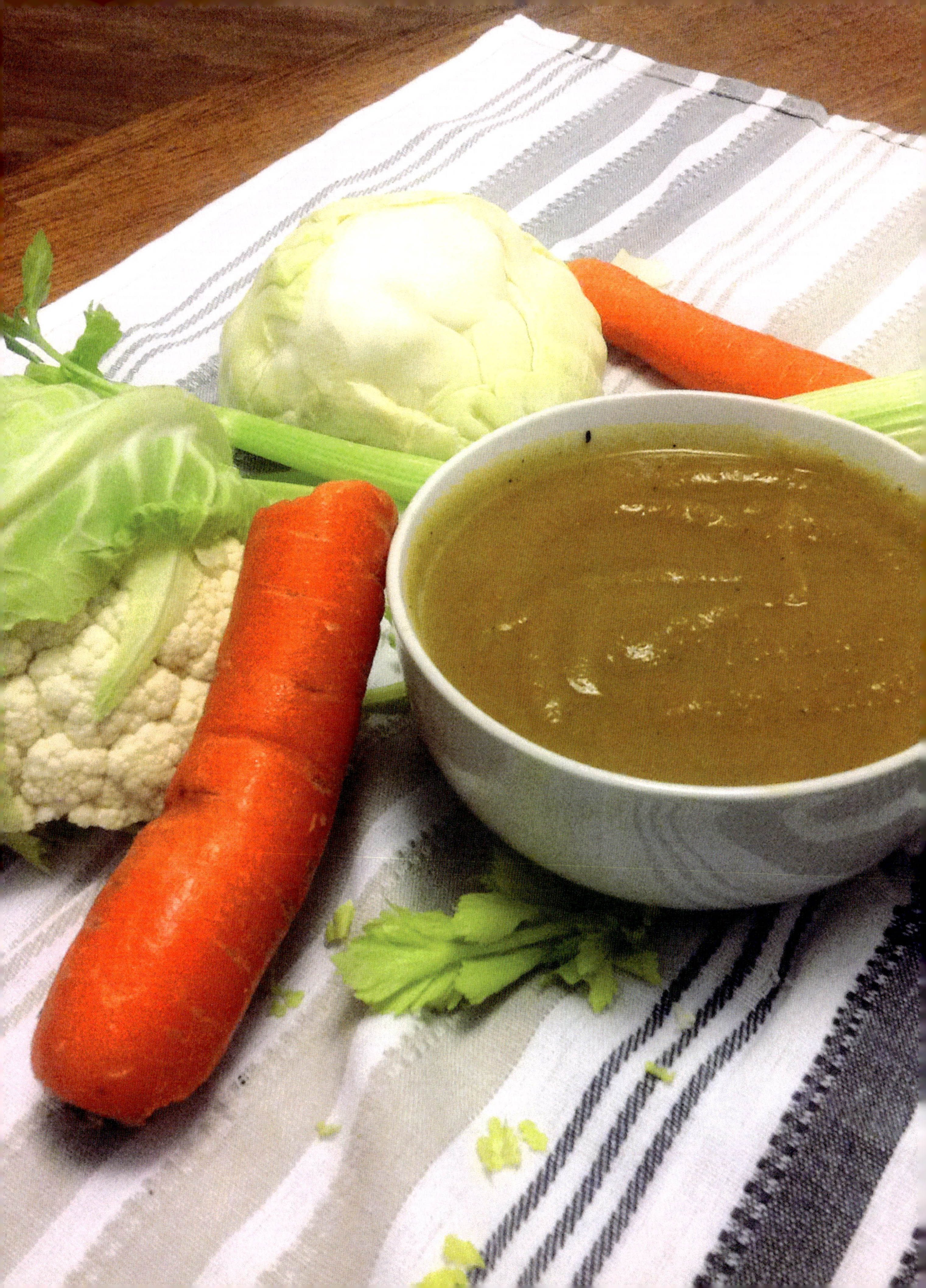

MAMA'S PEA SOUP WITH GAMMON

SERVES 4

INGREDIENTS

- 500G YELLOW SPLIT PEAS
- 3-4 CARROTS
- 1 ONION
- MINT LEAVES
- 2 FRESH TOMATOES
- 500 G GAMMON JOINT
- 1 LARGE POTATO

This soup is heartwarming, filling and savoury. A perfect meal for cold winter nights or comfort food... I'm getting hungry just thinking about it.

METHOD

(Soak split peas overnight, drain them before use)

1. Place the following in a large casserole and cover with water:
   - Peeled tomatoes, cut in half
   - Onions cut in half
   - Peeled and sliced carrots
   - Gammon
   - Peeled and cut potato
   - Mint leaves

2. Boil until gammon is tender. Once done, separate gammon and blend all the vegetables in the casserole.

3. Place gammon back into casserole dish with the blended vegetables.

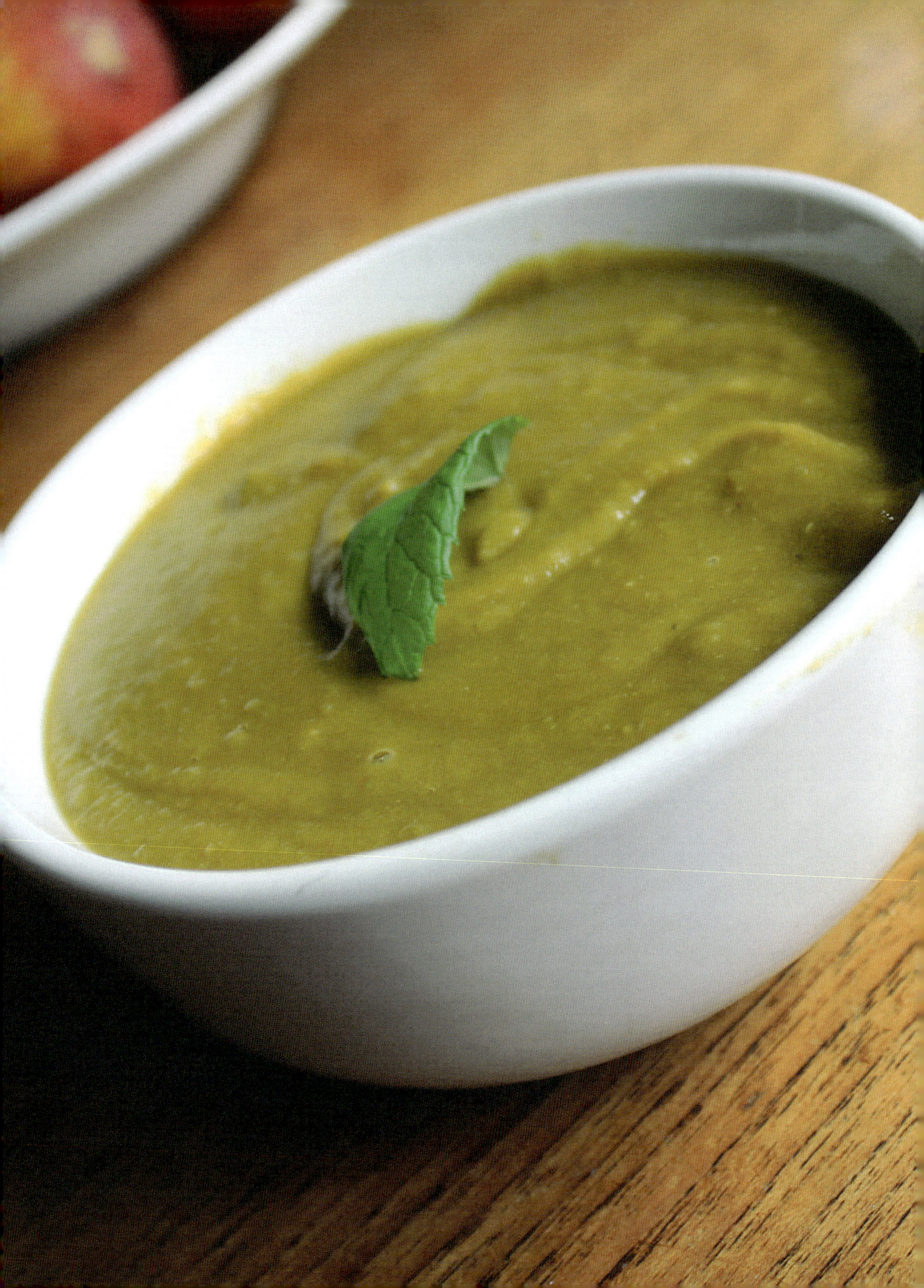

MAMA'S CALAMARES FRITOS
FRIED SQUID RINGS

SERVES 4

INGREDIENTS

- 3 - 4 FRESH SQUID OR 1 KG PREPARED SQUID RINGS
- OLIVE OIL
- PLAIN FLOUR
- SALT
- LEMON
- MILK

TIP
The milk will prevent the squid rings from spitting oil when placed in the frying pan.

Found on most, if not all menus in Gibraltar, the calamares are delicious with a simple lemon dressing or even a pot of alioli dip. Soft and fluffy, this is a definite yes on my list.

METHOD

Quick and easy and one of people's favourite dishes.

1. Wash and clean out the squid entirely, removing all ink, spine and innards.

2. Cut into rings, season with salt and leave in a dish to one side covered in milk.

3. Pour some flour on a large plate and some oil in a pan. Heat up the oil on a medium heat and in the meantime, transfer your rings one by one into the flour, covering them entirely. Place them in the frying pan.

4. Fry them until golden and serve with a large slice of lemon to squeeze over.

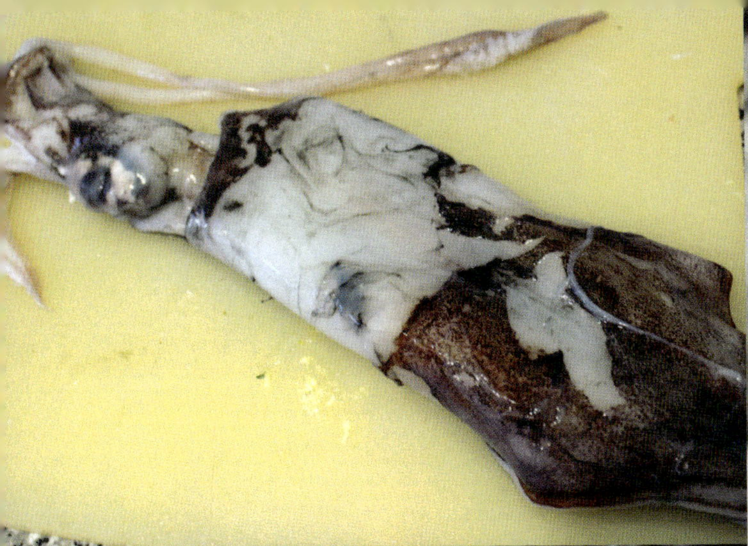
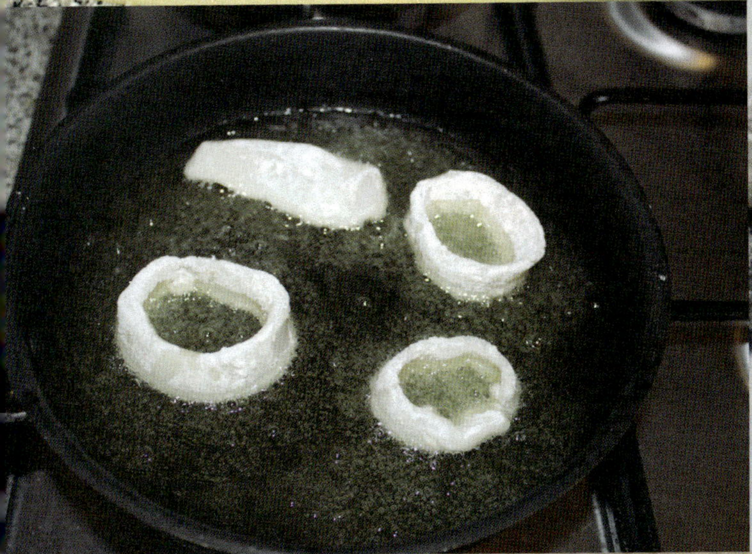
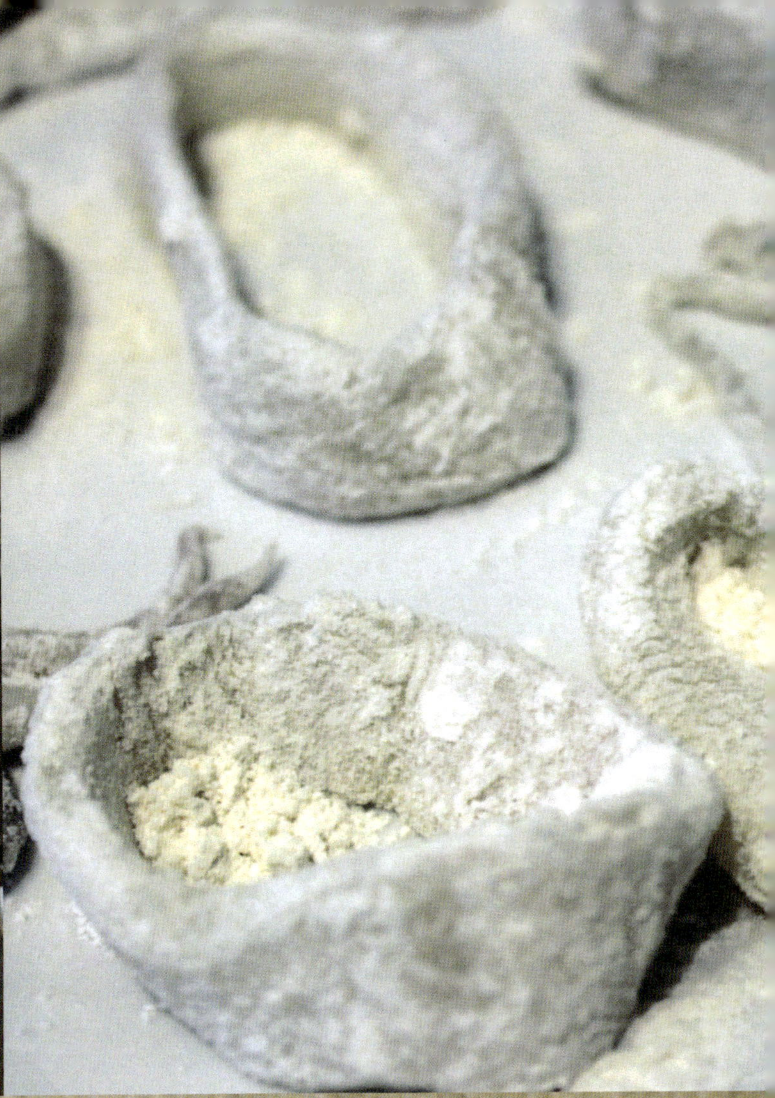
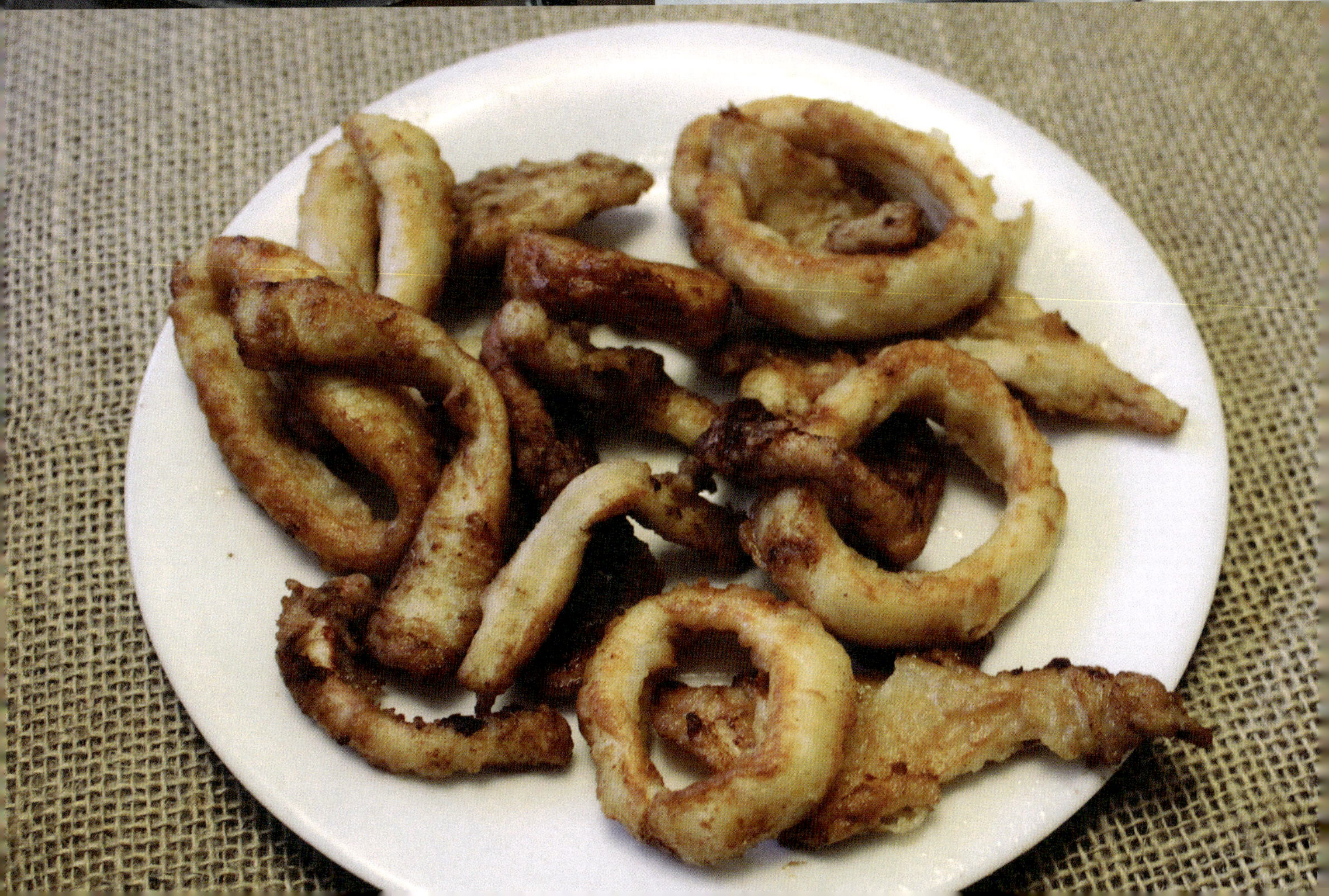

MAMA'S GAMBAS PIL PIL
GARLIC AND CHILLI PRAWNS

SERVES 4

INGREDIENTS

- 1 KG MEDIUM SIZED UNCOOKED PRAWNS OR SHRIMPS
- 100 ML OLIVE OIL
- 3 GARLIC CLOVES
- SAFFRON AND YELLOW FOOD COLOURING POWDER *(OR PAPRIKA)*
- SALT
- 3 SMALL DRIED CHILLIES
- DRY WHITE WINE

Prawns are unbelievably popular in Gibraltar and as they are full of flavour, there are just so many ways to cook them. One culturally inspired dish is Prawns Pil Pil, a spicy, garlic dish, served in a terracotta bowl.

METHOD

1. Peel the prawns, season with salt and place on the side.

2. Heat a pan with oil and fry the chilli and chopped garlic until softened. Add the prawns and cook on medium heat.

3. Pour in a splash of white wine for flavour.

4. Prawns will change colour and curl up meaning they are cooked. At this stage add in the saffron and powder and allow to cook for a bit longer but don't let the juices reduce. *(Careful not to overcook as they will become rubbery)*

5. Pour into a bowl and serve with some crusty bread.

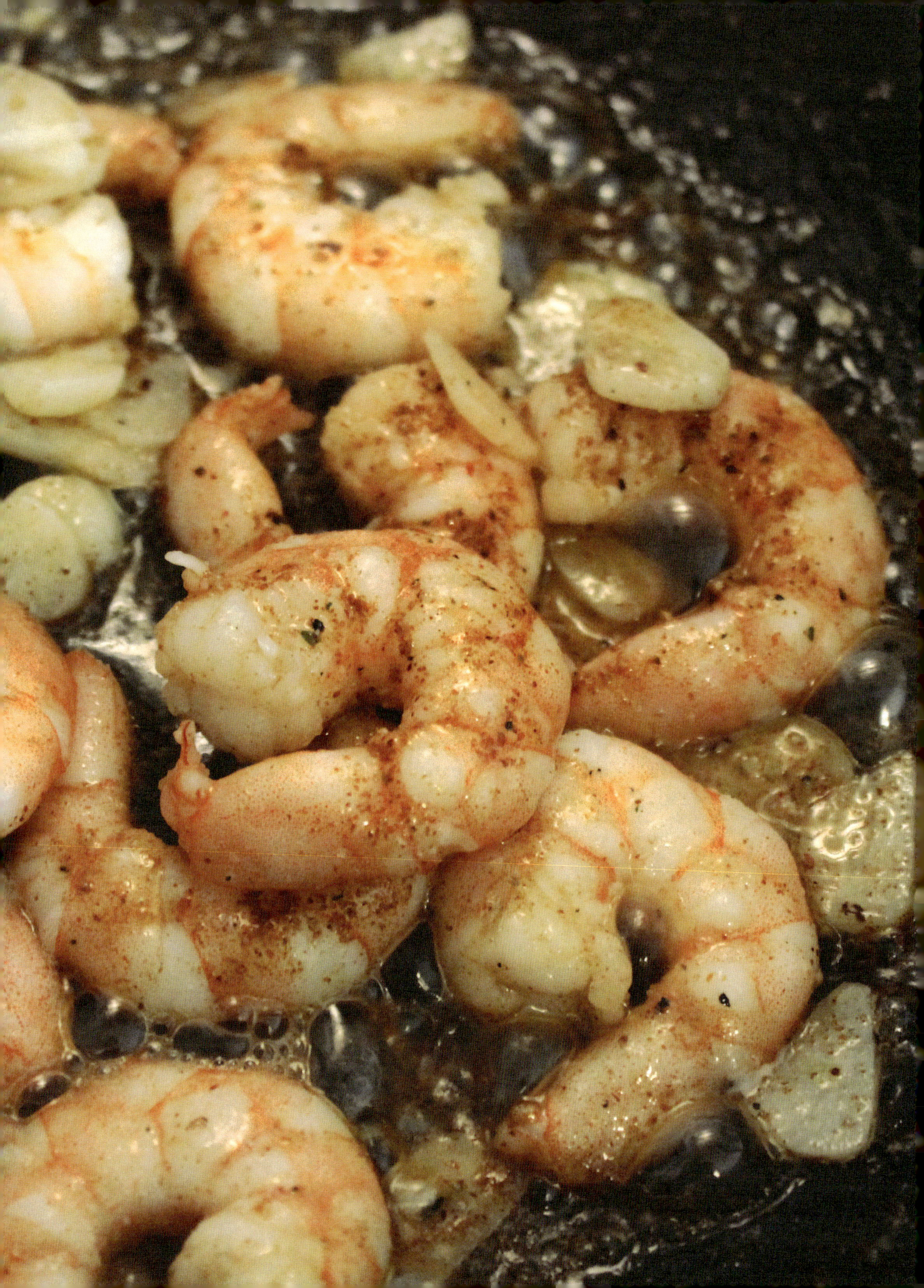

BATTER-DIP PRAWNS

SERVES 2

INGREDIENTS

- 500G PRAWNS
- 1 EGG
- 80 ML WATER
- 1/2 TSP GARLIC SALT
- 1/4 TSP BAKING POWDER
- 65 G SELF RAISING FLOUR
- OIL

METHOD

1. Shell the prawns, wash and devein them. Spear each one on a cocktail stick and set aside. In a bowl, beat the egg with the water and add the garlic salt and baking powder. Beat in the flour making a thick batter. Allow to set for 1 hour before using.

2. Dip the prawns, cocktail stick and all, into the batter and fry them until golden, then place them on a kitchen towel to drain the excess oil.

(I personally like to squeeze some lemon juice over them)

RECIPE BY ROSEMARIE MAÑASCO

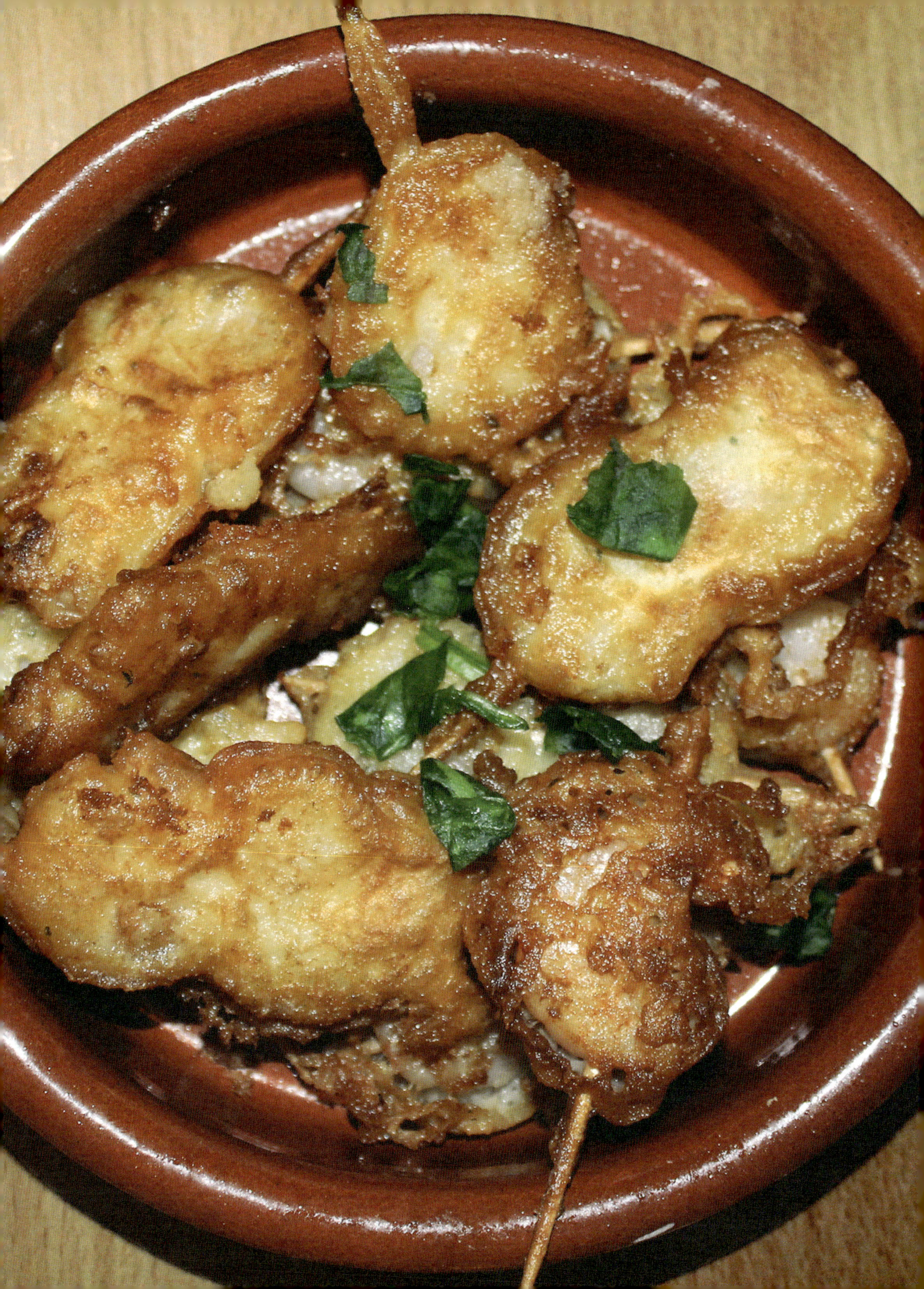

MAINS

POULTRY

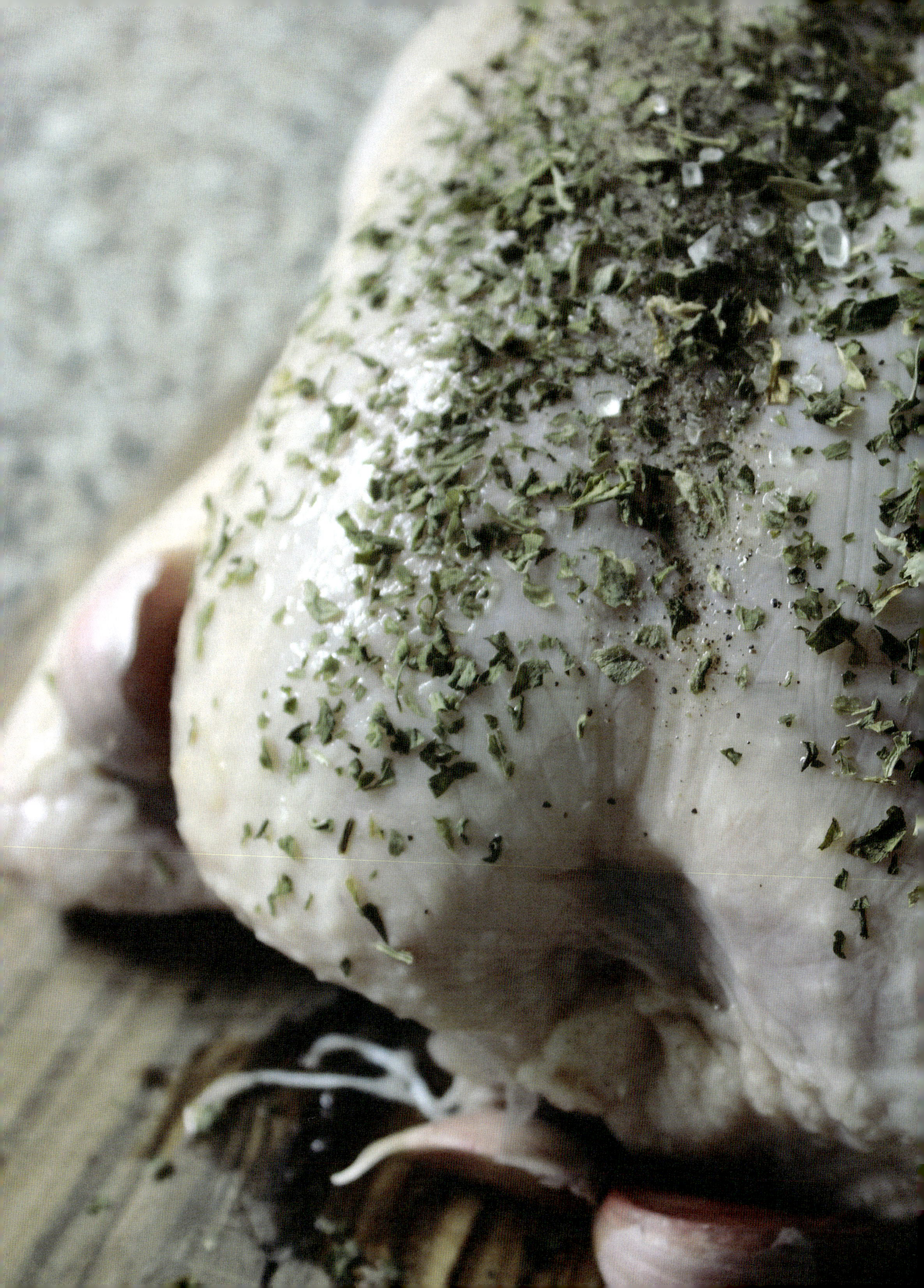

MAMA'S CHICKEN AND CHORIZO PINCHITOS

SERVES 1

INGREDIENTS

- 4 SMALL CHORIZO
- 1 CHICKEN BREAST
- RED BELL PEPPER
- 1 LARGE TOMATO
- HANDFUL OF RICE *(PER PERSON)*
- 1 SPRING ONION
- FRESH SPINACH
- SALT
- PEPPER

Where there's a barbecue you will most likely find pinchitos. Succulent, tender and full of flavour, these can be cooked indoors, in your oven or grill or over the hot coal of a barbecue on a beautiful summer's day. Sounds wonderful, doesn't it?

METHOD

1. In a large pan boil your rice.

2. Dice your chicken breast into large pieces and do the same to your peppers.

3. Season the chicken with salt and pepper and begin to prepare the skewers. Lay out your skewers with chorizo, chicken and peppers and continue to do so until all the stick is used up. Place to one side.

4. Scoop out the inside of your tomato, leaving the skin and a thin layer of tomato.

5. Place the tomato you scooped out to one side and put the hollow tomato along with the skewer on an oven dish or tray and grill until the chicken is cooked and no longer pink.

6. Once your rice is ready, drain and mix with the tomato you scooped out. Fry this in your pan with salt and pepper and serve inside your grilled tomato.

7. Chop your spring onion into small pieces and garnish. Wash a handful of fresh spinach and lay this on your plate, by now your chicken should be ready or close to ready.

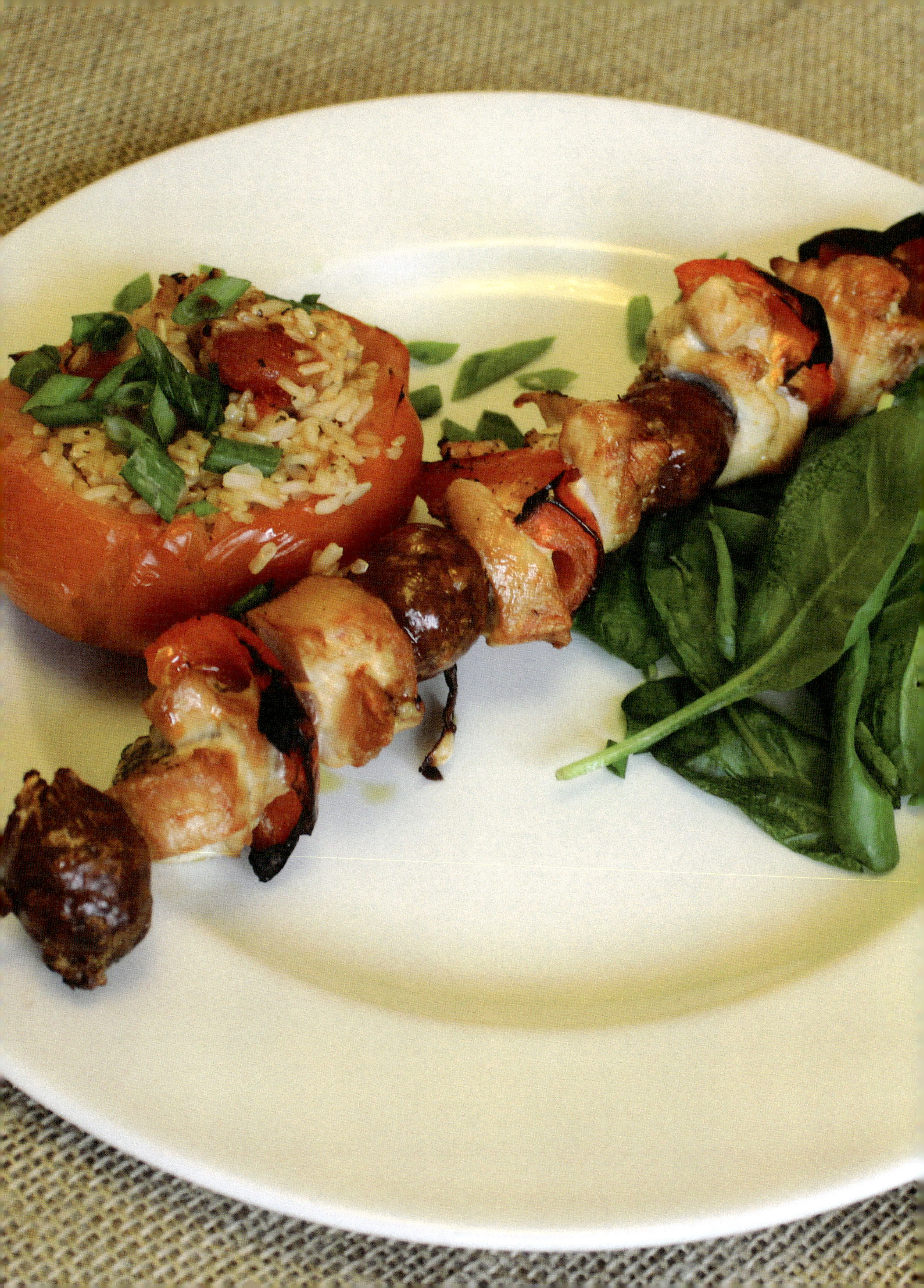

MAMA'S POLLO AL AJILLO
GARLIC CHICKEN

SERVES 2

INGREDIENTS

- 500G CHICKEN THIGHS OR 2 DICED CHICKEN BREASTS
- 6 GARLIC CLOVES
- FRESH / DRIED ROSEMARY
- FRESH / DRIED THYME
- SALT
- BLACK PEPPER
- OLIVE OIL
- SPLASH OF WHITE WINE

METHOD

1. Begin by thoroughly cleaning your chicken thighs or chicken breasts and seasoning them with plenty of salt and pepper.

2. In a large pan, heat up a generous pouring of oil and place your seasoned chicken thighs or diced breast. Fry your chicken until it becomes a golden colour all around.

3. Crush your whole garlic cloves and add them to the pan along with the rosemary and thyme. Stir and continue cooking everything together until the chicken is cooked through and the outside is a dark brown colour.

4. Add a splash of white wine and stir everything together to blend all the flavours. Allow the wine to reduce and serve.

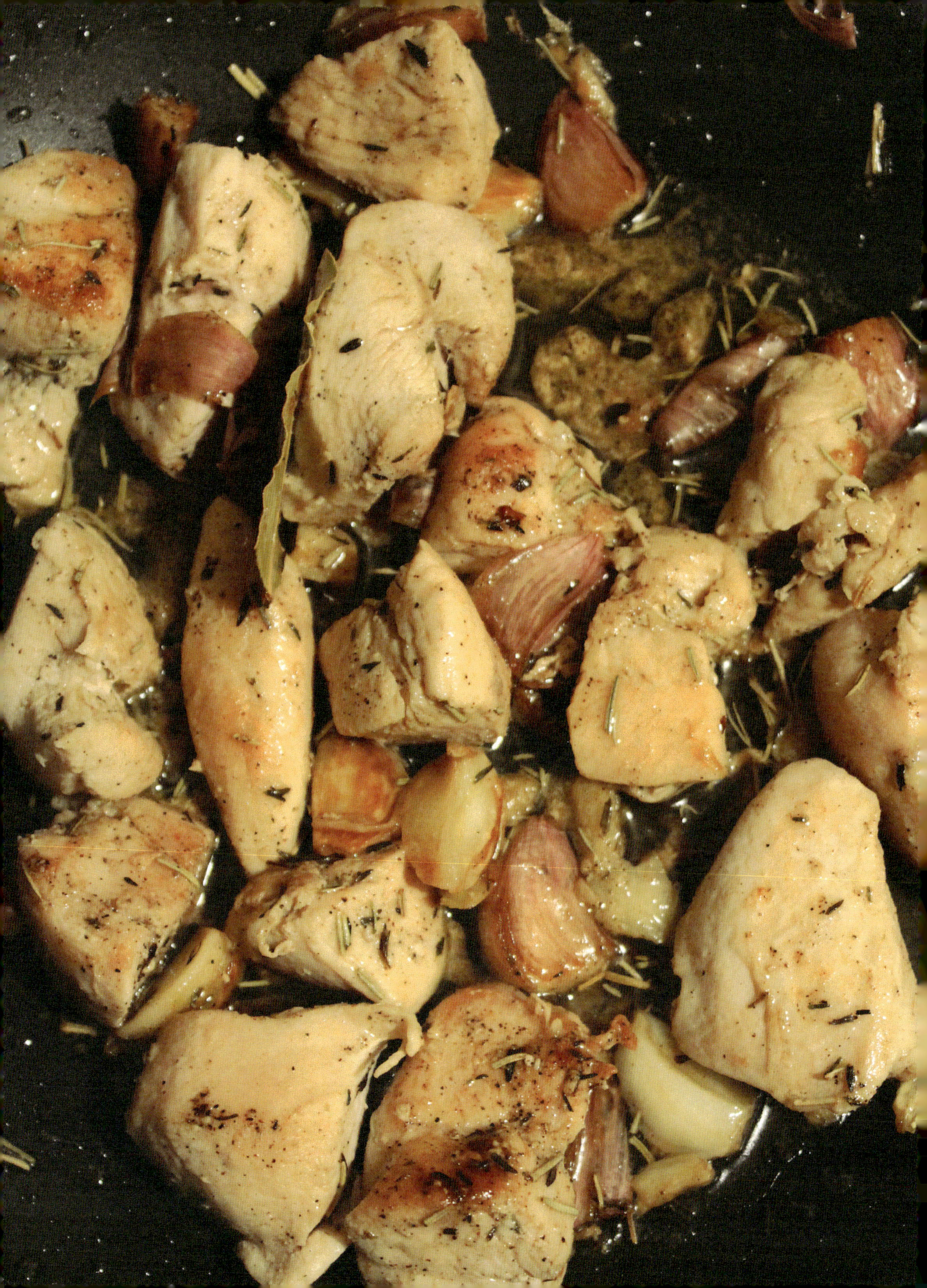

MAMA'S CHICKEN EMPANADO
CHICKEN ESCALOPES

SERVES 2

INGREDIENTS

- 2 LARGE CHICKEN BREASTS
- 2 GARLIC CLOVES
- FRESH PARSLEY
- SALT
- BLACK PEPPER
- PLAIN FLOUR
- 2 - 4 EGGS
- BREADCRUMBS
- SUNFLOWER OR OLIVE OIL

Undoubtedly one of the most recognised local dishes. So simple to make but tastes wonderful in a sandwich, with chips, mash, or on its own as a tapas dish.

METHOD

1. Prepare three separate plates, one with plenty of flour, one with plenty of breadcrumbs *(start with half a packet and refill as you need to)* and a separate plate with two cracked eggs, scrambled together. Season your eggs with finely chopped parsley, thinly chopped garlic and salt and pepper.

2. Wash your chicken breast and fillet your chicken into thin slices.

3. Once filleted, the fun, but messy stage begins. One at a time, cover your chicken slices with the egg, then flour, back into the egg and finally in breadcrumbs. Continue the process until all your chicken slices are finished.

4. Pour a generous amount of oil in a frying pan and fry your chicken, flipping it over occasionally until both sides are golden.

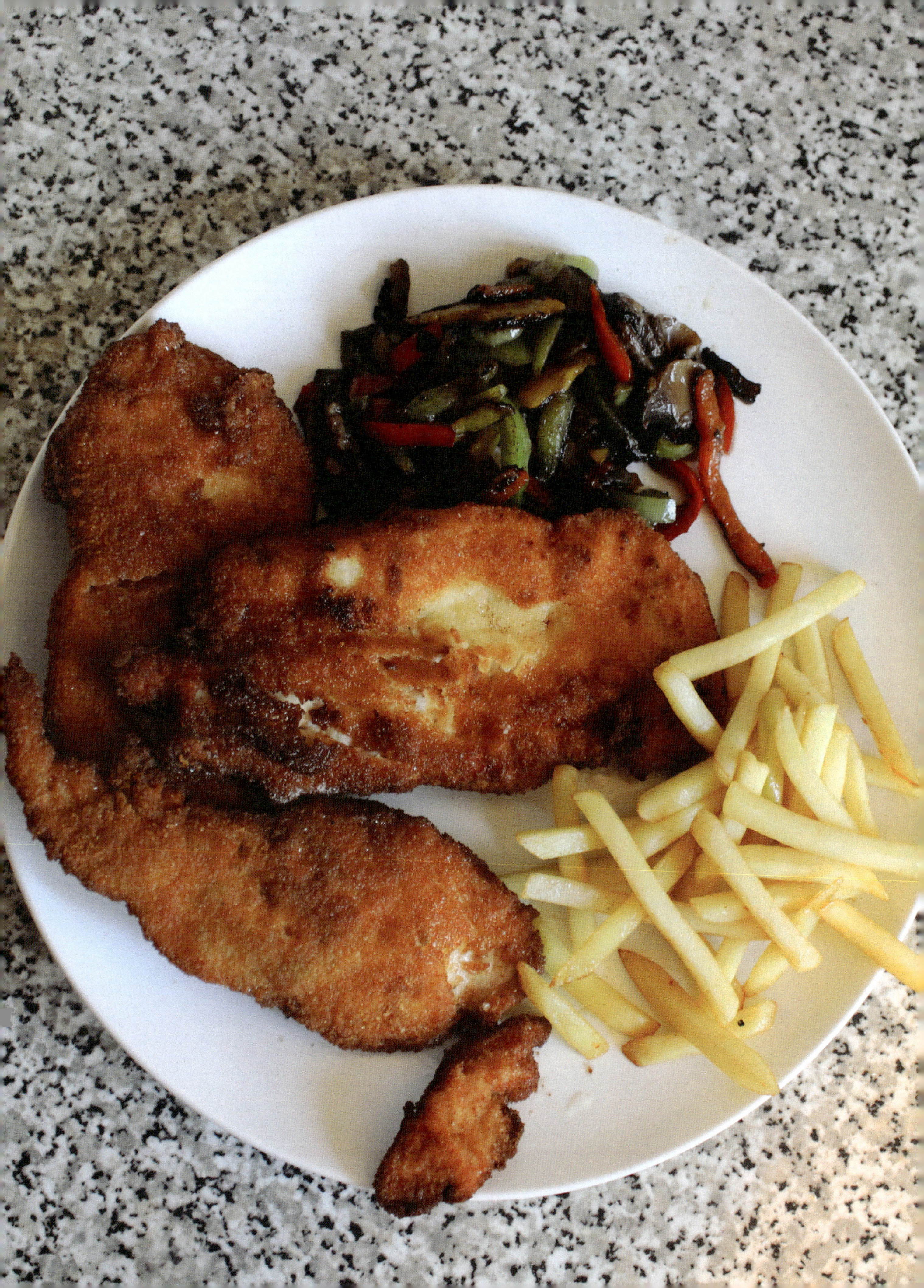

ARROZ CON POLLO
CHICKEN AND RICE

SERVES 3

INGREDIENTS

- 200 G CHICKEN BREAST
- 2 GARLIC CLOVES
- 2-3 TOMATOES
- 2 PEPPERS
- RICE *(HANDFUL PER PERSON)*
- SAFFRON
- HALF LEMON
- BAY LEAF
- SALT

Like many dishes in Gibraltar, various cultures have inspired the cuisine we eat today, none more than the neighbours across the border. The arroz con pollo is for those not too fond of fish, or looking to try something different.

METHOD

1. Boil the kettle and leave to one side.

2. Chop your garlic, tomatoes and peppers into small pieces and fry in olive oil; this is known as a *refrito*.

3. Once you have done so and the vegetables are softened, add in your diced chicken and cook. When the chicken is ready pour the boiled water into the pan filling it up about half way and add in the bay leaf, salt, saffron and a handful of rice per person. Stir the ingredients together and leave on a low heat until the water is reduced.

4. Stir occasionally to keep your rice from sticking if the water has evaporated and the rice is still not ready, feel free to add more water.

5. Once ready serve with a lemon or squeeze over some lemon juice.

BY LORRAINE LAGUEA

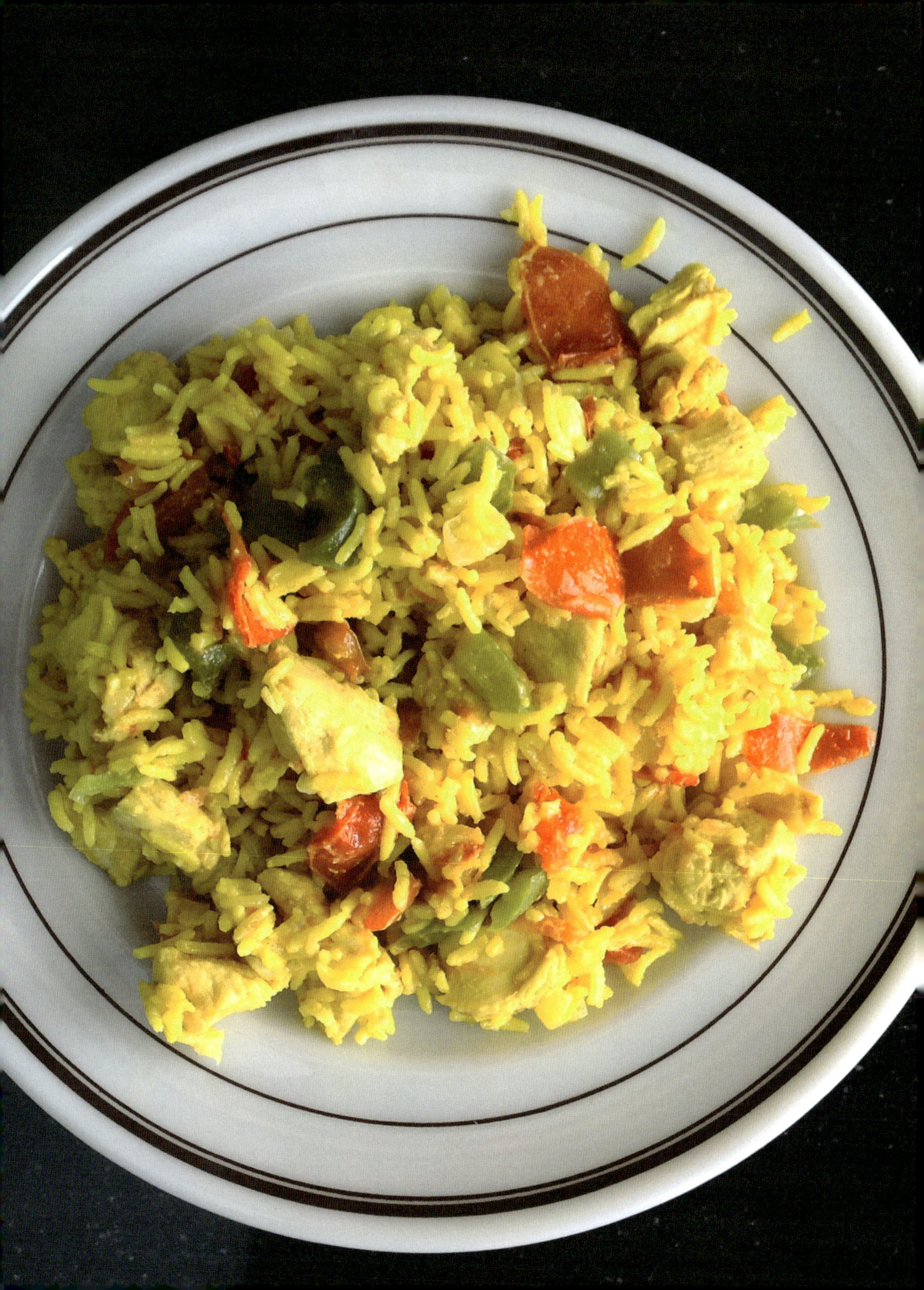

POLLO EN TOMATE
CHICKEN IN TOMATO SAUCE

SERVES 3

INGREDIENTS

- 3 CHICKEN BREASTS, CUT IN HALF
- 560 G JAR FRIED TOMATOES
- 1 GREEN PEPPER
- 1 BAY LEAF
- 2 SLICED CARROTS
- 1 CUBED MEDIUM POTATO
- 2 GARLIC CLOVES
- 1 CHOPPED ONION
- 1/2 GLASS WHITE WINE
- DASH CAYENNE PEPPER

METHOD

1. Heat some oil in the frying pan and seal the pieces of chicken breasts. Once sealed place this in your pressure cooker.

2. In the same oil used for the chicken breasts sauté the onions, garlic, carrots, potatoes and whole green pepper. Cook for a while, when onions are of a golden colour pour in your wine, tomatoes and bay leaf. Stir and place into pressure cooker or casserole dish, adding the dash of cayenne pepper, salt and black pepper to taste. Add water to cover. Cook for 20 to 25 minutes in the pressure cooker, or partially covered in your casserole dish until the chicken is tender, topping up with water as required.

3. Boil macaroni and use them as a bed for the chicken breasts and tomato sauce.

RECIPE BY ROSEMARIE MAÑASCO

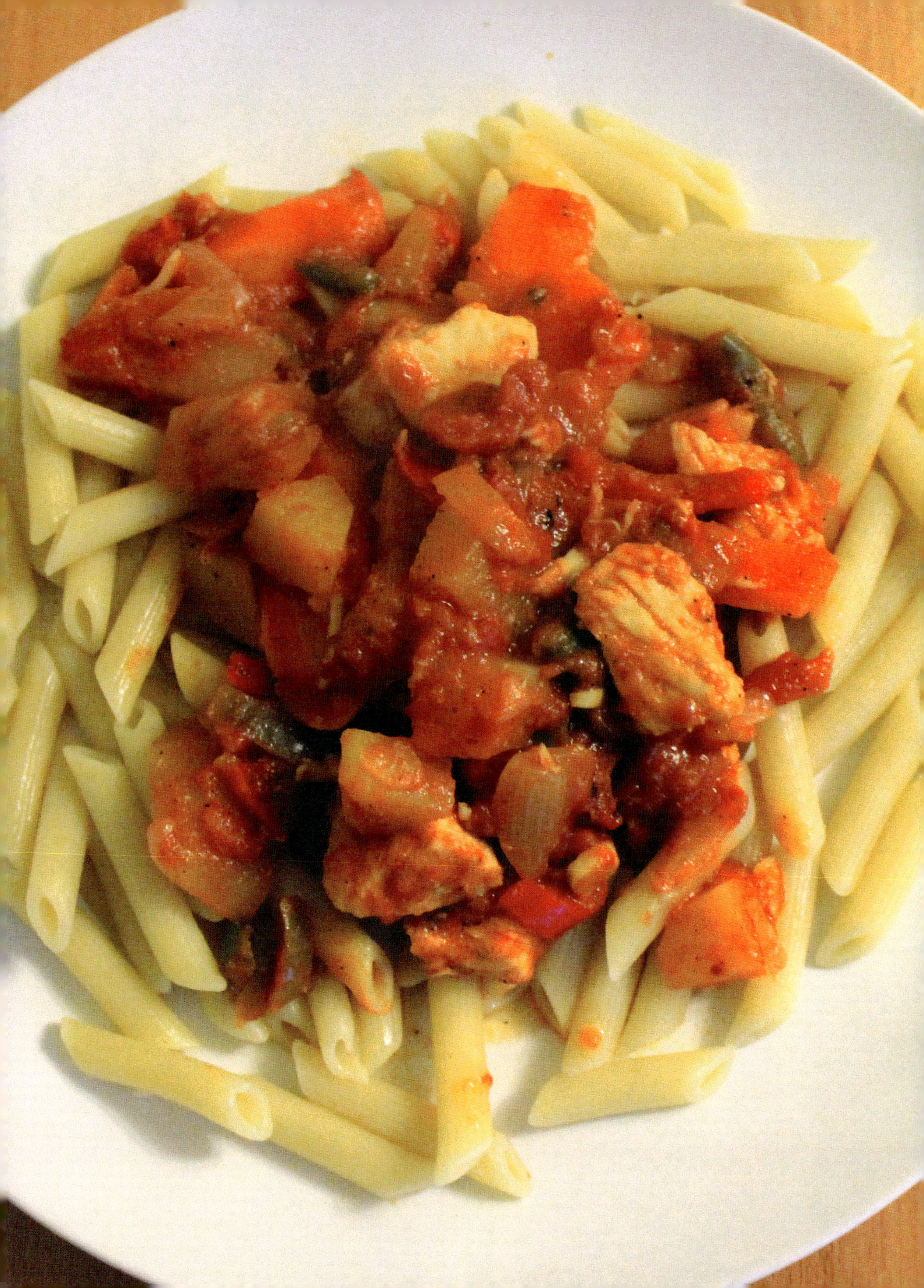

MAMA'S CHICKEN FAJITAS

SERVES 2

INGREDIENTS

- 6-8 FLOUR WRAPS
- 2 CHICKEN BREASTS
- 1/2 ONION
- 1/2 RED AND 1/2 GREEN AND 1/2 YELLOW PEPPER
- 400 G RED KIDNEY BEANS
- OLIVE OIL
- FAJITA MIX / SPICES
- 400 G CHOPPED TOMATOES OR 3 - 4 WHOLE TOMATOES
- CHILLIES
- CHEESE OF CHOICE
- LEMON JUICE
- LETTUCE LEAVES

METHOD

1. Grab yourself a grill pan or frying pan and place it on a medium – high heat.

2. Begin by slicing your chicken fillets into thin strips. Do this to your peppers, remember to halve them and de-seed them, add onions and place everything in a large bowl.

3. Once you have your ingredients in the bowl, mix in your fajita spices.

4. When ready, place everything onto your grill or pan and drizzle over some olive oil. Stir occasionally so that it doesn't burn or stick to the pan and make sure everything is cooked properly so that there is no pink chicken through.

5. Once the chicken is ready, drain and add in your red kidney beans, lower your heat and leave for a bit.

6. Place your wraps in the microwave for 30 seconds so they warm up and soften, grate some cheese and place everything on separate plates and bowls so everyone can enjoy preparing their own fajitas as they like it.

7. If you would like you can also cut some lettuce leaves to add in alongside the cheese.

8. If you like some homemade salsa simply chop some tomatoes and chillies and mix together well with a little coriander.

SUGGESTION
Drizzle some lemon juice and mix in if you prefer a slightly bitter taste.

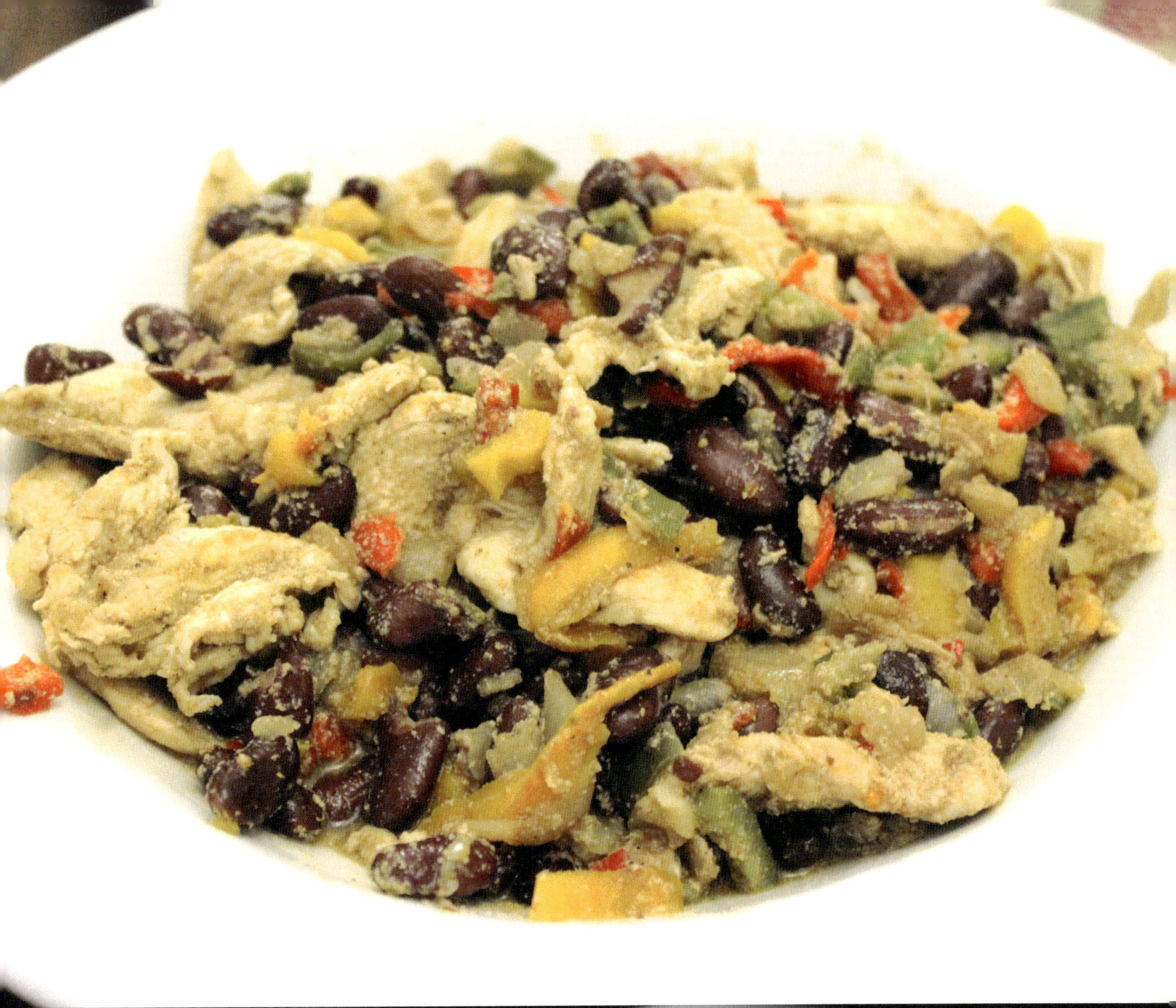
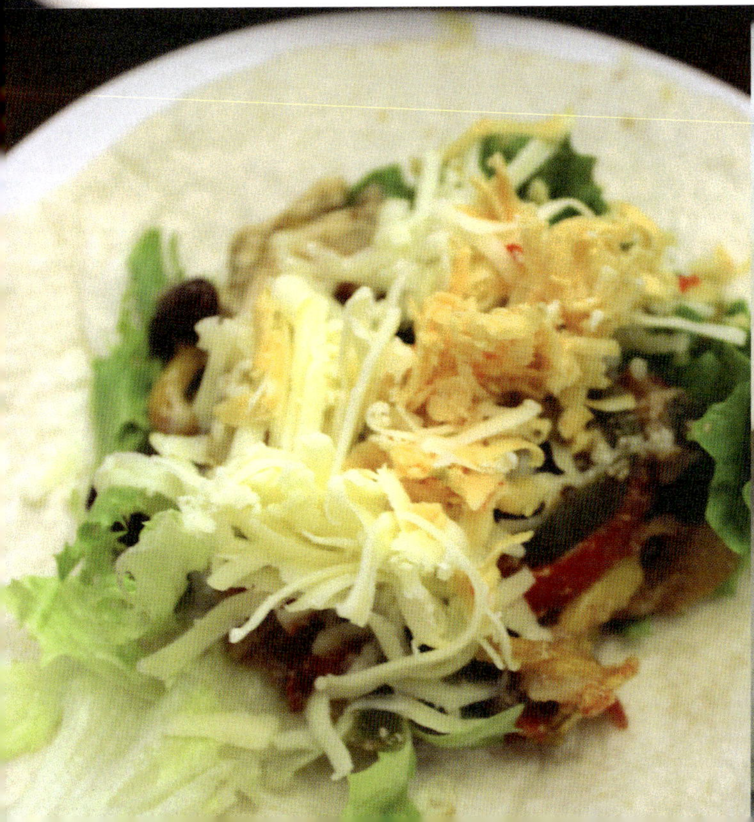
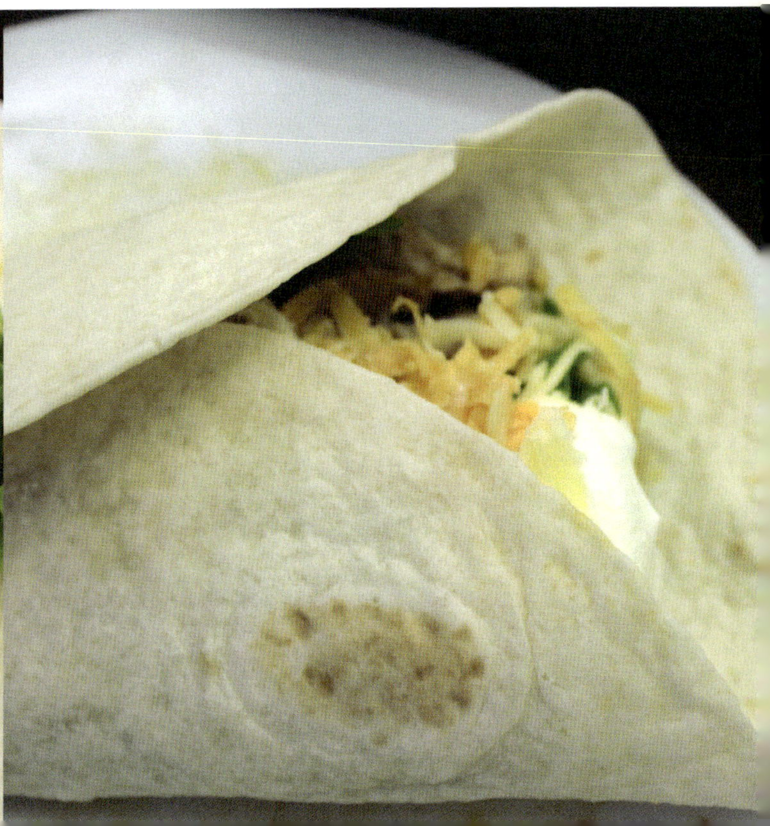

MAMA'S CHICKEN IN WHITE WINE AND SAFFRON WITH RICE

SERVES 1

INGREDIENTS

- 3 DRUMSTICKS *(PER PERSON)*
- 1 ONION
- 1 GARLIC CLOVE
- RICE *(HANDFUL PER PERSON)*
- 1/2 GLASS WHITE WINE
- BASIL
- SAFFRON

The saffron and white wine blend together perfectly with the vegetables to give you a juicy chicken full of flavour that falls off the bone.

METHOD

1. Chop the garlic and onion and fry in a large pan with a bit of oil or butter. Stir occasionally as this burns very easily. Meanwhile boil a full kettle of water. Once this has boiled and the onion and garlic are soft add in the drumsticks, pour enough water into the pan to cover the chicken and season.

2. Add the rest of the ingredients except for the rice.

3. Leave partially covered for 30 – 45 minutes stirring occasionally. Check the chicken is thoroughly cooked through and not pink.

4. Boil some rice, then serve.

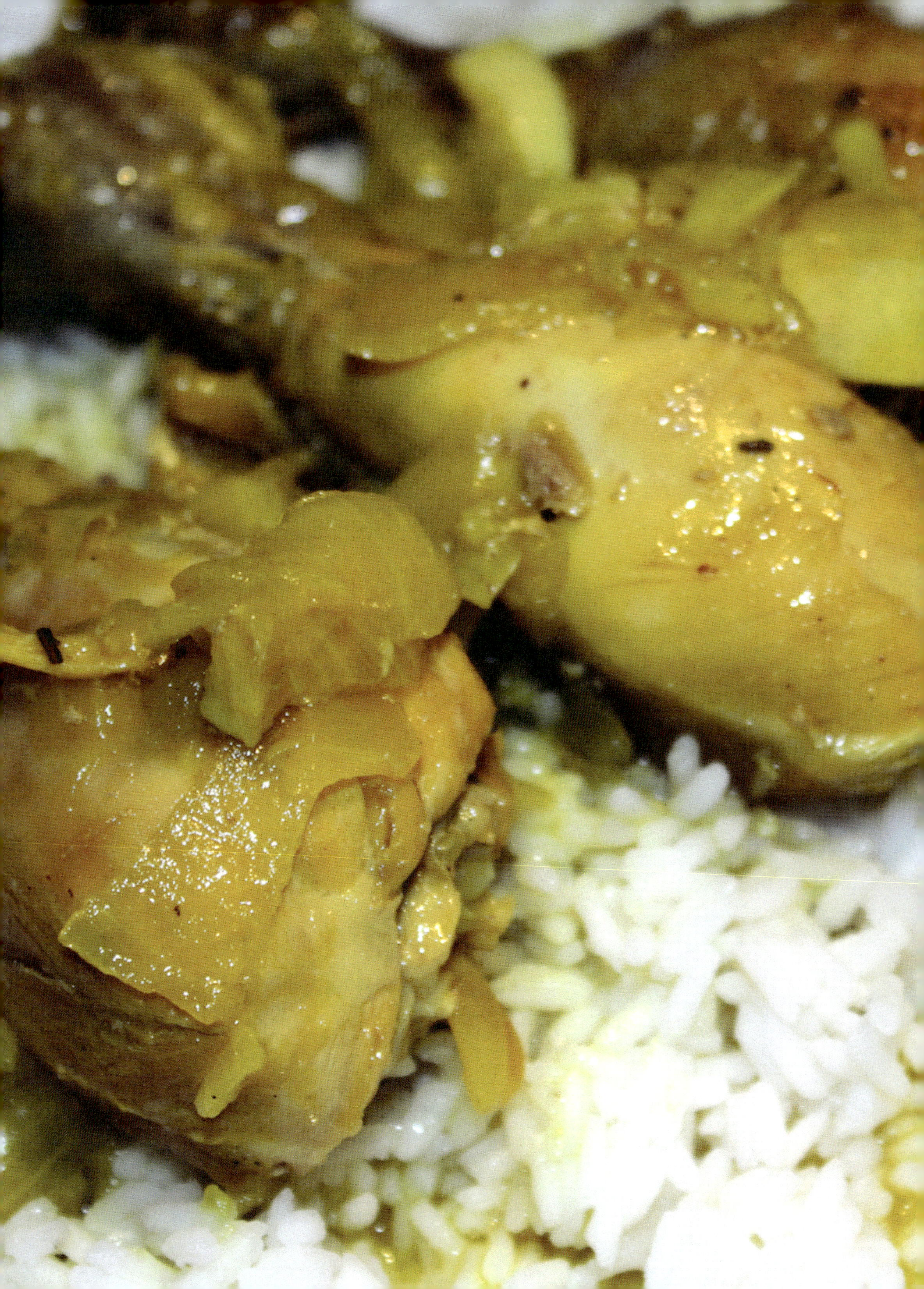

MAMA'S CREAMY MUSHROOM, CHICKEN AND PANCETTA

SERVES 1

INGREDIENTS

- 300 G BABY NEW POTATOES
- PARSLEY
- OLIVE OIL
- 150 ML SINGLE CREAM
- 1/4 GLASS WHITE WINE (DRY)
- PLAIN FLOUR
- 200 G MUSHROOMS
- 2 GARLIC CLOVES
- LEMON JUICE
- 50 G GREEN BEANS
- 100 G PANCETTA
- 1 CHICKEN BREAST

METHOD

1. Begin by opening and draining your baby new potatoes. If your potatoes are whole, cut them in half and place them in a bowl, dress with oil and mix with either fresh *(preferably)* or dry parsley. Leave to one side.

2. Chop your green beans and garlic and place to one side. As for mushrooms, chop them very finely but leaving 2 or 3 aside to slice thinly instead of chopping.

3. Now dice your chicken breast into small pieces or slices as you prefer and fry in a large pan with a bit of oil. Once the chicken is seared, almost cooked, add in your pancetta and vegetables *(except the potatoes)*.

4. The potatoes can now be fried in a separate pan with a bit of salt and pepper.

5. Stir fry all your ingredients together and add a 1/4 wine glass of dry white wine to your chicken pan and allow to cook together. When ready pour in your single cream and stir. If you notice that the sauce is too runny, thicken with a bit of flour, adding small amounts and stirring thoroughly, so that it mixes in well and you avoid lumps.

6. Leave on a very low heat for a minute whilst the potatoes cook a little more and serve.

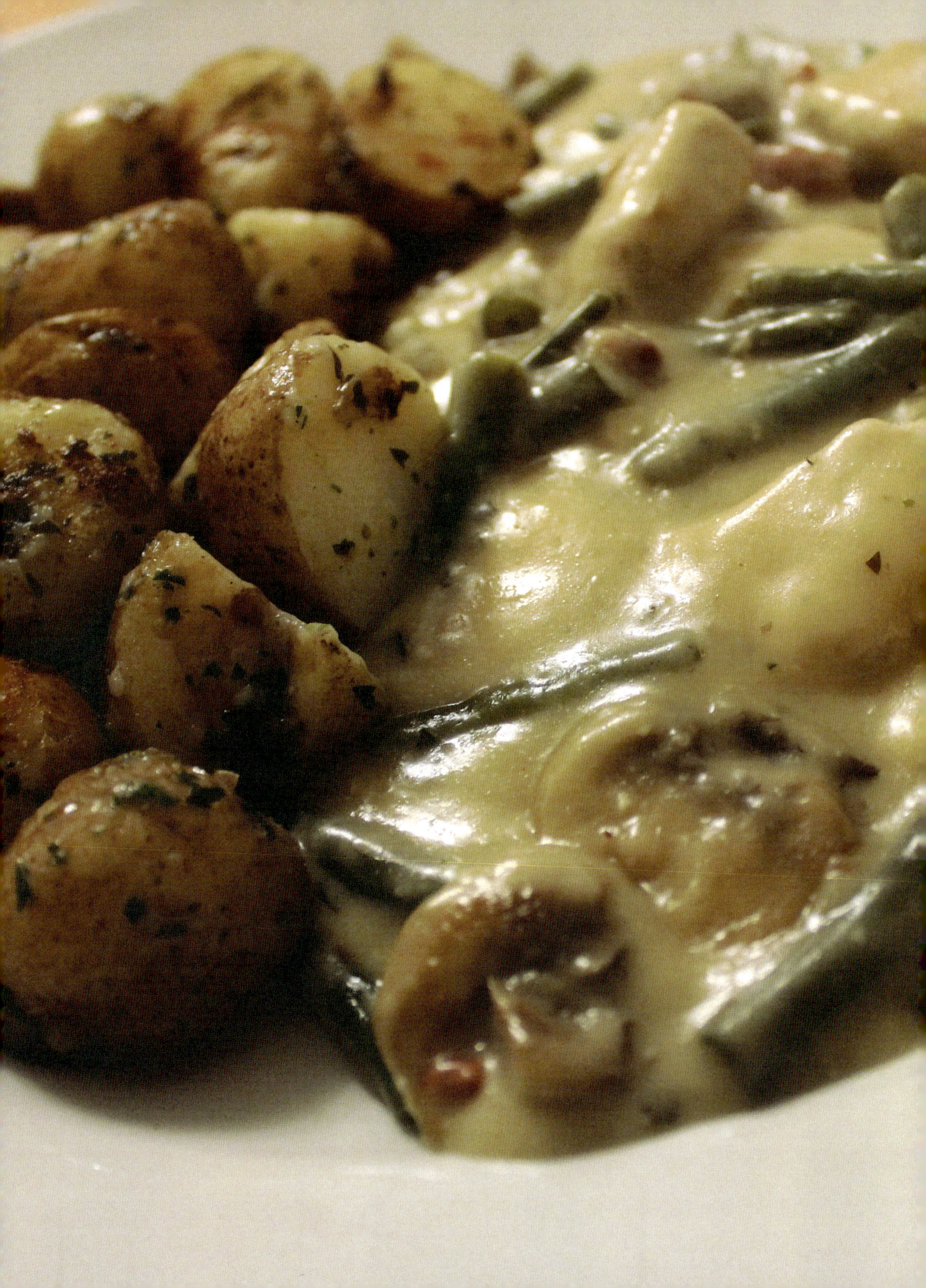

MEAT

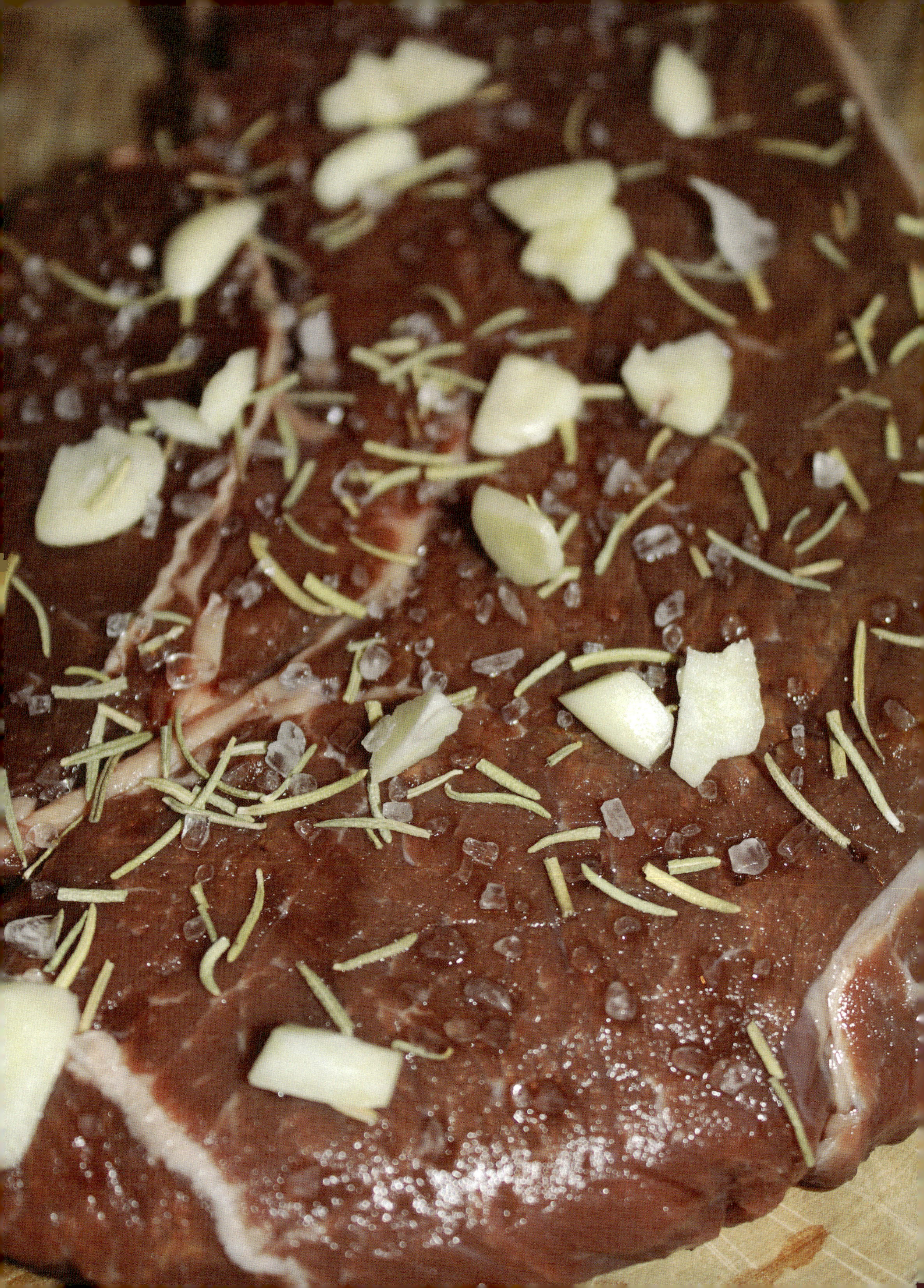

MAMA'S EASY BBQ PULLED PORK PARCELS

SERVES 1

INGREDIENTS

- 350G UNSMOKED GAMMON JOINT
- HP HONEY BBQ WOODSMOKE SAUCE
- 2 EGGS
- 2 SMALL POTATOES
- 1 PUFF PASTRY SHEET

METHOD

For this recipe I used unsmoked gammon joint, although bone-in pork shoulder would also work

1. Cover your gammon joint with your chosen BBQ sauce. *(I chose sticky honey BBQ sauce)*.

2. Place this in the oven at 200°C for 20 minutes, then change to grill mode and grill for 5 – 10 minutes, turning your joint over so every side is crispy.

3. Whilst the joint is in the oven, chop two small potatoes into small cubes and fry.

4. Once your joint is ready, remove from the oven and using two forks pull your pork apart.

5. In a frying pan, pour in your pork and squeeze over some more BBQ sauce, fry for 2 – 5 minutes to ensure everything is cooked throughout and slightly crisp the now shredded pork.

6. Drain your chips and mix with two whisked eggs.

7. Lay your puff pastry on a baking tray, and spread your chip and egg mix, with your BBQ pork over on half of your pastry. Cover with the rest of your pastry and seal. Brush over with any leftover egg you have.

8. Place in the oven for 20 – 25 minutes until puffed and golden.

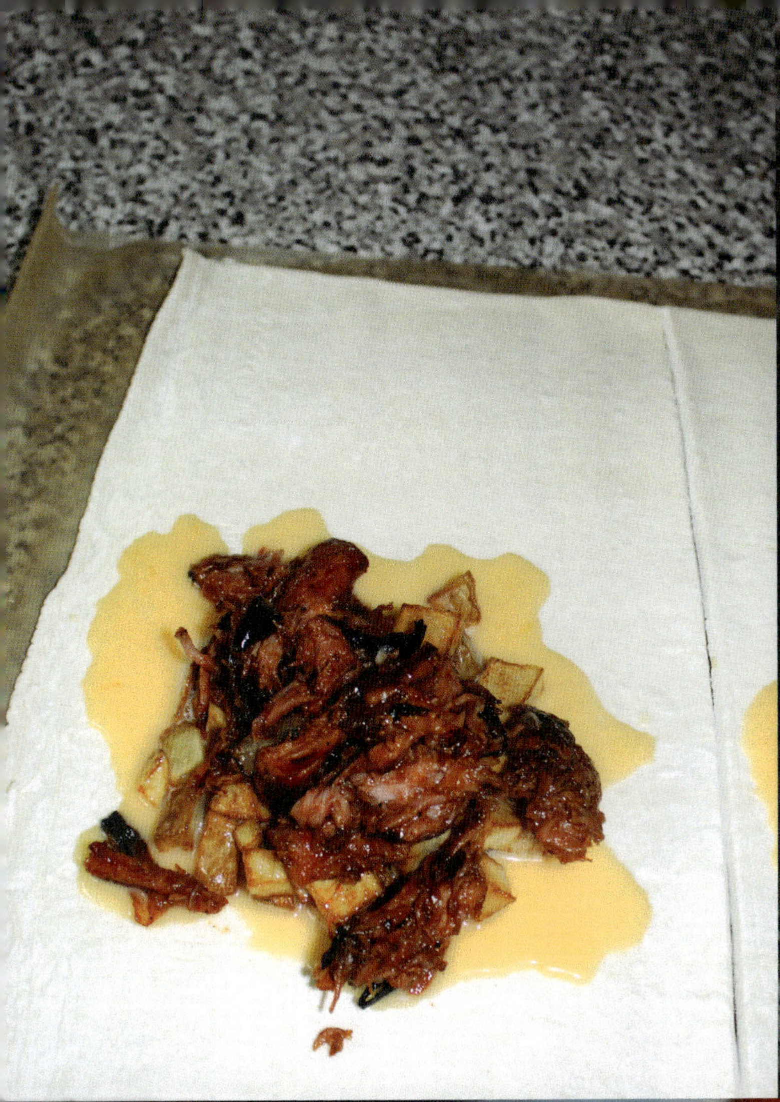
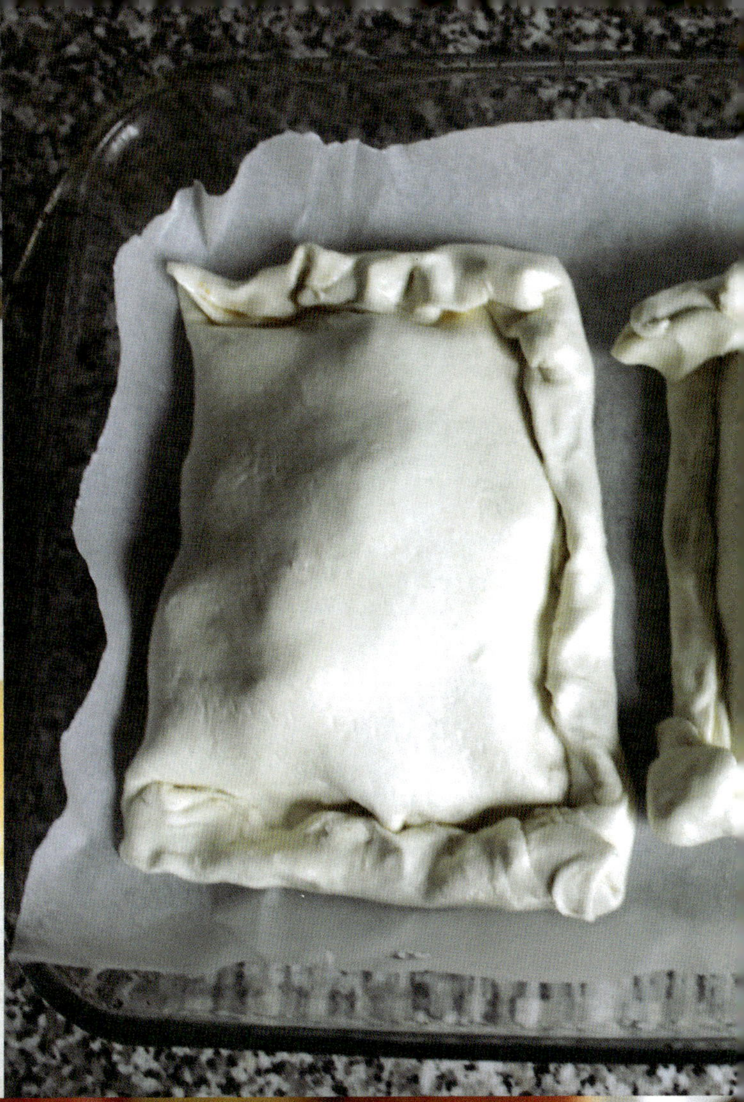
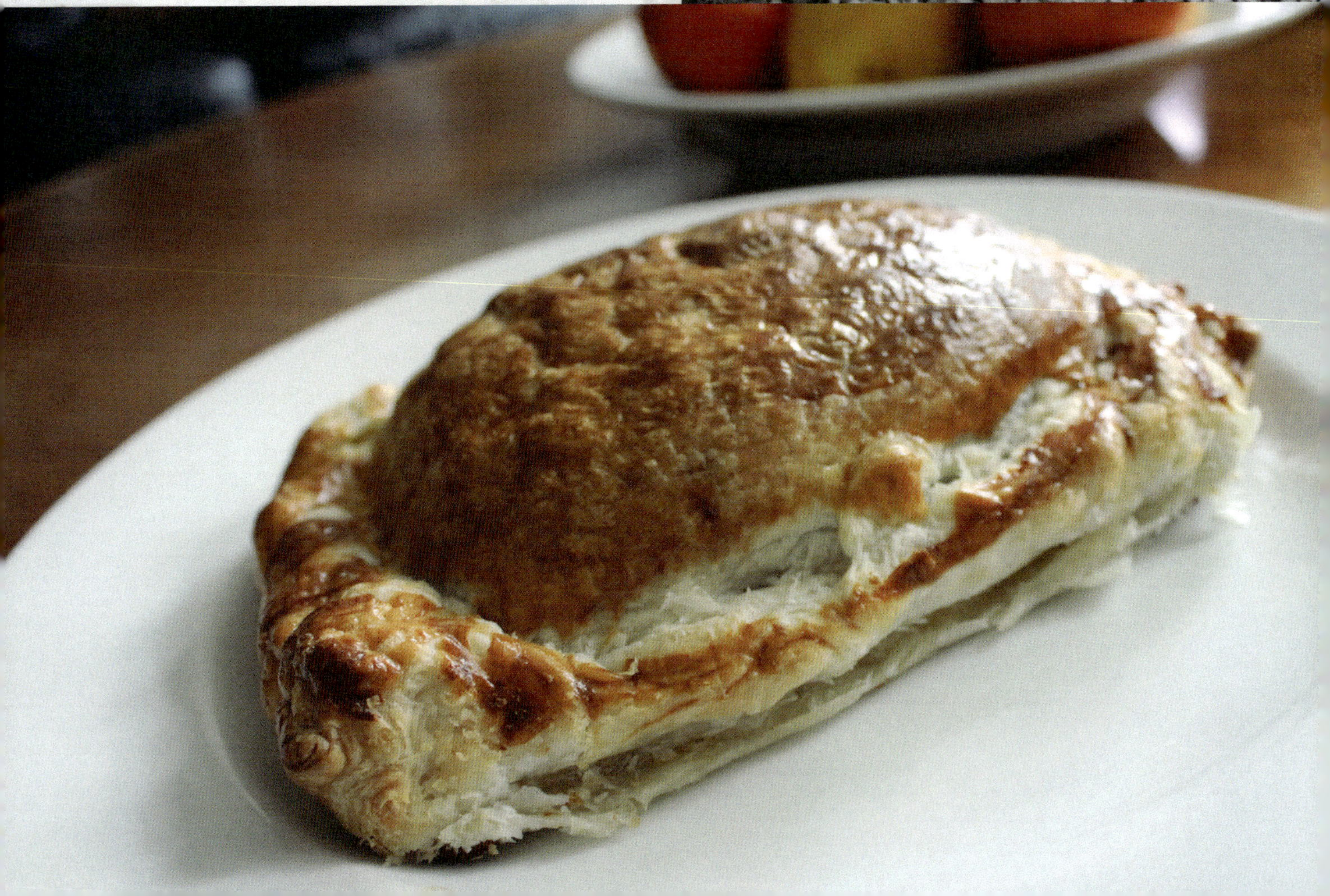

ALBONDIGÓN
MEATLOAF

SERVES 2

INGREDIENTS

- 500 G MINCED BEEF
- 2 EGGS
- 100 G GRATED CHEESE
- 5 LARGE GARLIC CLOVES *(FOR LOAF)*
- 2 - 3 GARLIC CLOVES *(FOR SAUCE)*
- 1/4 ONION
- 1/4 GREEN OR RED PEPPER
- 1 LARGE TIN PASSATA
- 1 TSP TOMATO PUREE
- CHOPPED PARSLEY
- HOT SAUCE
- BREADCRUMBS *(A HANDFUL)*
- FLOUR
- DRY WHITE WINE *(HALF A WINE GLASS)*
- 600 ML WATER

METHOD

1. Mix all your ingredients together and shape into a bread loaf, roll your loaf in flour and sauté on all sides for a few minutes by frying lightly in a pan.

2. Remove when sealed and in a large casserole gently fry 3 large garlic cloves in olive oil, add a large tin of passata, a little wine, about a quarter of a pint of water, then season and bring to the boil.

3. Simmer for about 10 minutes before adding the meatloaf into the casserole with the tomato sauce.

4. Stir often so that the loaf does not stick to the bottom of the casserole. Simmer on low heat for about 20 minutes and turn the loaf around continuing to cook for another 15 or 20 minutes until done.

BY ANA MARIA MORRO

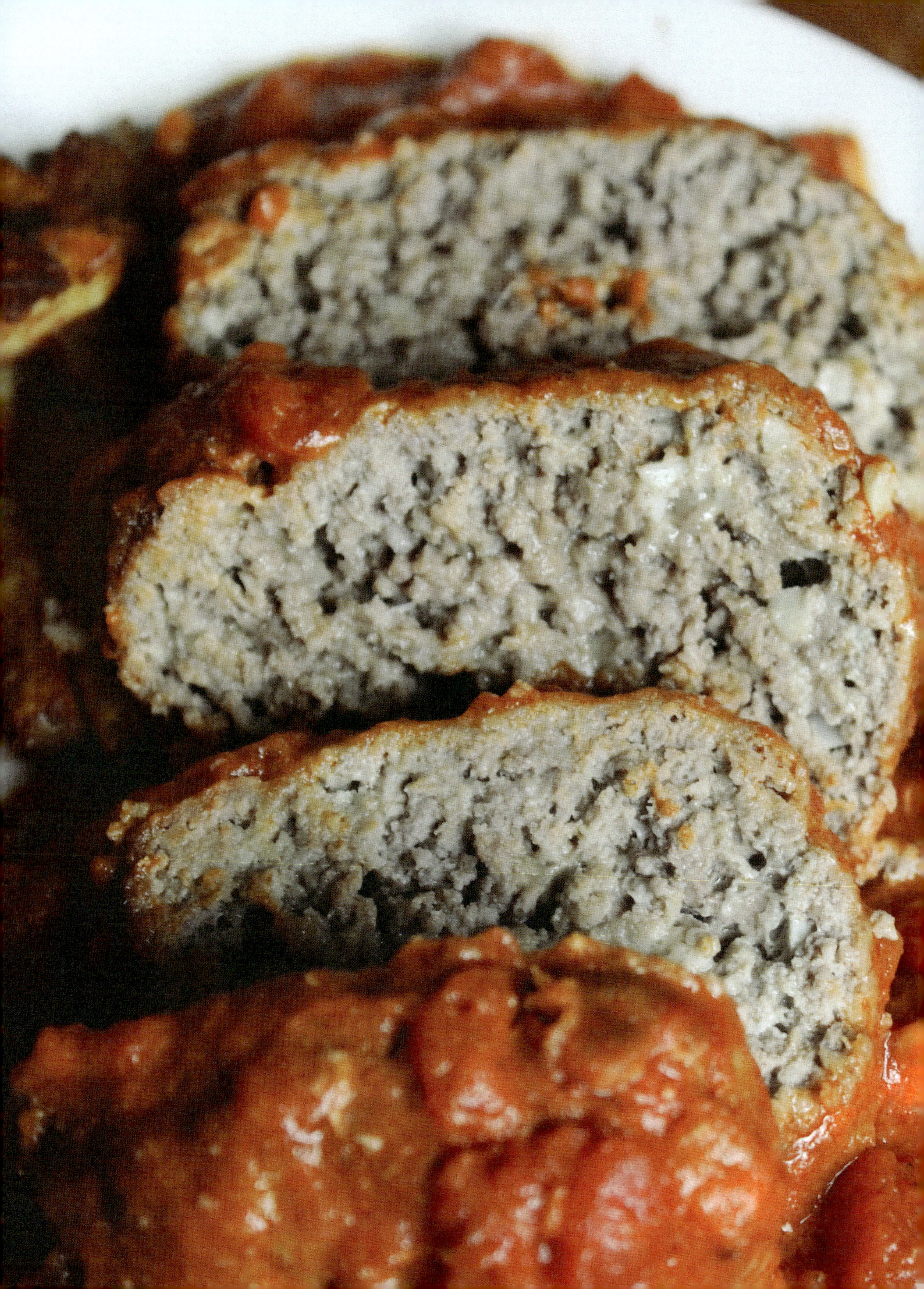

MUM'S PINCHITOS
MOROCCAN KEBABS

SERVES 4

INGREDIENTS

- 500 G LEAN BEEF / LAMB
- 2 GARLIC CLOVES
- FRESH PARSLEY
- 2 TSP SALT
- PINCHITO SPICE MIXTURE
- 3 TSP OLIVE OIL
- 1 RED PEPPER
- 1 GREEN PEPPER
- 1/2 ONION

These spicy beef kebabs are an absolute favourite at barbecues. Spices and marinated meats can be bought from local Moroccan butchers, so why not give it a try yourself.

METHOD

1. Begin by dicing your meat and mixing them with your spices and oil, enough to marinade your meat entirely. Chop the garlic and parsley very finely and add to the marinated meat.

2. Slice your peppers into cubes and attempt to do the same with your onion leaving them as semi large slices. Now, skewer the meat, try to have 3 to 4 cubes on a stick, alternating between the meat, pepper and onion.

3. Lay the pinchitos on a barbecue or on foil under a grill and cook under a high heat rotating as necessary until cooked. This should take about 6 - 8 minutes.

BY LORRAINE LAGUEA

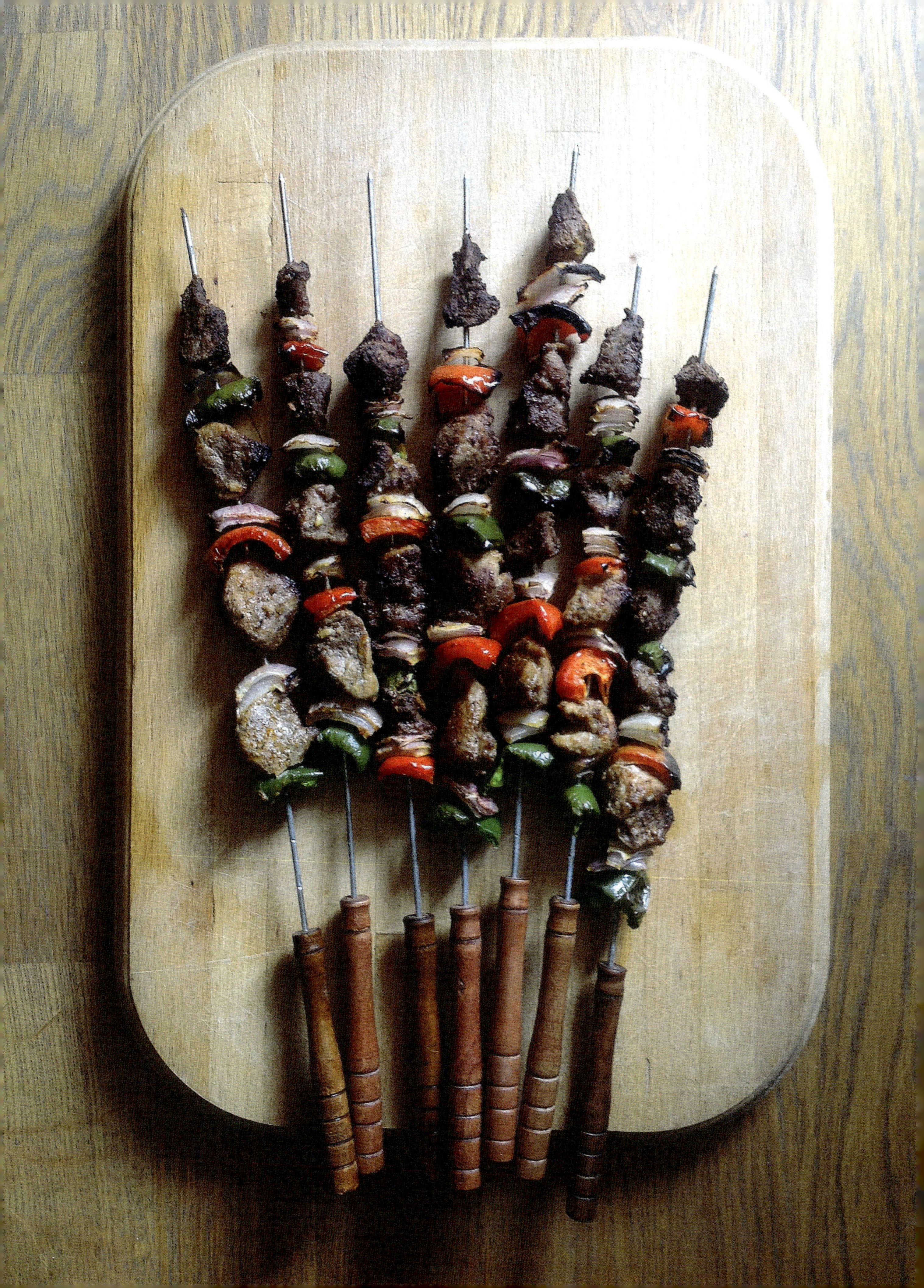

MAMA'S COTTAGE PIE

SERVES 3

INGREDIENTS

- 2 LARGE POTATOES
- BUTTER
- A SPLASH OF MILK
- 250G MINCED MEAT
- 1 ONION
- 1 GARLIC CLOVE
- 1 CARROT
- 1 LEEK
- 1 BEEF STOCK CUBE
- 2 TBSP BUTTER
- CHEESE
  (RED LEICESTER OR ANY OTHER OF YOUR CHOICE)

METHOD

1. Boil the potatoes; once boiled, add butter and milk and mash until lovely and smooth.

2. Melt the butter and lightly fry chopped onions, garlic, finely sliced carrot and leek. When soft, add your minced meat along with a sprinkle of beef stock and season with salt and pepper.

3. In a small oven dish lay the meat mixture and cover with the mashed potatoes.

4. Grate your cheese and sprinkle over the mashed potato. Grill until cheese is golden.

SUGGESTION

If you prefer adding an extra layer why not try boiling an egg or two, slicing into thin circles and layering that in-between the meat and potatoes.

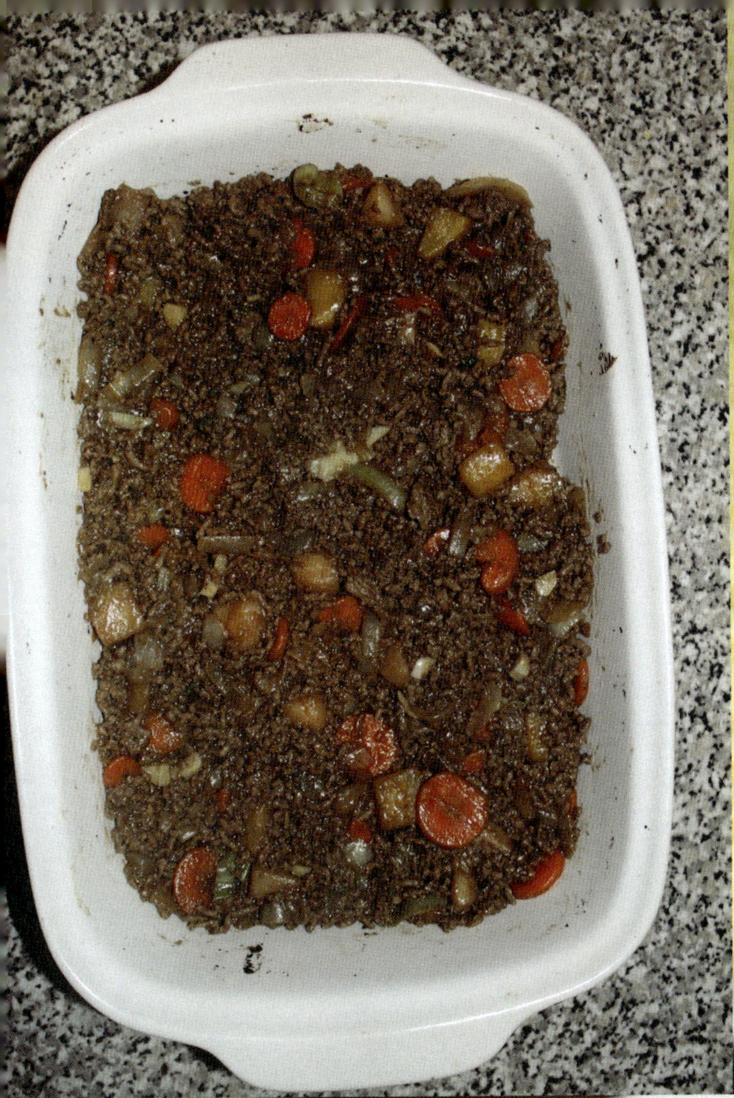
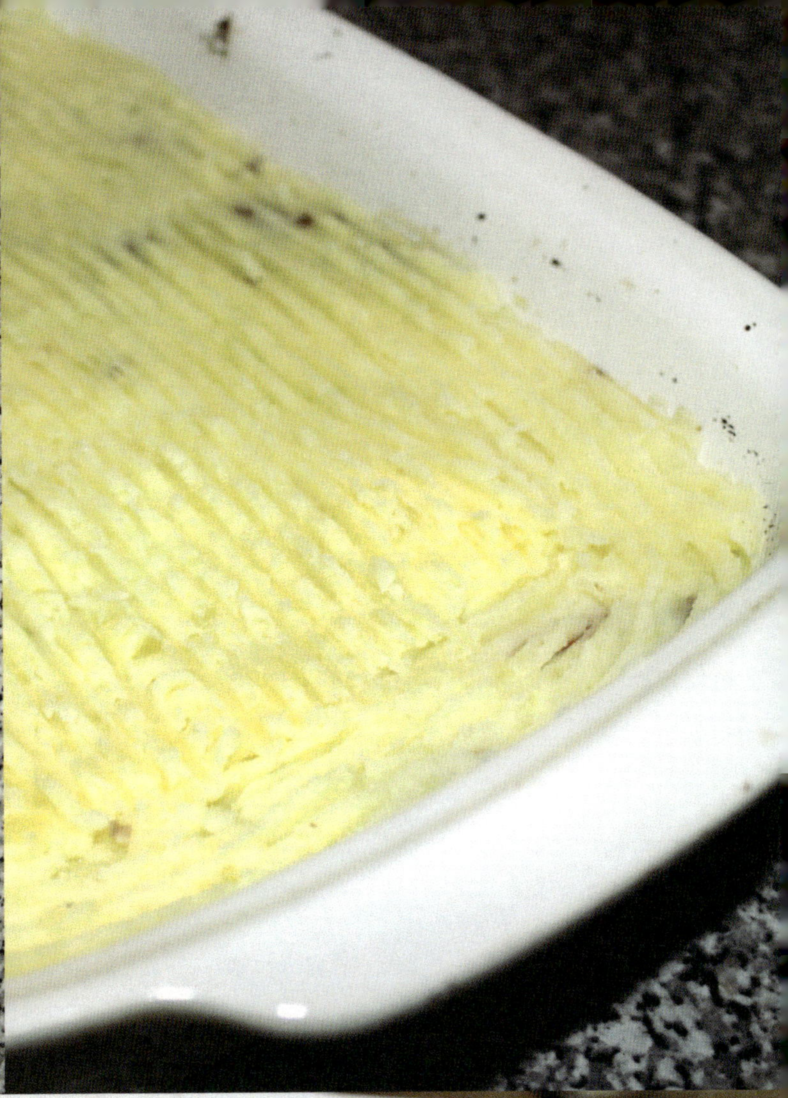
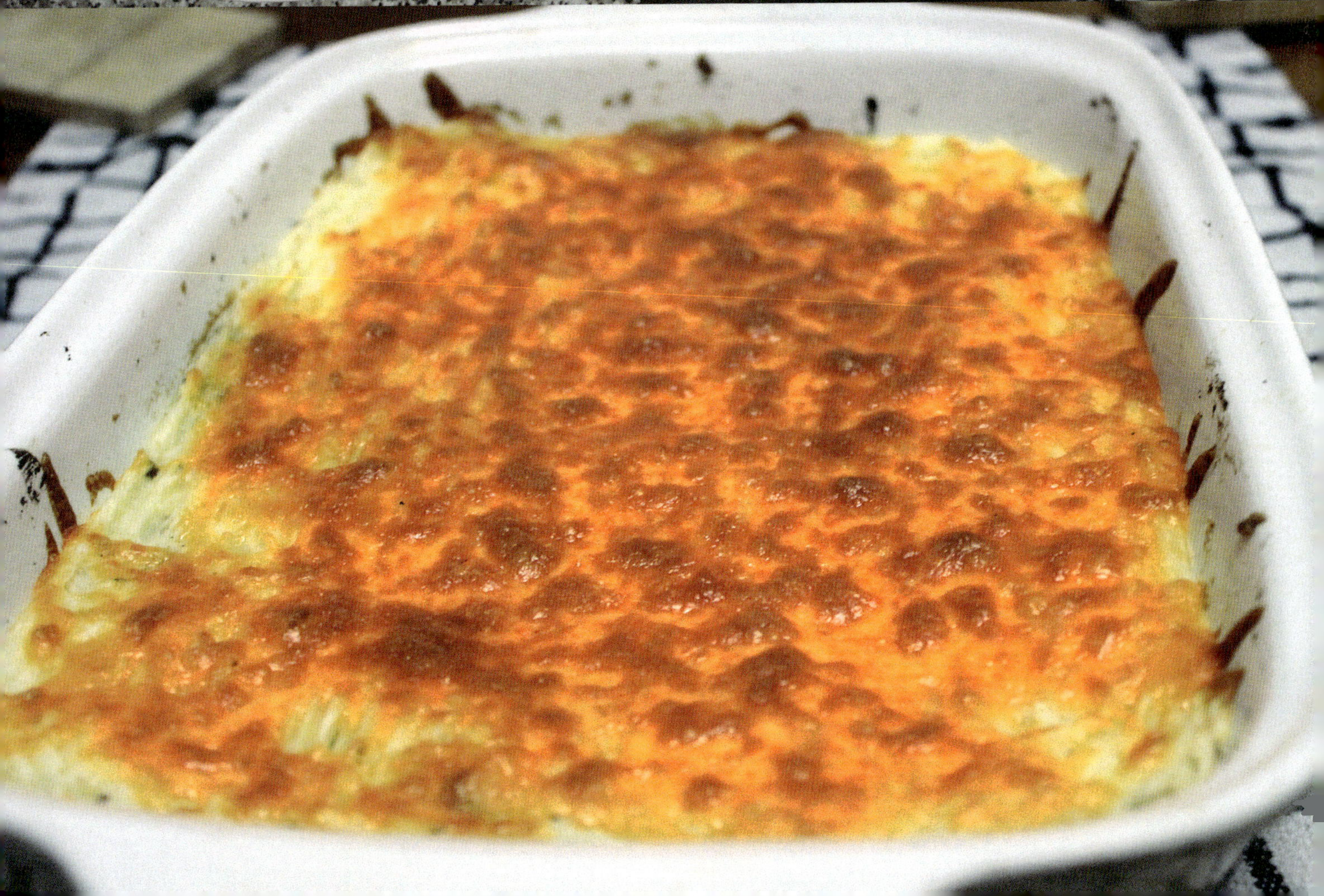

MAMA'S POTAJE DE BERZA

MAMA'S GIBRALTARIAN STEW

SERVES 5

INGREDIENTS

- 500 G PORK COLLAR
- 500 G STEWING STEAK
- 1 PIG'S TROTTER
  (CUT INTO FOUR)
- 110 G PORK BELLY
- 110 G BLACK PUDDING
- 110 G CHORIZO
- 2 GARLIC CLOVES
- 1 MEDIUM ONION
- 2 FRESH TOMATOES
- 1 LARGE PUMPKIN SLICE
- 5 POTATOES
- 400 G BUTTER BEANS
- 400 G CHICKPEAS
- 1/2 KG RUNNER BEANS
- LARGE BUNCH FRESH MINT
- 1 TSP PAPRIKA
- 8 WHOLE BLACK PEPPERCORNS
- 1 TSP CUMIN POWDER

METHOD

1. In a pressure cooker, place your pork collar, stewing steak, pig's trotter, pork belly, chorizo, whole, peeled garlic cloves, one onion cut in two, tomatoes cut in two, pumpkin, chopped mint, teaspoon of paprika, eight whole black peppercorns and one teaspoon of cumin powder.

2. Cover your ingredients with boiling water and season with salt. This should take 45 minutes in a pressure cooker, or alternatively cook until tender in a casserole dish, continually topping up with water.

3. Once everything is tender, remove the meat, pig's trotters and chorizo and blend the remaining vegetables. Add your runner beans cut into two or three pieces, chickpeas, butter beans, black pudding and potatoes to your blended pan. Cook for 15 minutes in a pressure cooker and remove from the heat. Alternatively, place in a casserole dish, partially covered for 30 - 40 minutes or until tender, topping up with water as required.

4. Place your meat and chorizo back in with all your ingredients once everything is tender and soft.

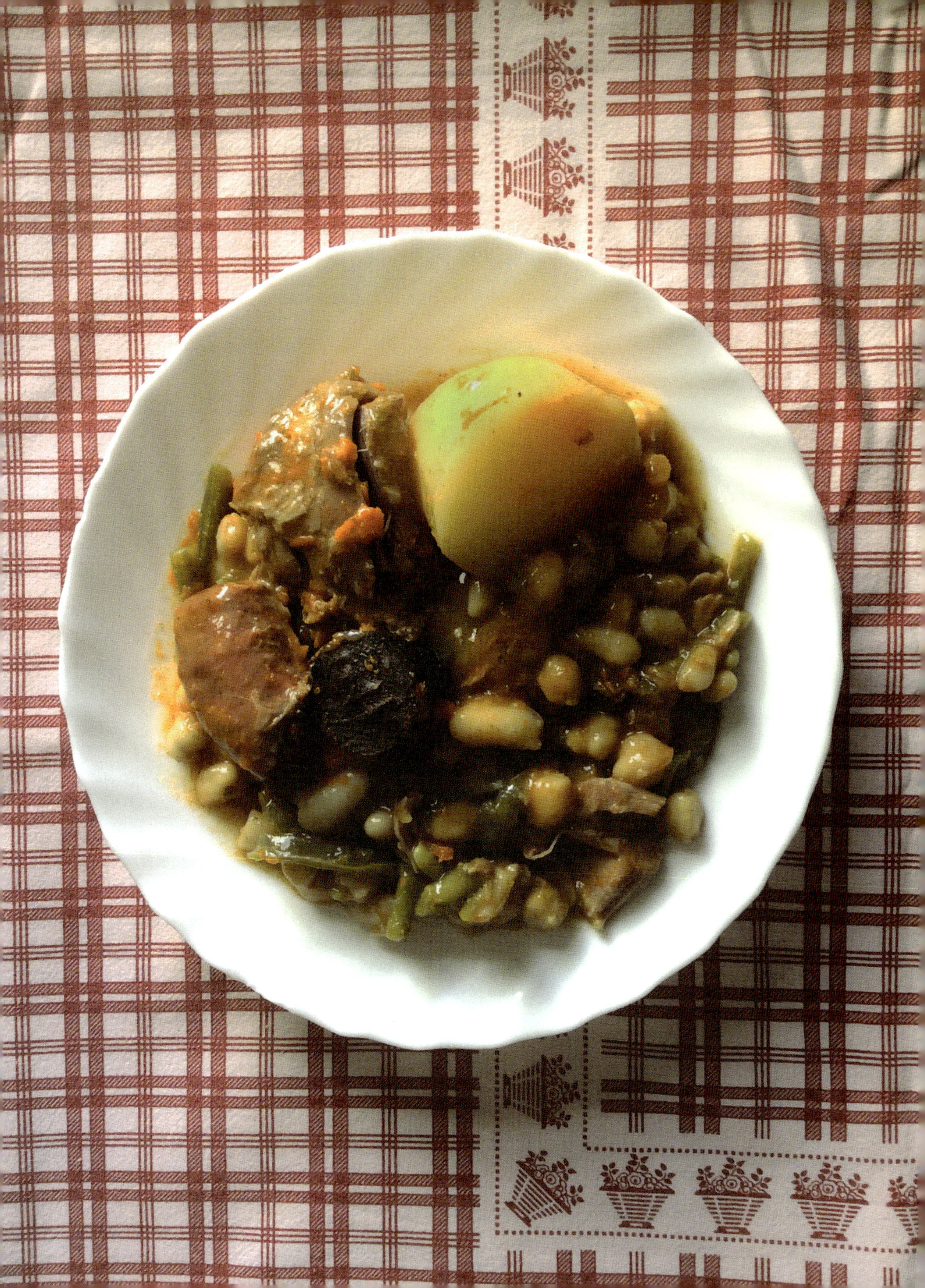

MUM'S CROQUETAS
MUM'S BACON CROQUETTES

SERVES 3

INGREDIENTS

- 5 MEDIUM POTATOES
- 200 G SMOKED BACON
- 1/4 RED ONION
- 3 EGGS
- FRESH CHOPPED PARSLEY
- 75 G BREADCRUMBS
- SALT
- GROUND BLACK PEPPER
- OLIVE OIL

These tasty croquettes are so easy and quick to make you'll have no excuse. They are perfect for snacking, parties and great for kids to enjoy.

METHOD

1. Dice and boil your potatoes until soft. Whilst your potatoes are boiling, dice your smoked bacon *(you can always buy pre diced bacon)* and fry without oil until fully cooked but not crispy.

2. When your bacon is ready, remove all the excess fat from your pan. Your potatoes should now be ready, drain all water from your boiled potatoes and mash.

3. Mix your bacon and potatoes together and season with salt, pepper and a pinch of parsley. Allow to cool and add a beaten egg to your mixture. *(Allowing it to cool will prevent the egg cooking).* The potato mixture should be a pasty consistency. If you feel this is not the case add a handful of breadcrumbs.

4. Prepare two separate bowls, one with 2 beaten eggs and the other with breadcrumbs.

5. Assemble your croquettes by shaping a tablespoon of your potato mixture in your hands and rolling into a flattened ball.

6. Heat a frying pan with enough oil to cover the base of the pan. Fry your croquettes on both flattened sides until golden brown. Place on a paper kitchen towel to drain any excess oil.

BY LORRAINE LAGUEA

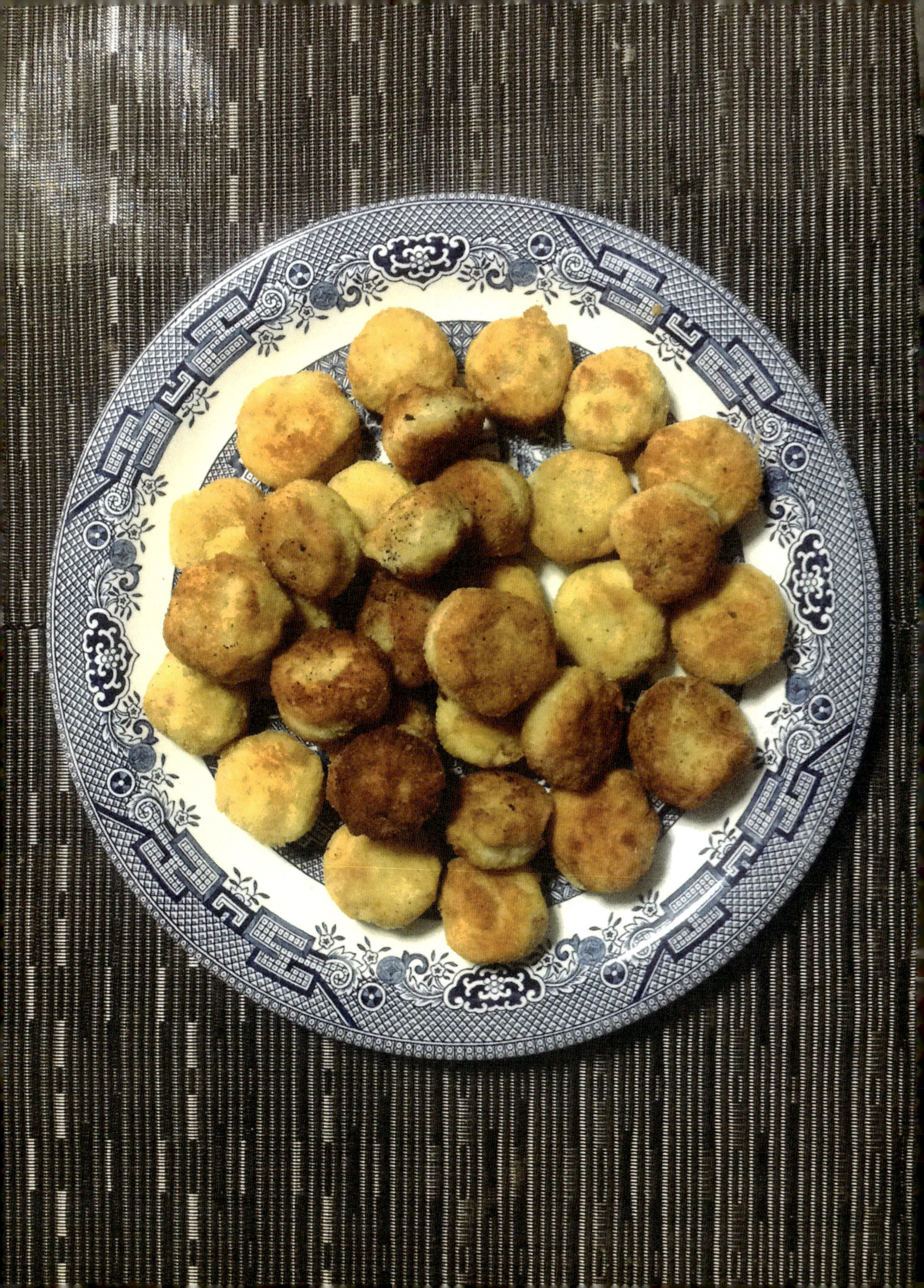

MAMA'S ALBÓNDIGAS
MEATBALLS

SERVES 2

INGREDIENTS

- 400 G MINCED BEEF
- 2 GARLIC CLOVES
- SPINACH LEAVES (HANDFUL)
- 1 SMALL ONION
- 60 G PASTA
- SALT
- GROUND BLACK PEPPER
- OREGANO
- BASIL
- OLIVE OIL
- 1 TIN CHOPPED TOMATOES
- SUN-DRIED TOMATOES (OPTIONAL)

TIP
If when preparing your tomato sauce it tastes too sharp, mix in a teaspoon or two of sugar.

Meatballs are great on their own or in a rich tomato sauce and a few slices of bread, but I've made an alternative and used tagliatelle pasta.

METHOD

1. Preheat your oven to 200°C
2. Fill up a kettle and bring to the boil.
3. Chop your garlic, onion and spinach into small pieces and place in a large bowl, mix together with the mince beef and season with salt, basil, pepper and a bit of oil.
4. With clean hands, knead together all the ingredients. Grab small pieces of your mixture and roll into balls, squishing together as you roll. Place these on a baking tray. You should end up with 14 or so meatballs.
5. Place these in the center of the oven for 10 – 15 minutes.
6. In a large pan pour your chopped tomatoes and add in a few pieces of sun-dried tomatoes, if using. Season with salt and oregano and place over a medium – low heat.
7. In a separate pan, boil 2 – 3 handfuls of pasta and season with a pinch of salt and a tablespoon of oil so the pasta doesn't stick together.
8. Once the meatballs in the oven are ready, add *(with juices optional)* to your tomato sauce pan. Stir and allow to sit until your pasta is ready, so flavours can mix together nicely. Simmer, to reduce any excess juices from the sauce to avoid it being too runny.
9. Once your pasta is ready drain and serve.

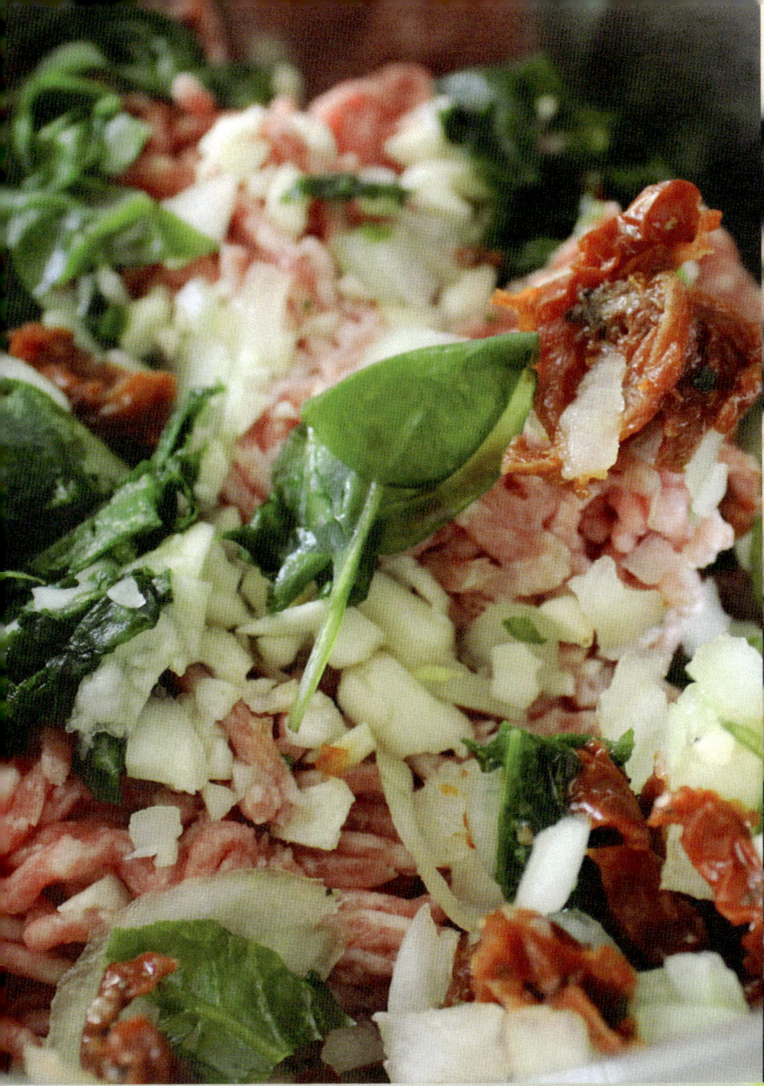
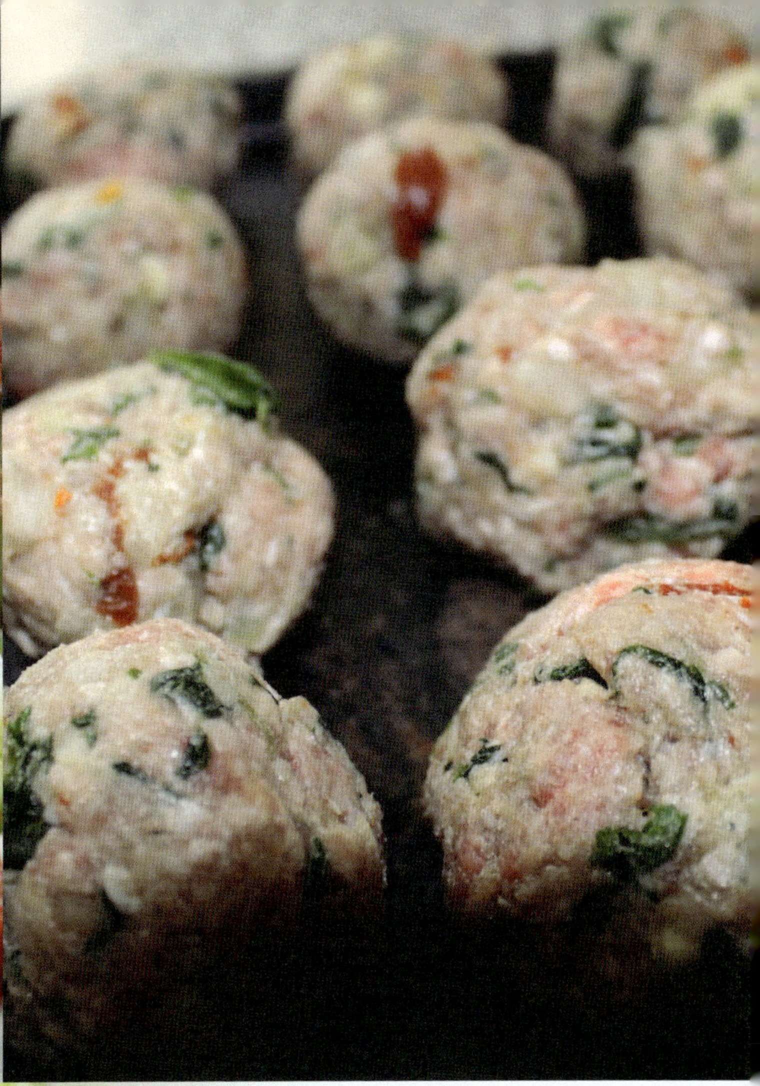
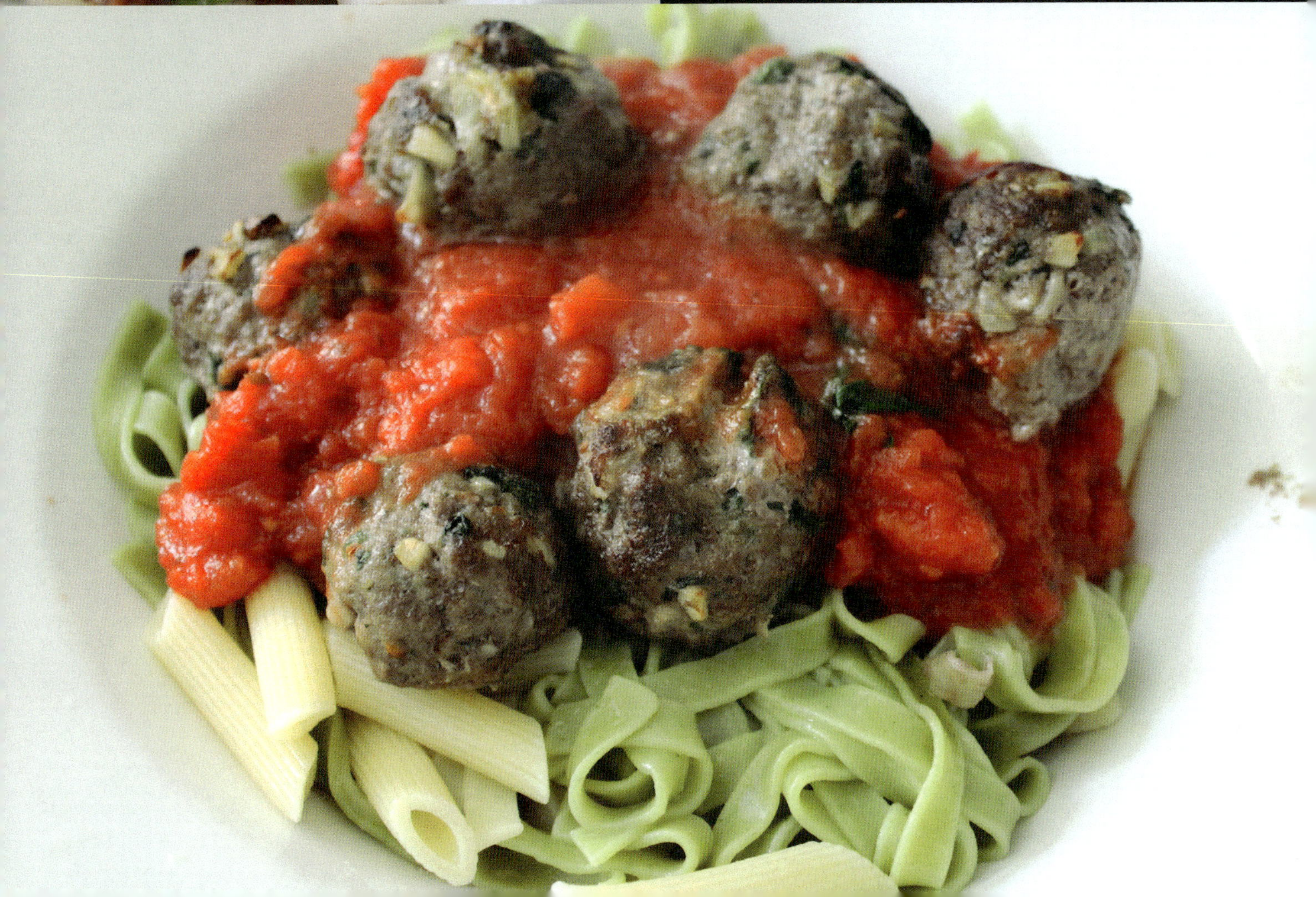

MAMA'S CHORIZO, SPINACH, TOMATO AND CHEESE STUFFED AUBERGINES

SERVES 1

INGREDIENTS

- 1 LARGE AUBERGINE
- OLIVE OIL
- GROUND BLACK PEPPER
- 65 G DICED CHORIZO
- 1 LARGE TOMATO
- SPINACH LEAVES *(HANDFUL)*
- 50 G CHEDDAR CHEESE
- SALT

METHOD

1. Preheat the oven to 200°C.

2. Cut your aubergine in half lengthwise and scoop some of the flesh out of the middle of the aubergine halves. Chop the flesh and put to one side.

3. Place the aubergine halves onto a baking tray and season with salt and ground black pepper, pour some oil over and place in the oven for 8-10 minutes.

4. Whilst that is in the oven, fry the chorizo for a couple minutes and add in the chopped aubergines, tomato and spinach and cook for 2 to 3 minutes with olive oil.

5. Remove the aubergines from the oven and fill the halves with your mixture, grate some cheese and sprinkle over. Place back in the oven for 5 – 8 minutes until soft.

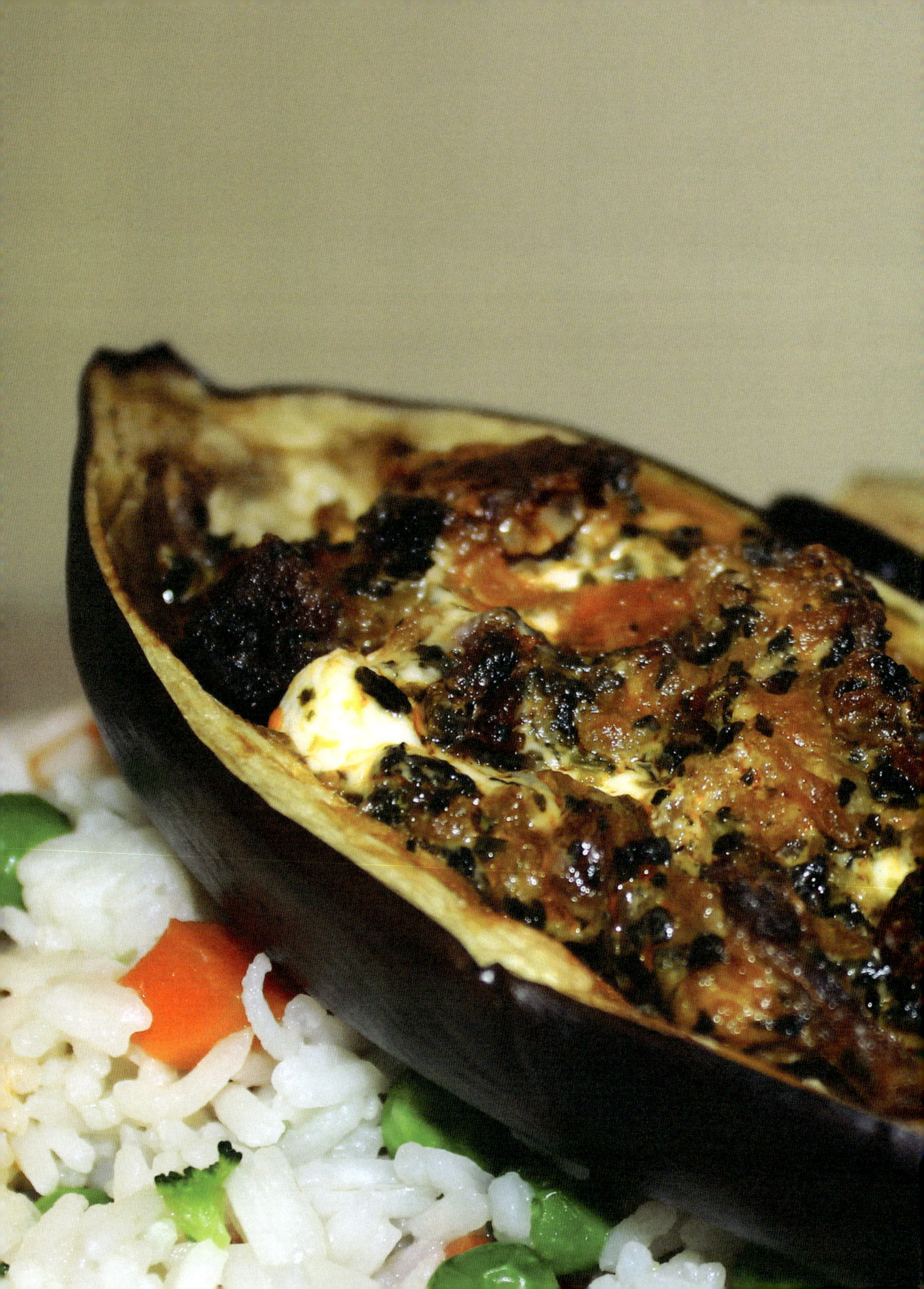

MAMA'S PORK, CHORIZO AND BROCCOLI TART

SERVES 2

INGREDIENTS

- 300 G PORK LOIN STEAKS
- 200 G BROCCOLI
- 65 G CHORIZO
- PUFF PASTRY
- 1 ONION
- 2 GARLIC CLOVES
- 400 G CHOPPED TOMATOES
- SALT
- FRESH BASIL LEAVES

Why not try something different with your puff pastry and fill it with pork, chorizo and broccoli? A sort of Spanish inspired Vol-au-Vent.

METHOD

1. Begin by chopping and boiling the broccoli in a pan and preheating your oven to 200°C.

2. Chop the garlic and onions very finely and fry in a bit of oil.

3. Once you see that the onion and garlic have softened, dice the chorizo and pork and fry together.

4. When cooked, add in the chopped tomatoes and season with salt and basil. By now the broccoli should have been boiled and ready to drain, add this to your mix.

5. Stir and leave on a low heat for the flavours to mix together for a couple of minutes.

6. Remove your mixture from the heat and create a cup shaped pouch with your puff pastry. Fill with you mixture.

7. Place in the centre of the oven and leave for 20 minutes or until you see the pastries are ready, risen and golden but not burning.

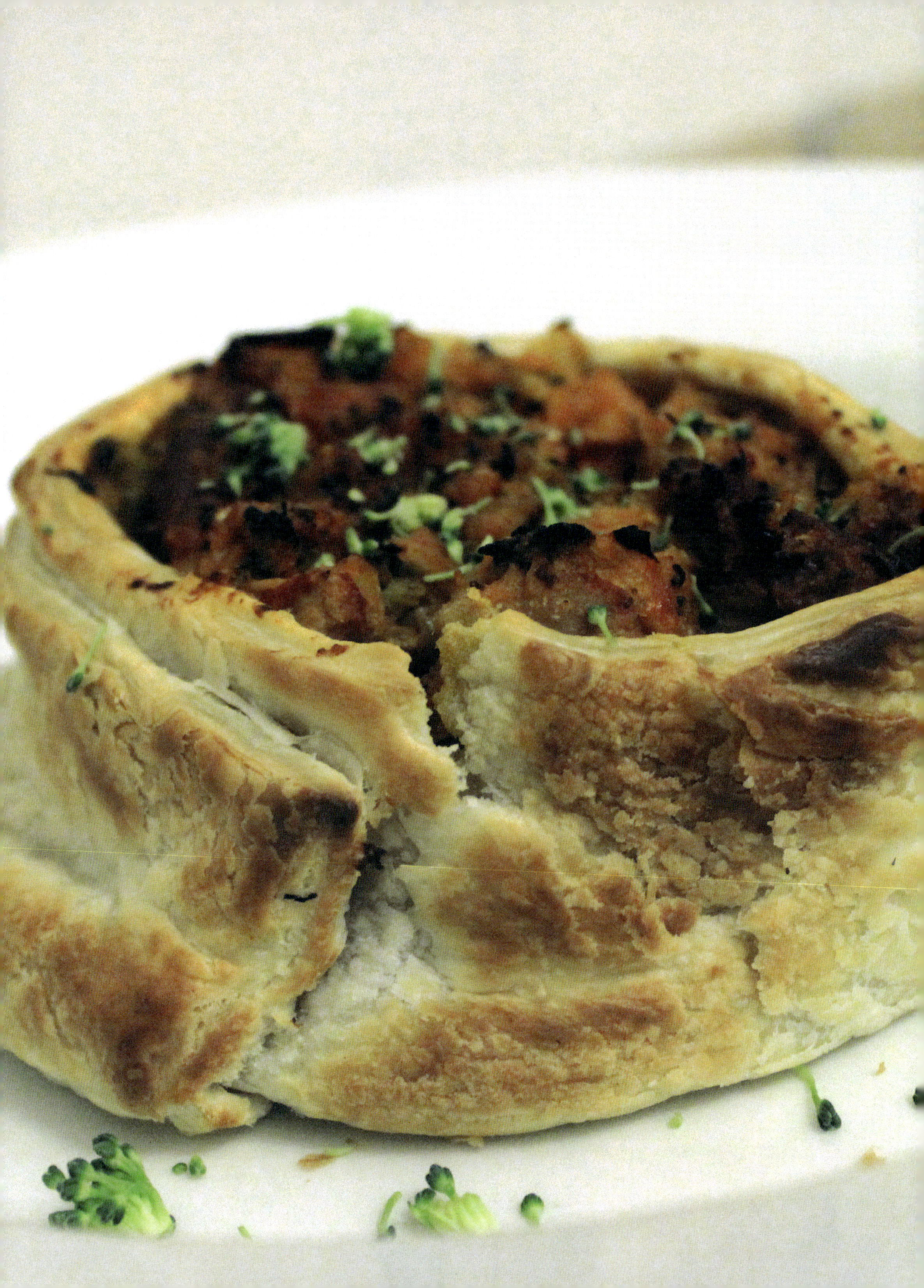

MAMA'S ROLITOS
BEEF OLIVES

SERVES 2

INGREDIENTS

- 5 THIN SLICES BEEF
- 1 ROASTED RED PEPPER
- 2 SLICES OF HAM
- 2 BOILED EGGS
- GREEN OR BLACK PITTED OLIVES
- 3 MEDIUM POTATOES
- 1 TBSP BUTTER
- SPLASH MILK

SAUCE

- 100 G ALMONDS
- PARSLEY
- BREADCRUMBS (HANDFUL)
- 400 G CHOPPED TOMATOES
- 3 CLOVES OF GARLIC
- 1 LARGE ONION
- GLASS OF WHITE WINE
- OIL
- SALT
- PEPPER
- WATER

TIP
Use a cocktail stick to keep your rolled up beef and stuffing in one piece.

Rolitos are a Gibraltarian treasure. They can be tricky to prepare, but believe them when they say, everything good is worth waiting for.

METHOD

1. Boil your eggs and finely dice, along with your peppers, ham and olives.

2. Once everything is finely chopped, mix it together in a large bowl and begin to roll your beef. Place a spoon or two of the stuffing, depending on the size of the slice of beef, along the middle and roll. Use a cocktail stick at each end to keep it from unrolling.

3. Leave your beef to one side and begin with the sauce. Finely chop your garlic and onion and fry until the onion is translucent. When ready, add the chopped tomatoes and the rest of the ingredients.

4. Add your beef to the pan and leave for 15 - 20 minutes until everything is cooked through. If you see the sauce is thickening too much, add water until you get a consistency you are happy with.

5. Whilst the rolitos are stewing, wash and dice your potatoes and boil until soft, then mash with butter and milk.

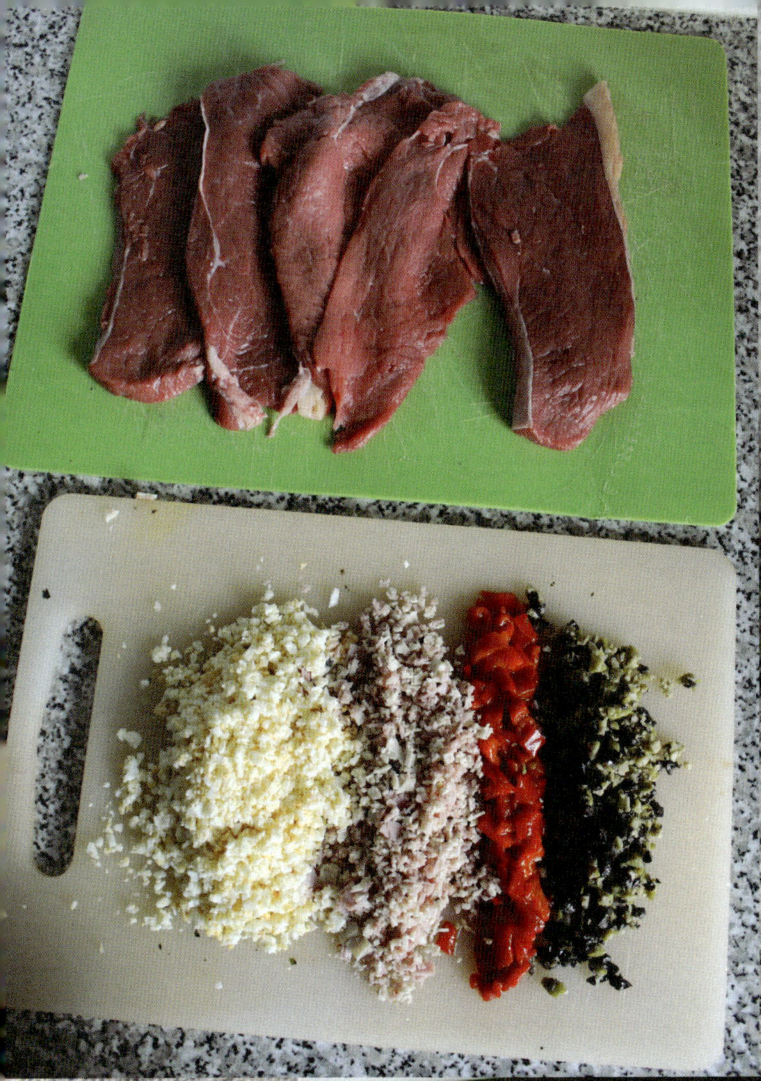
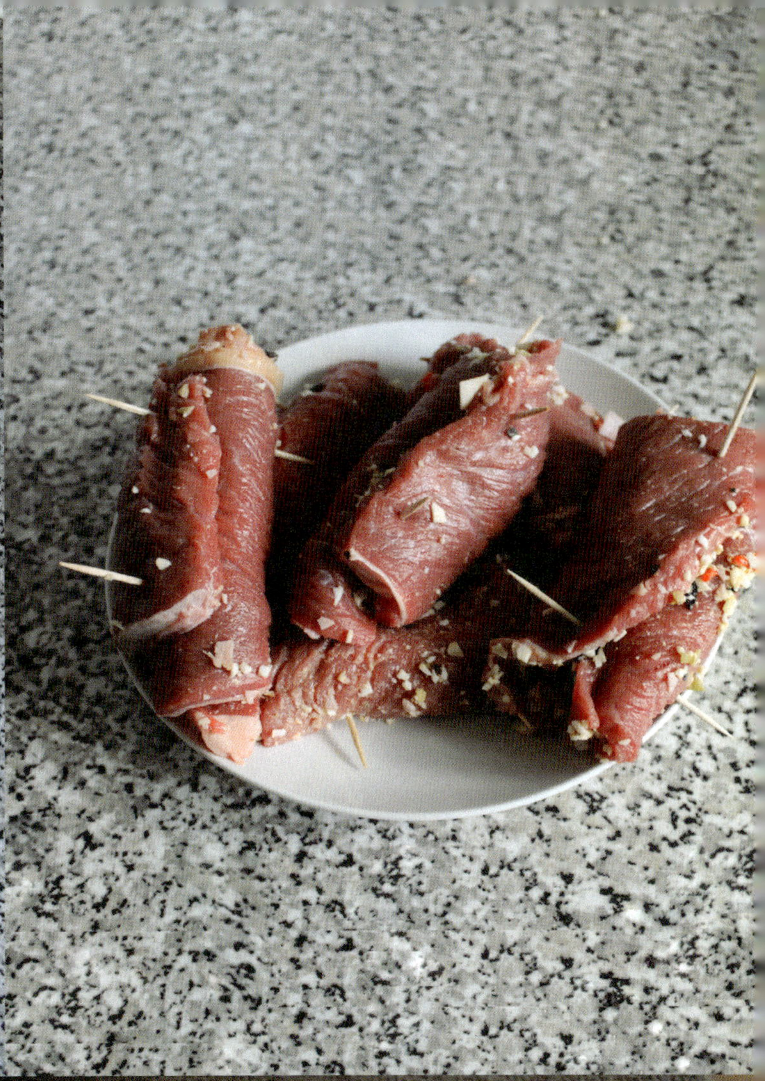
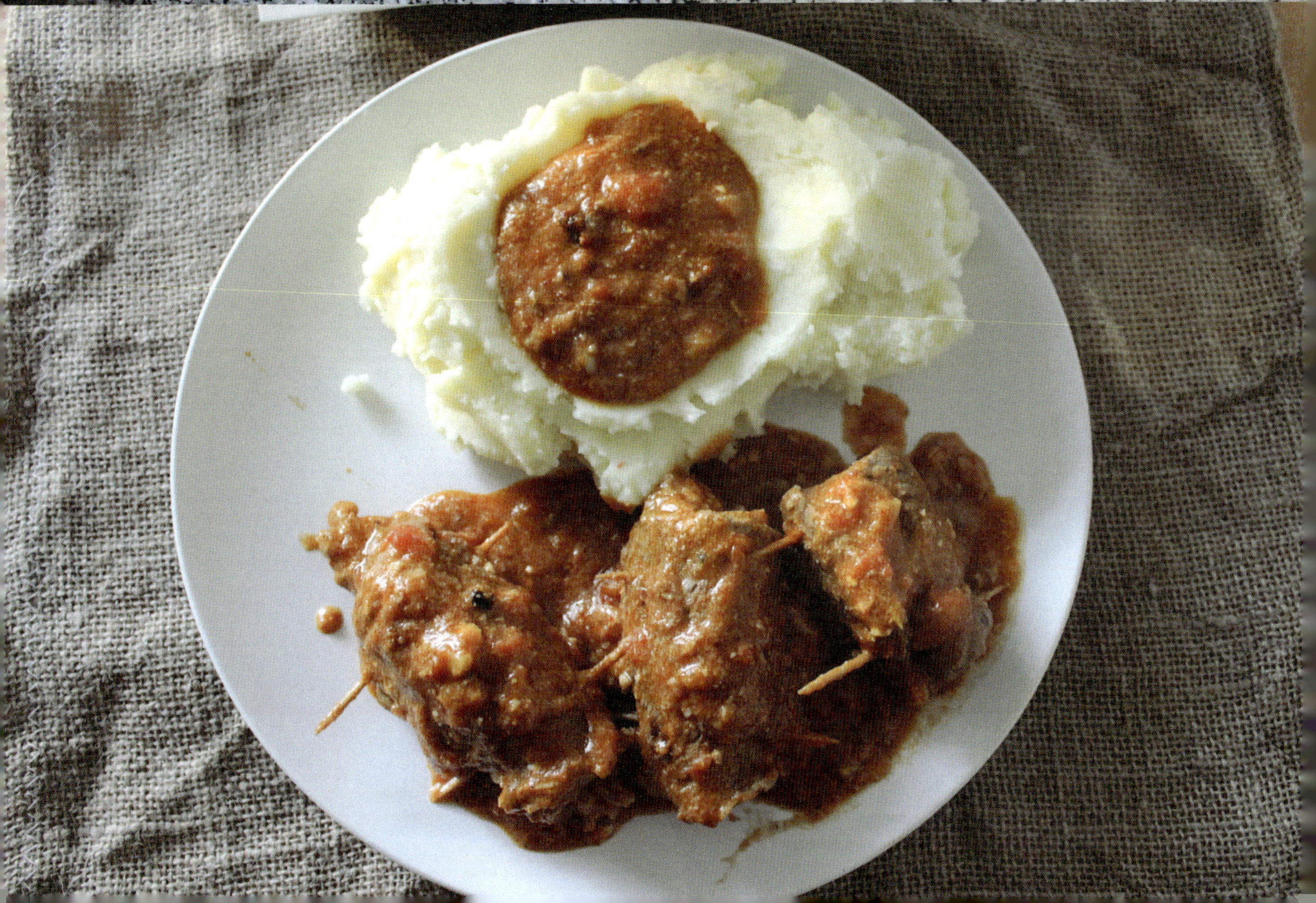

MAMA'S HUEVOS A LA FLAMENCA

SERVES 1

INGREDIENTS

- 1 EGG
- 227 G TIN CHOPPED TOMATOES *(TOMATE TRITURADO)*
- 145 G PEAS
- 1 POTATO
- 65 G CHORIZO CHUNKS
- 1/2 ONION
- 2 GARLIC CLOVES
- OLIVE OIL

A very traditional Spanish dish, this recipe differs throughout Spain and no doubt Gibraltar may have its own version inspired by the multitude of cultures and generations.

METHOD

1. Dice the potatoes into smaller pieces and fry in oil until soft.

2. As the potatoes are frying, chop the onions and garlic into small pieces. Fry a separate pan, until soft and add in the chopped tomatoes; cook together until simmering *(taste the tomato sauce, if it's too sharp add a teaspoon of sugar.)* Add in the peas and chorizo.

3. Once the chips are all ready, mix together with the tomato sauce and other ingredients.

4. Pour everything into a terracotta bowl.

5. Crack 1 egg in the centre of the dish and place in the oven at 180°C until the egg is cooked.

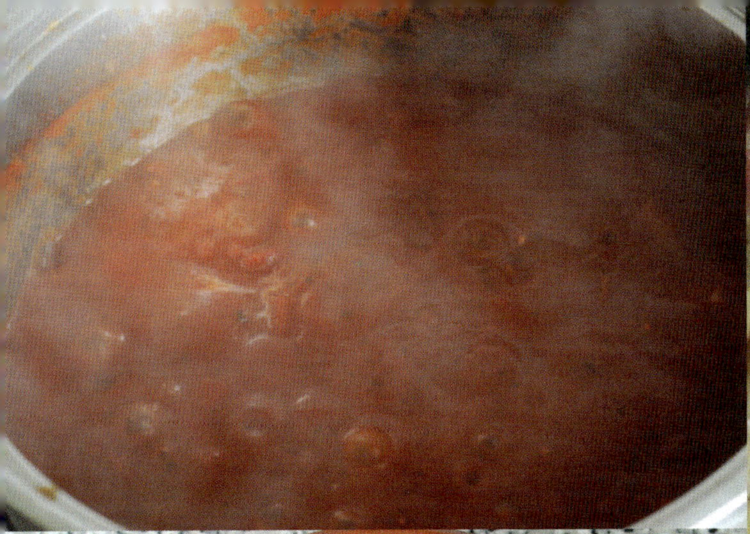
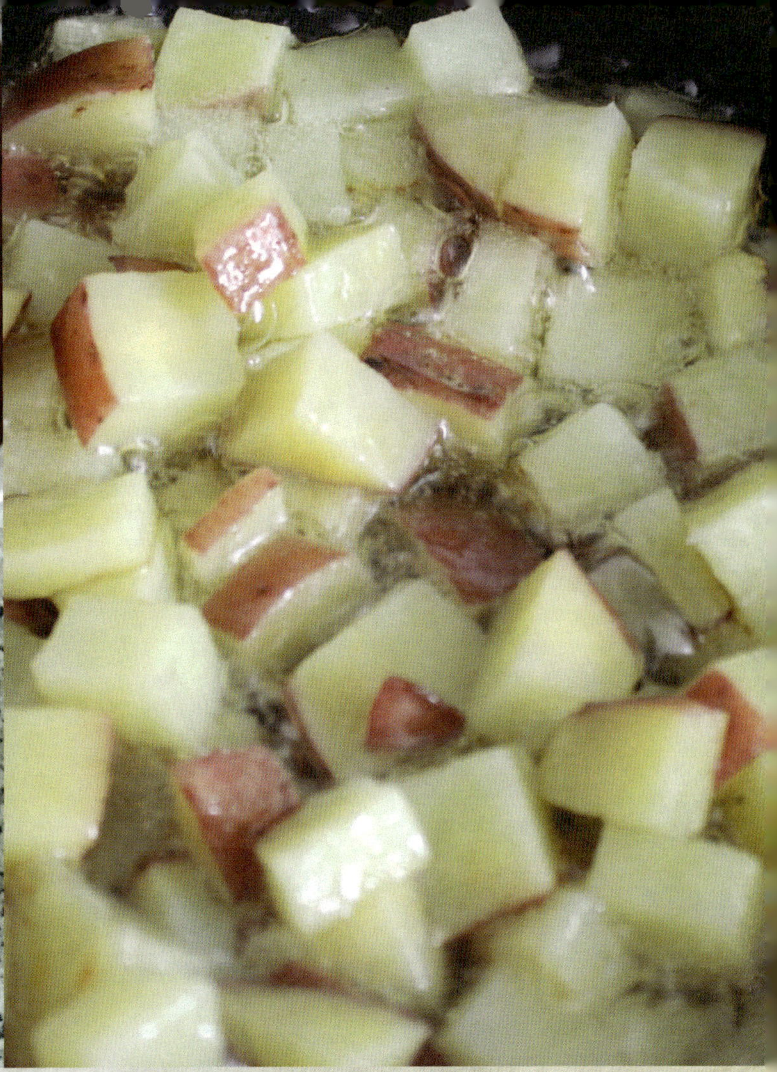
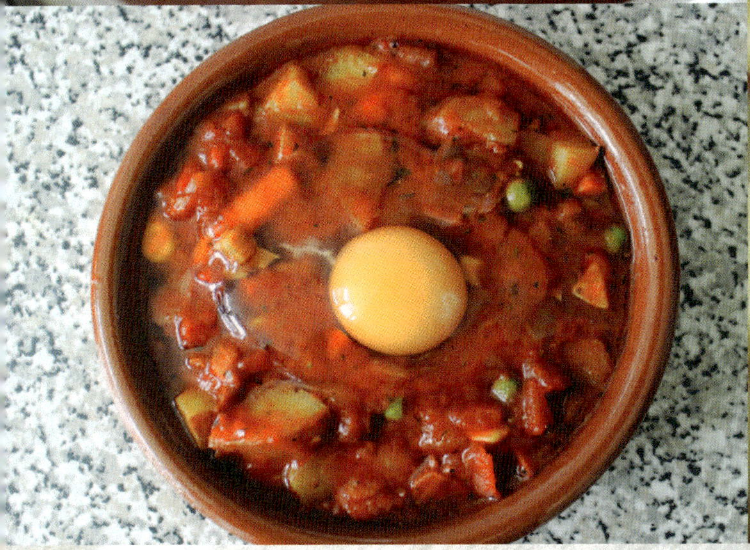
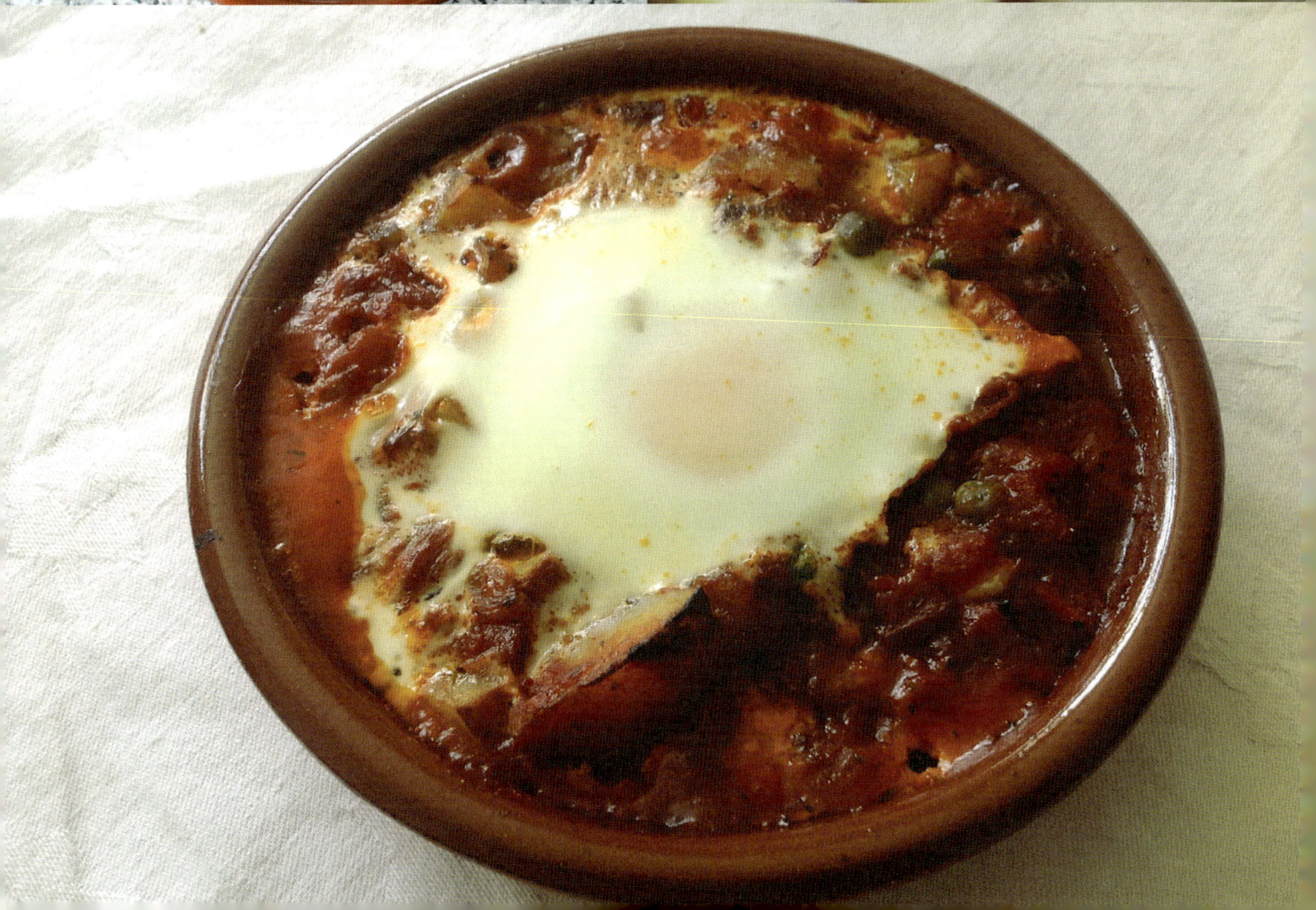

MAMA'S PEPPERONI AND SUN-DRIED TOMATO BURGERS

SERVES 2

INGREDIENTS

- 250 G MINCED BEEF
- 4 SUN-DRIED TOMATOES
- 1/2 ONION
- 1 GARLIC CLOVE
- 70 G PEPPERONI SLICES
- BURGER BUNS
- GRATED CHEESE
- FLOUR
- WATER
- BABY LEAF SALAD

Not your ordinary burger, this is full of flavour with a little peppery spice from the chopped up pepperoni slices. Finish it off with a layer of soft melted cheese and you have a winner.

METHOD

1. Chop all your ingredients and mix them in a large bowl, except for the burger buns and mixed salad leaves.

2. Squeeze and mix together all of the ingredients with your hands. Add a little flour and water to combine everything together and season with salt and pepper.

3. Grab a handful of your mixture and flatten together to produce a burger like shape. Place your burger to one side, you should be able to create two large burgers or a few smaller ones.

4. Once you have your burger shapes ready, simply fry on a medium heat or place on a baking tray and grill.

5. Serve in your buns with grated cheese and salad leaves.

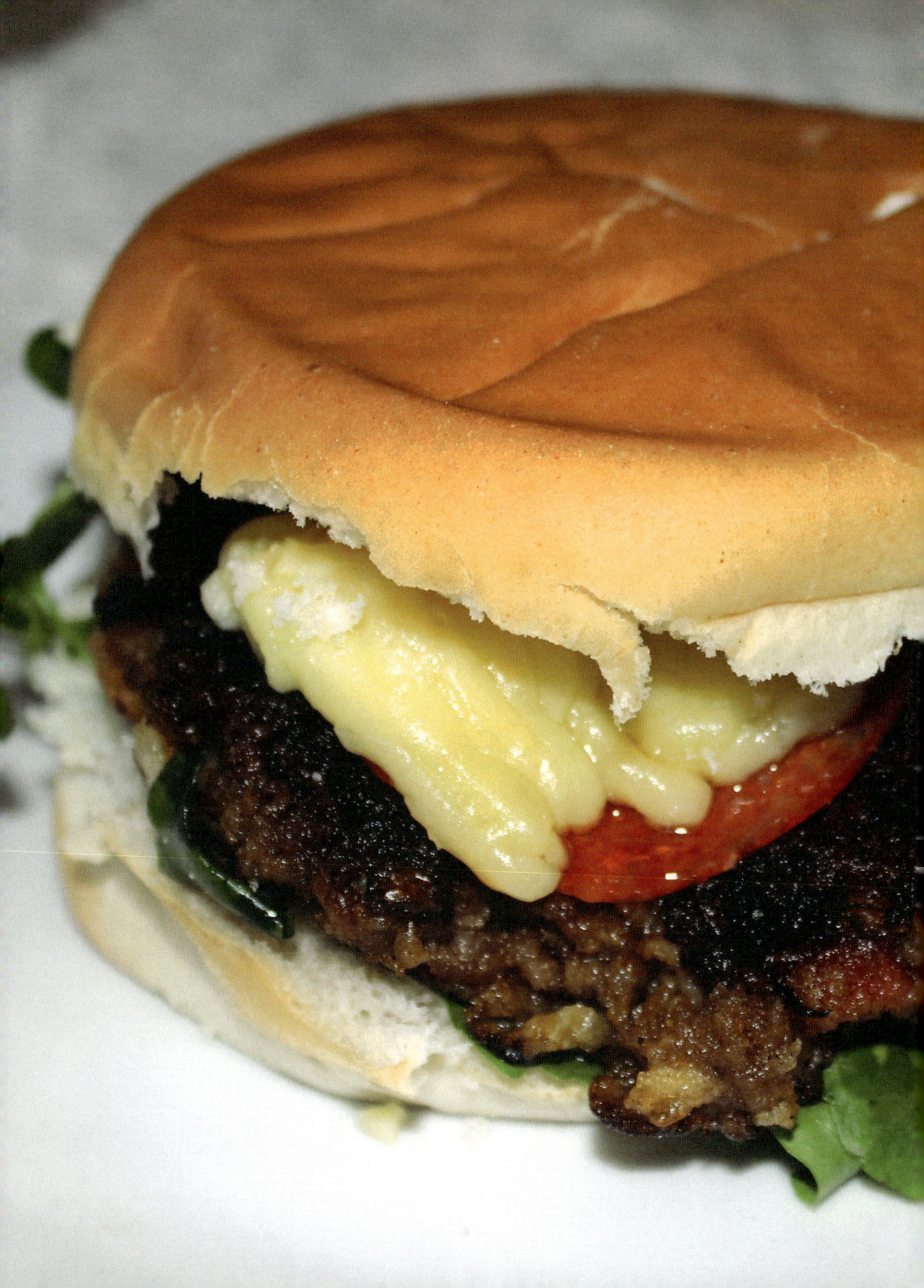

MAMA'S CANNELLONI RELLENOS

STUFFED CANNELLONI

SERVES 4

INGREDIENTS

- 100 G MORTADELLA
- 100 G HAM
- 100 G CHEDDAR CHEESE
- 2 EGGS
  (HARD BOILED)
- 180 G OLIVES
- 400 G CHOPPED TOMATOES
  (TOMATE TITURADO)
- 1/2 LARGE ONION OR 1 SMALL ONE
- OIL
- 250 G CANNELLONI PASTA

There's nothing better than Mama's Cannelloni, the sweet flavour of the chopped tomatoes and minced up meat and olives make them perfect any day.

METHOD

1. Cut the ham, eggs, mortadella and olives and blend together until it forms a paste; use this to fill the pasta.

2. Chop the onion and fry; once soft mix with the tomatoes adding some herbs if you wish.

3. Pour some tomato sauce on the bottom of the oven dish and place the now stuffed pasta on top. Finish off by pouring the rest of the tomato sauce over everything. Cover with foil and place in the oven at 225°C – 250°C for 30 minutes.

4. Once the time has passed uncover the dish, grate some cheese over the top and return to the oven for a further 10 minutes or until golden.

SUGGESTION

Perfect recipe to make with all that left over Christmas food. Simply mince everything together and continue the recipe as normal.

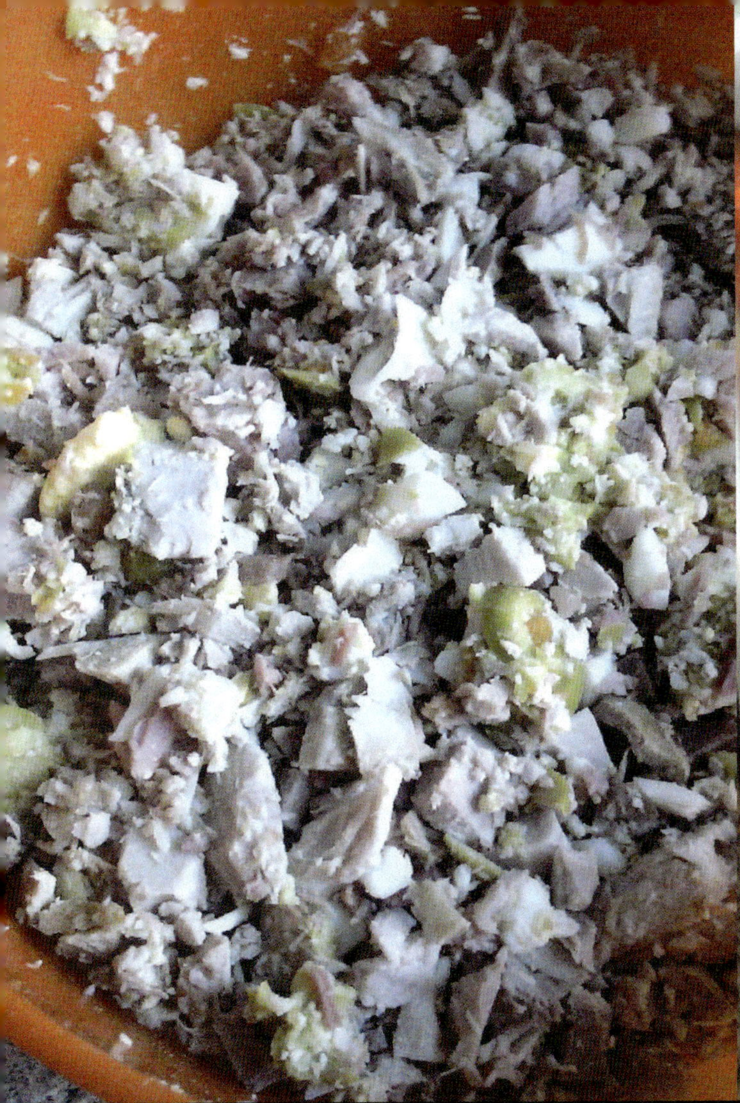
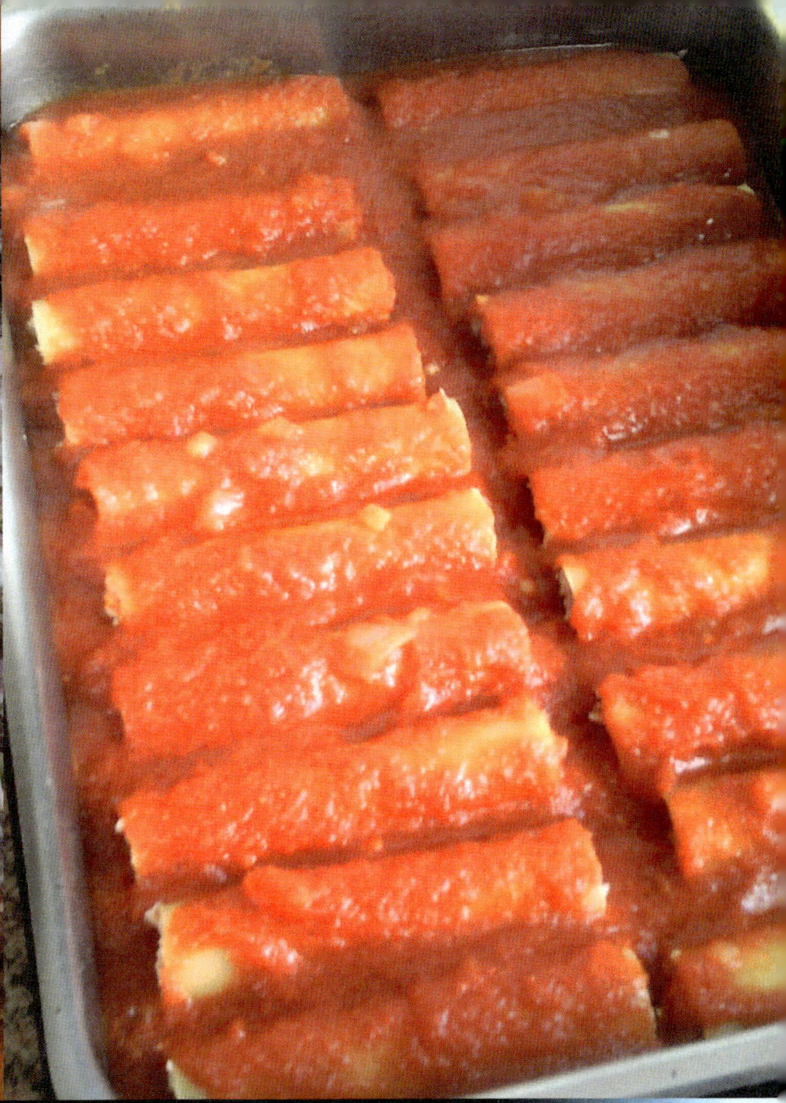
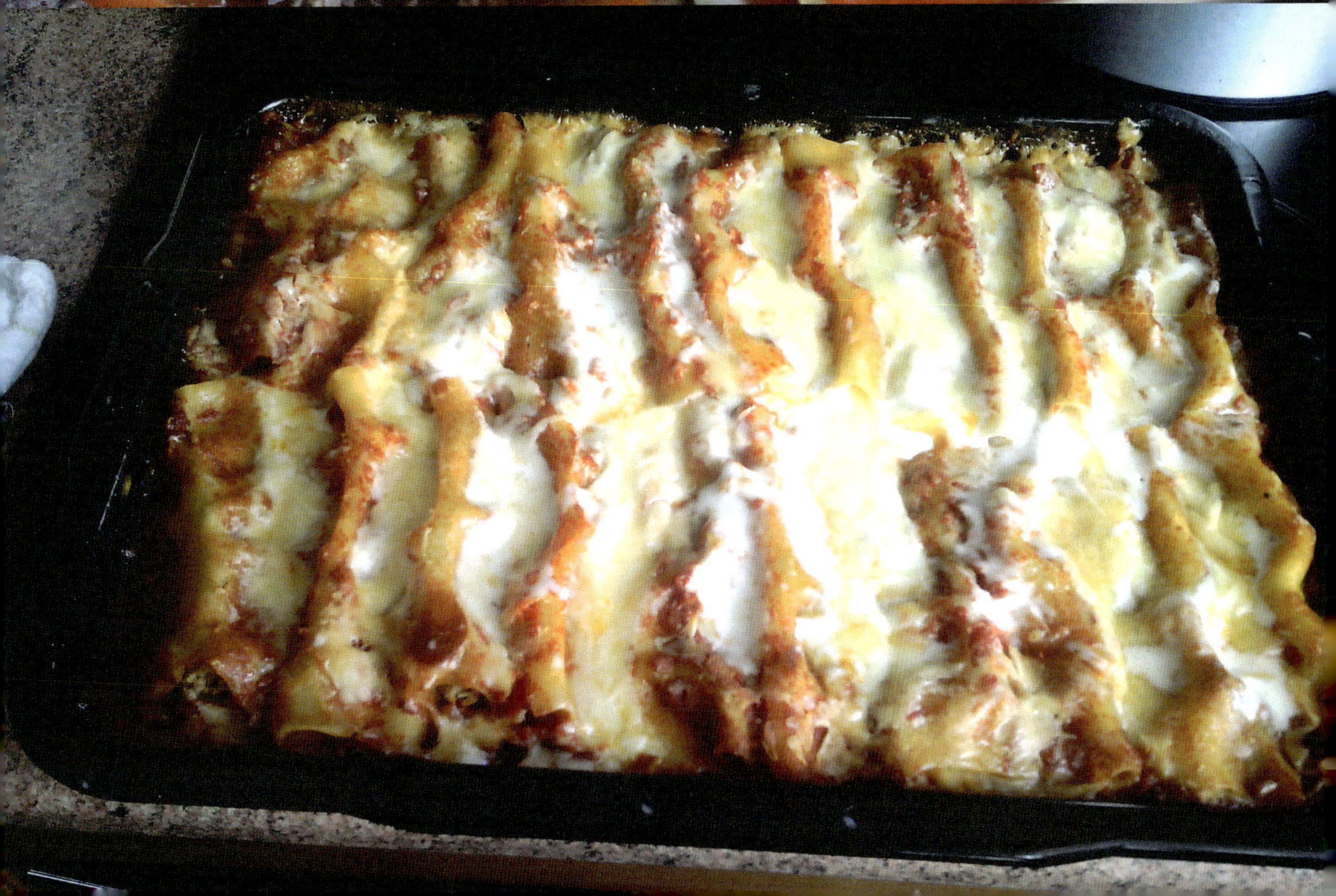

FISH

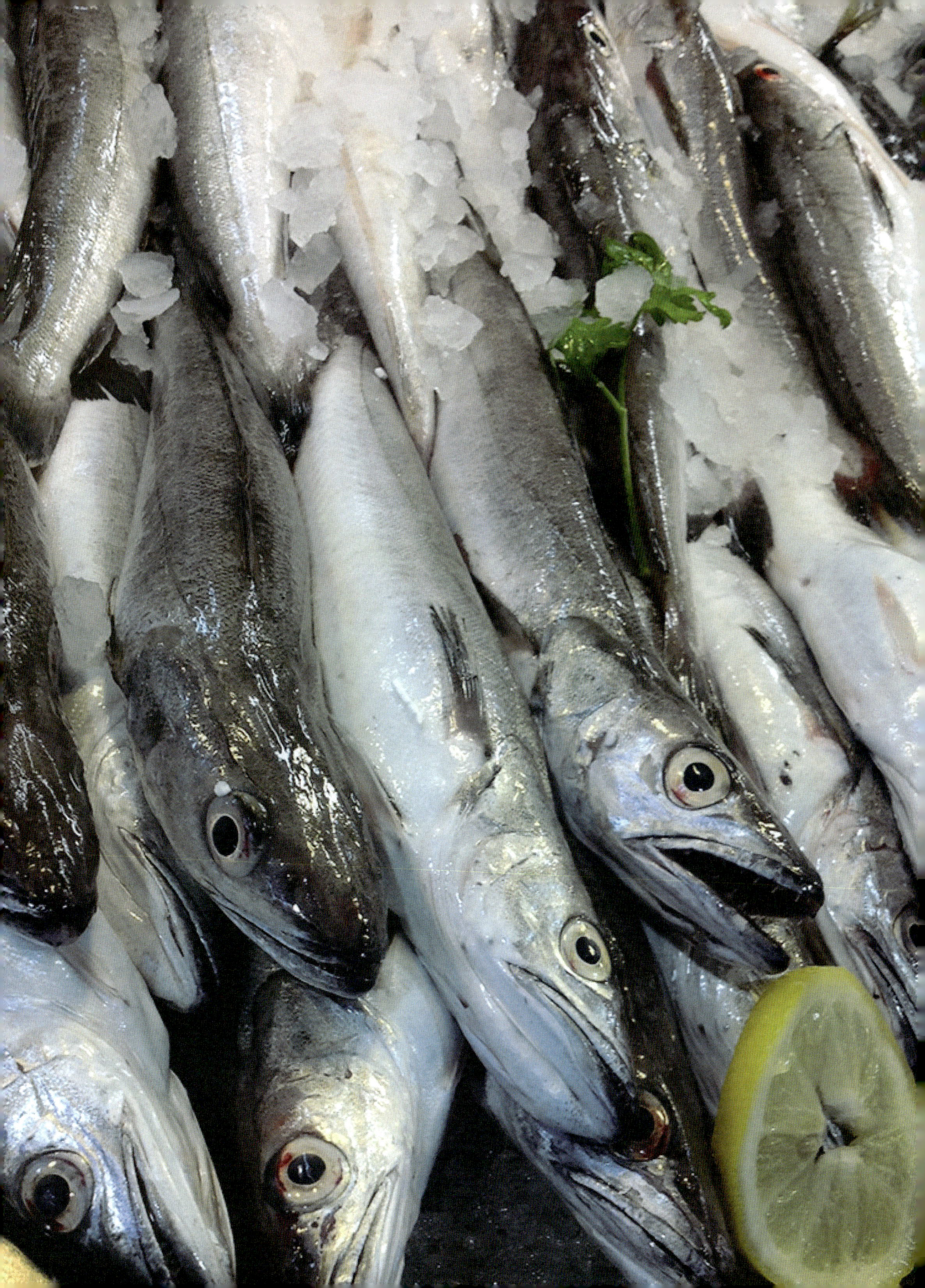

MUM'S PRAWN STUFFED SQUID AND RICE

SERVES 3

INGREDIENTS

- 2 SQUID / CALAMARES (PER PERSON)

SAUCE

- OLIVE OIL
- 1 GREEN PEPPER
- 1 ONION
- 2 - 3 GARLIC CLOVES
- 4 FRESH TOMATOES
- 1 BAY LEAF
- 1 CHICKEN STOCK
- SAFFRON
- 1/2 GLASS WHITE WINE

STUFFING

- 500 G KING PRAWNS / LANGOSTINOS
- 3 GARLIC CLOVES
- CHILLI FLAKES
- OREGANO

Fish for everyone! Gibraltar is surrounded by water so it's no surprise each family may have their own way of cooking seafood, but here's a dish I thoroughly enjoy.

METHOD

Clean your squid and prawns thoroughly.

1. Begin my making the base of your sauce *(refrito)*. Chop your ingredients and pour everything except for the tomatoes into a hot pan with a tablespoon of olive oil and cook until soft, once that's ready add in your tomatoes and continue to cook and stir until the tomatoes are soft and pureed.

2. When your **refrito** is ready place it to one side and move on to your squid and prawns.

3. For the stuffing, fry the garlic in a little olive oil and add your prawns and the squid tentacles, leaving the clean and hollow body of the squid to one side.

4. Add the chilli, oregano, season with salt and pepper and fry until golden.

5. Once ready, stuff the hollow squid with your cooked stuffing ingredients and hold together with a cocktail stick.

6. To the **refrito,** add the wine, stock cube, diluted with boiling water, salt, pepper, saffron and add your stuffed squid, place on a medium heat for 30 minutes or until soft and add more water if necessary.

7. Once the squid is soft, add a handful of rice per person and add more water, cook until the rice is soft and ready.

BY LORRAINE LAGUEA

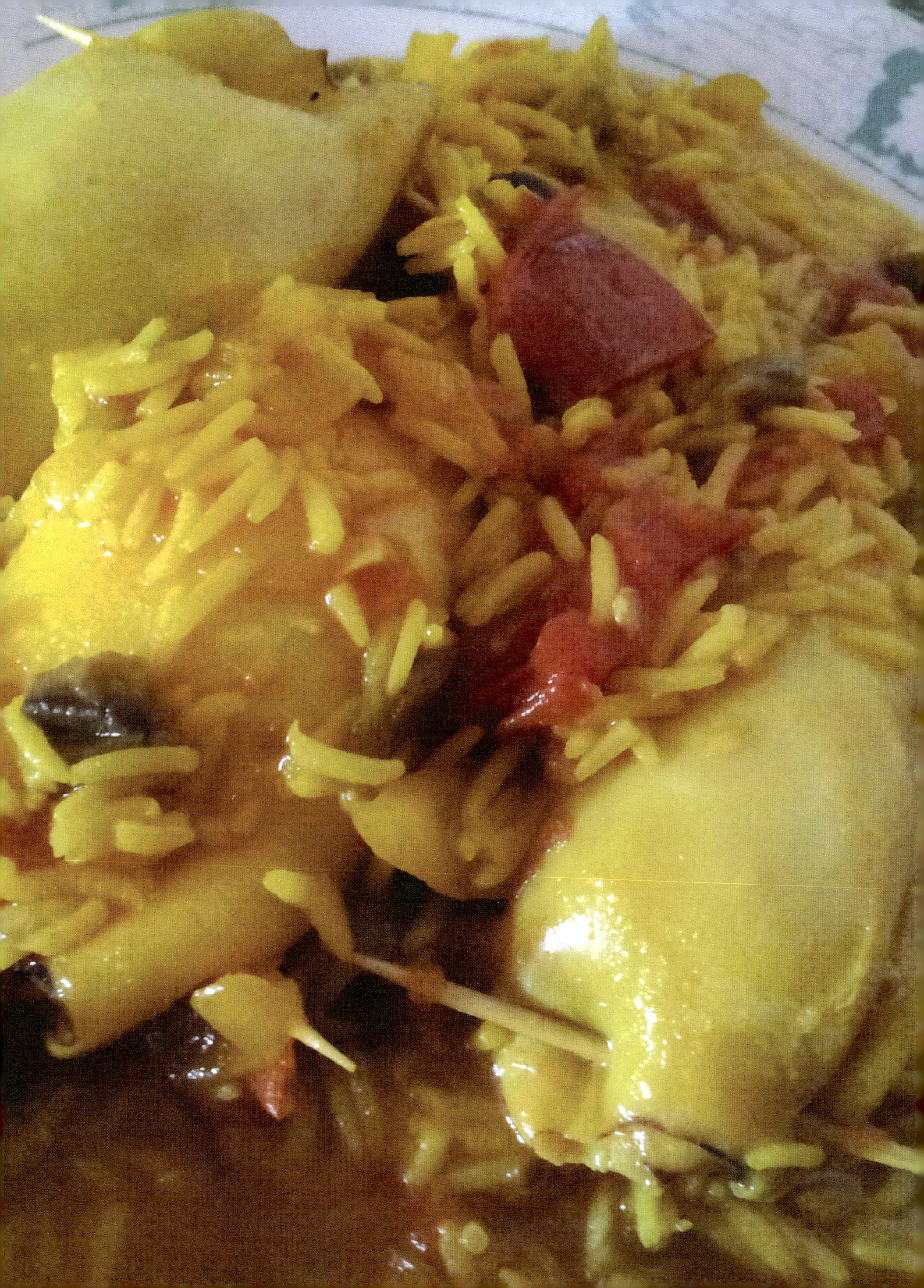

MAMA'S PARGO AL HORNO
OVEN BAKED RED BREAM

SERVES 2

INGREDIENTS

- 1.5 KG FISH
- 3 MEDIUM POTATOES
- 1 LARGE ONION
- 2 MEDIUM GREEN PEPPERS
- 4 LARGE TOMATOES
- 2 GARLIC CLOVES
- PARSLEY
- OIL
- WHITE WINE
- 1 LARGE LEMON

METHOD

1. Cut the potatoes into thick slices and parboil. Gut and descale the fish.

2. Cut the vegetables into quite large pieces and in a large frying pan place a tablespoon of olive oil. Fry the garlic, onions, tomatoes and pepper until soft.

3. In an oven dish place the fish, with the potatoes around the fish and add the fried vegetables with salt, a splash of wine and sliced lemon.

4. Place in oven at 200°C until fish is cooked and golden.

MAMA'S FISH À LA MEUNIÈRE

SERVES 1

INGREDIENTS

- SALMON, SOLE FISH OR PLAICE
- PARSLEY
- SPLASH WHITE WINE
- BREADCRUMBS
- OLIVE OIL

The simplest fish recipes are usually the best and this one does not faulter. The breadcrumbs soak up the white wine and the juices blending everything together as the fish cooks gently in the oven.

METHOD

1. Preheat your oven to 180°C – 200 .

2. Gut the fish and remove the skin. *(you can always ask the fishmonger to do this if you prefer.)*

3. Grab an oven dish, pour a little oil in the dish and place your fish on top, season with salt and pepper, chopped parsley, oil drizzled over and a little white wine.

4. Once you have done that lightly cover your whole fish with breadcrumbs, place in the centre of the oven for 15 to 20 minutes.

5. When the breadcrumbs are golden your fish is ready to eat.

   Serve with a side of boiled white rice if desired.

MAMA'S DORADA A LA SAL
SALTED SEA BREAM

SERVES 1

INGREDIENTS

- SEA BREAM
  (OR ANY WHOLE FISH)
- COARSE ROCK SALT
- FRESH PARSLEY BUNCH.

Although fish is eaten throughout the year, there is something special about eating it in the summer and with BBQ season in full swing one recipe to try is dorada a la sal. The thick layer of salt creates a coating that keeps the fish juicy and full of flavour. Make sure to ask your fishmonger to clean out the fish thoroughly.

METHOD

1. Stuff your fish with a few bunches of fresh parsley. Cover your fish *(I used sea bream)* in a thick layer of salt on both sides.

2. Wrap your fish in foil and place under the grill or on a BBQ for 20 – 30 minutes, rotating every so often.

3. When ready, remove the foil and separate the salt from the fish; it should peal off as a solid layer. Open your fish in half and enjoy.

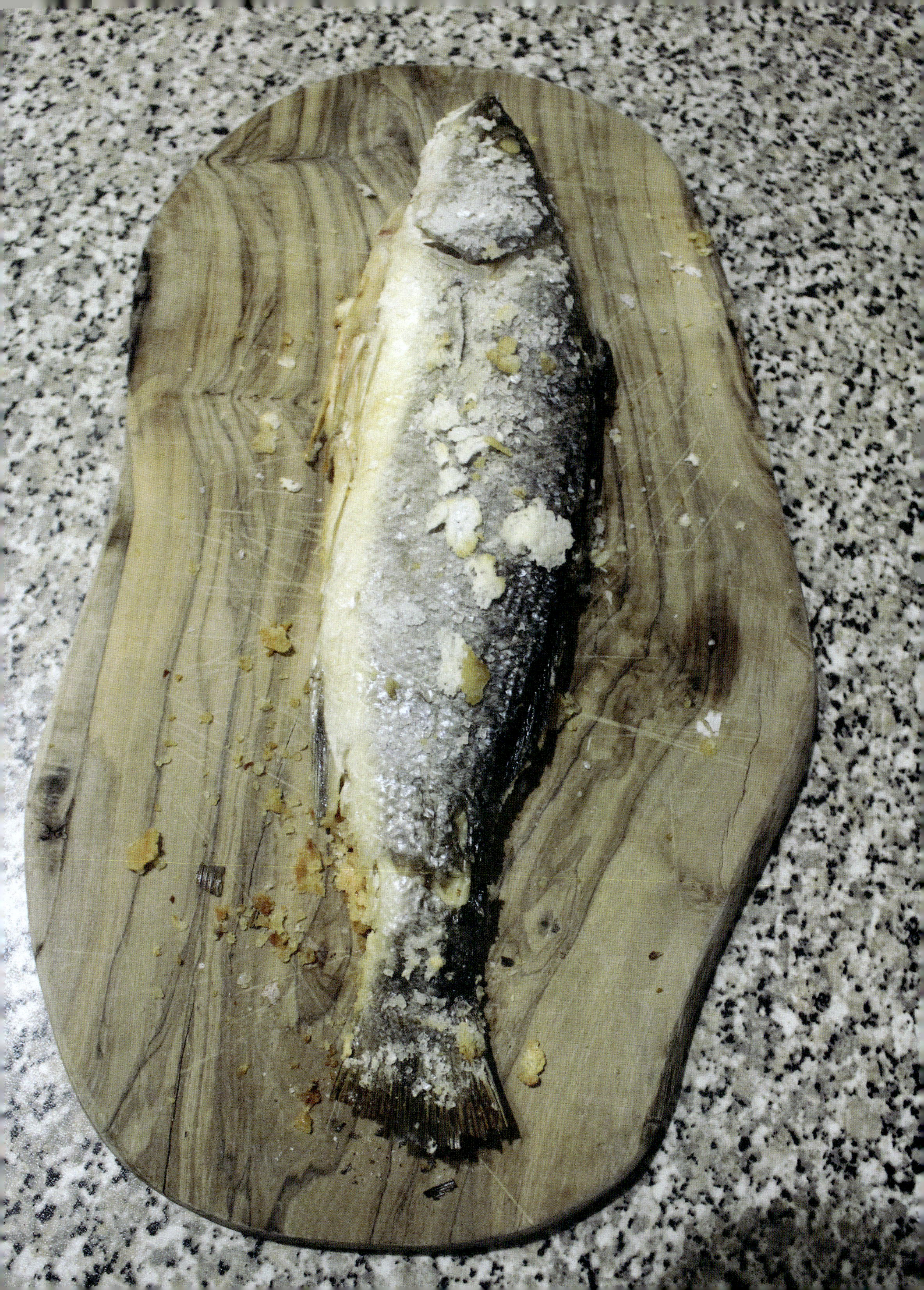

MAMA'S JIBIA GUISADA
GRANNY'S CUTTLEFISH STEW

SERVES 2

INGREDIENTS

- 1 KG JIBIA *(CUTTLEFISH)*
- 1 GARLIC CLOVE
- 1 LARGE ONION
- 5 - 6 TOMATOES
- 1 BAY LEAF
- SAFFRON
- SALT
- PEPPER
- 4 - 5 POTATOES
- 145 G PEAS

Growing up, I have always loved this dish, the soft cuttlefish makes it easy to eat and the fresh taste of the tomato and vegetables just makes having part of your five a day that much more enjoyable. You may want to keep a slice of bread close by...

METHOD

1. Make a *refrito* with the tomato, onion and garlic by chopping them up into small pieces and frying slowly in a pan with some oil.

2. When that is ready chop your cuttlefish into small pieces and add into your mix with some saffron and a bay leaf and cover with water. Cover the pan and leave to cook, checking the water level, and stir every now and again. *(If you have a pressure cooker simply cook it for 5 minutes.)*

3. Dice your potatoes and once the cuttlefish is soft add potatoes and peas and cover once again with water. Season with salt and pepper and leave until potatoes are ready. Stir occasionally and add a bit of water if required, so as to keep everything from drying out.

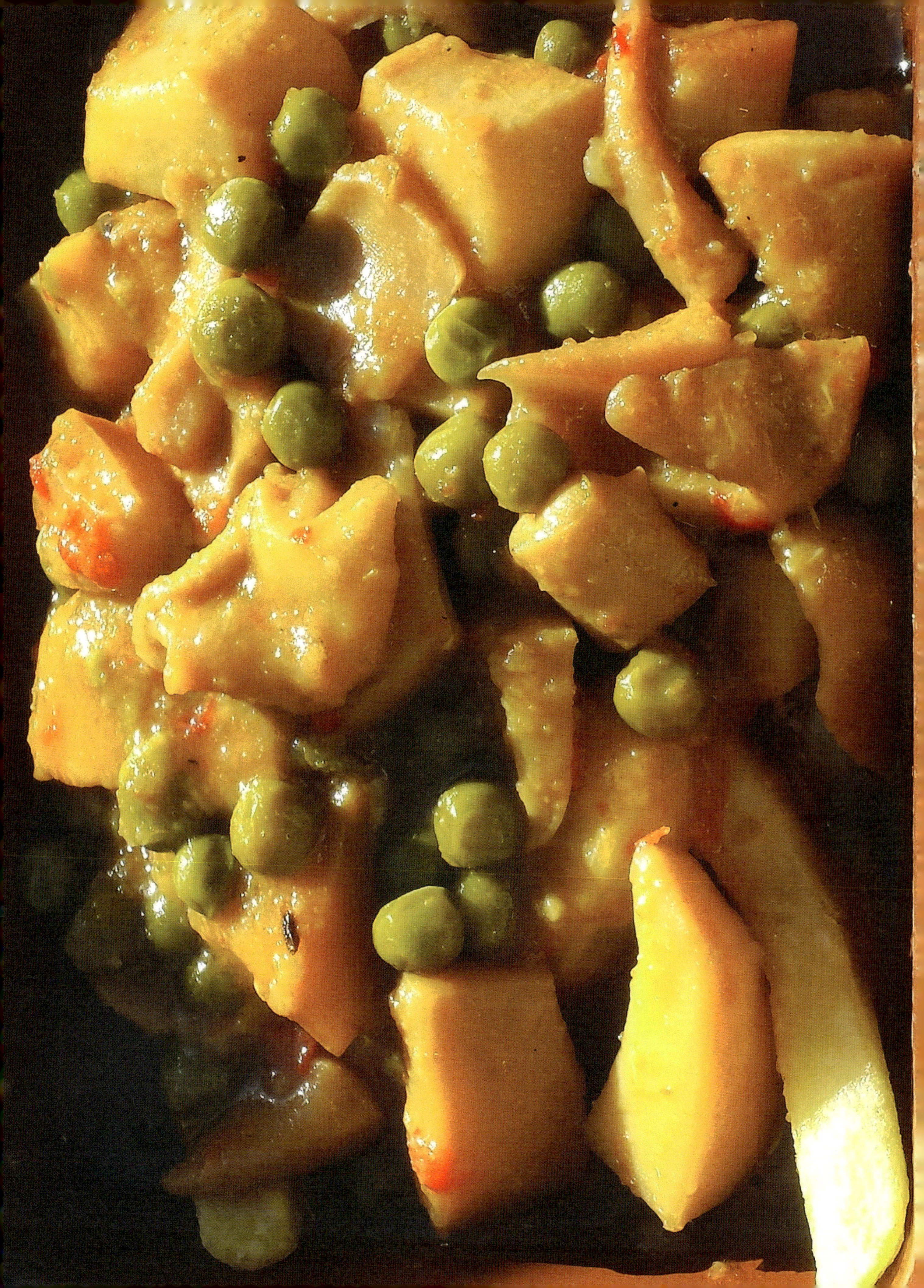

MAMA'S CALAMARES RELLENOS
STUFFED SQUID

SERVES 4

INGREDIENTS

- 2 LARGE CLEANED SQUID
- 3 EGGS
- 4 GARLIC CLOVES
- PARSLEY
- 250 G CHEESE
- BREADCRUMBS
- 6 LARGE TOMATOES
- 1 MEDIUM ONION

SUGGESTION
Do not overstuff your squid as they will shrink and the stuffing will expand.

We love stuffing! Mixing together all the tentacles with the stuffing and slow roasting the squid with the incredibly delicious nutty sauce (PAGE 99) makes this dish irresistibly mouthwatering.

METHOD

1. Preheat oven to 200°C

2. Prepare stuffing by mixing the eggs, two finely chopped garlic cloves, finely chopped parsley, grated cheese and 2 handfuls of breadcrumbs. Dice the squid tentacles and mix together with the stuffing.

3. Turn your squid inside out and stuff, up to 3 1/4 of the squid. Seal the opening with a cocktail stick.

4. Place to one side and prepare your sauce *(refrito)*. Fry your garlic, onion and tomatoes until nice and tender and blend together.

5. Place the stuffed squid in an oven dish and pour the sauce over. Cover with foil and cook in the oven for at least 30 minutes.

6. Remove the foil and check the squid is tender. If your squid is soft leave in the oven for a further 5 minutes with no foil or until golden brown.

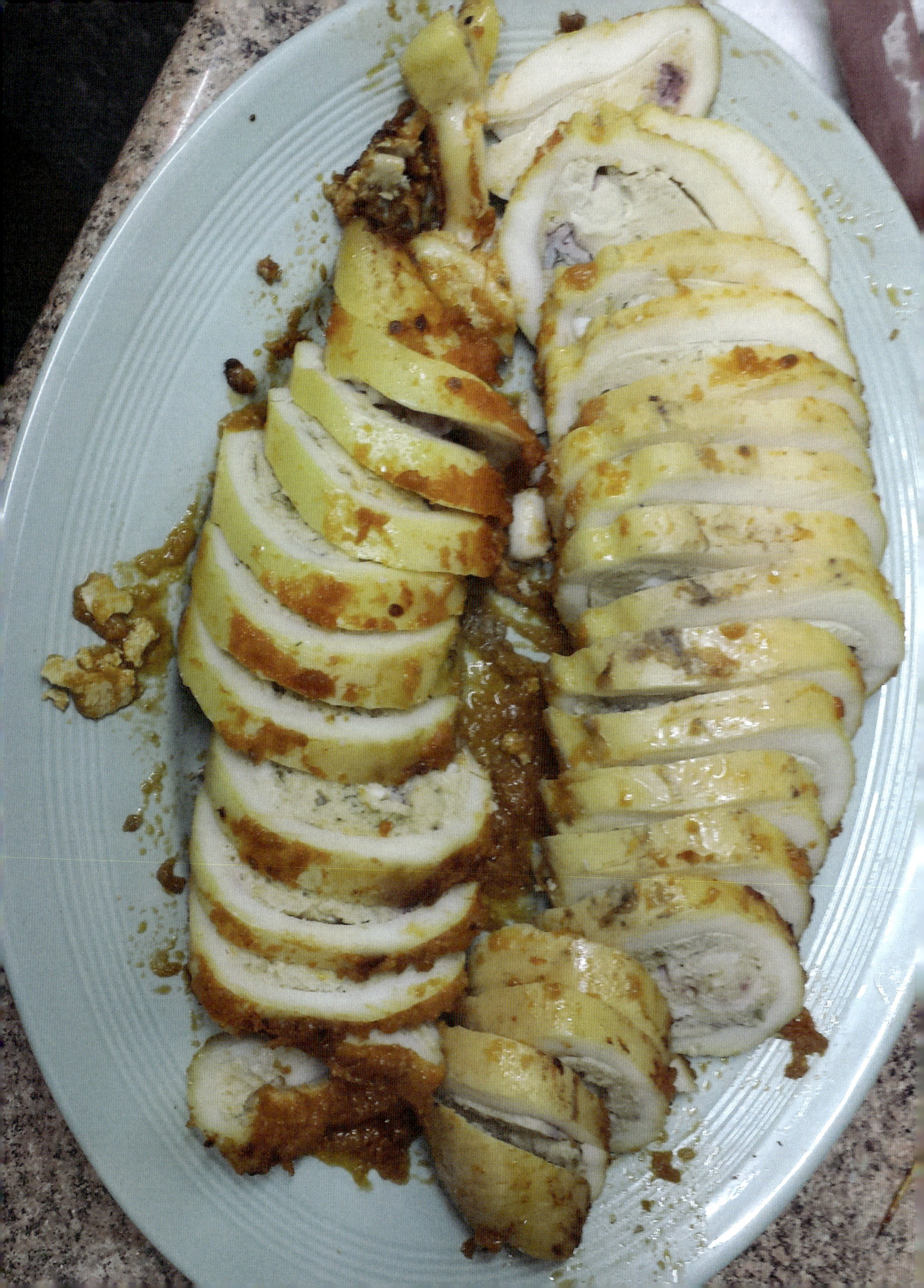

TUNA TURNER

SERVES 2

INGREDIENTS

- 1 SMALL ONION
- 160 G TIN OF TUNA
- PARSLEY
- 2 EGGS
- 100 G GRATED CHEESE
- 1 PACKET PUFF PASTRY

METHOD

1. Hard boil an egg in a small pan. Cut onion into small pieces and mix with tuna, along with the hard boiled egg and parsley.

2. Roll puff pastry into a rectangle, brush with a beaten egg and add grated cheese. Lay your tuna mixture on your pastry and roll into a swiss roll shape. Cut into slices of 2 centimetres.

3. Place pastry slices in dish and glaze with the remaining beaten egg. Bake in moderate oven at 175°C until golden brown.

BY MARIA LUISA

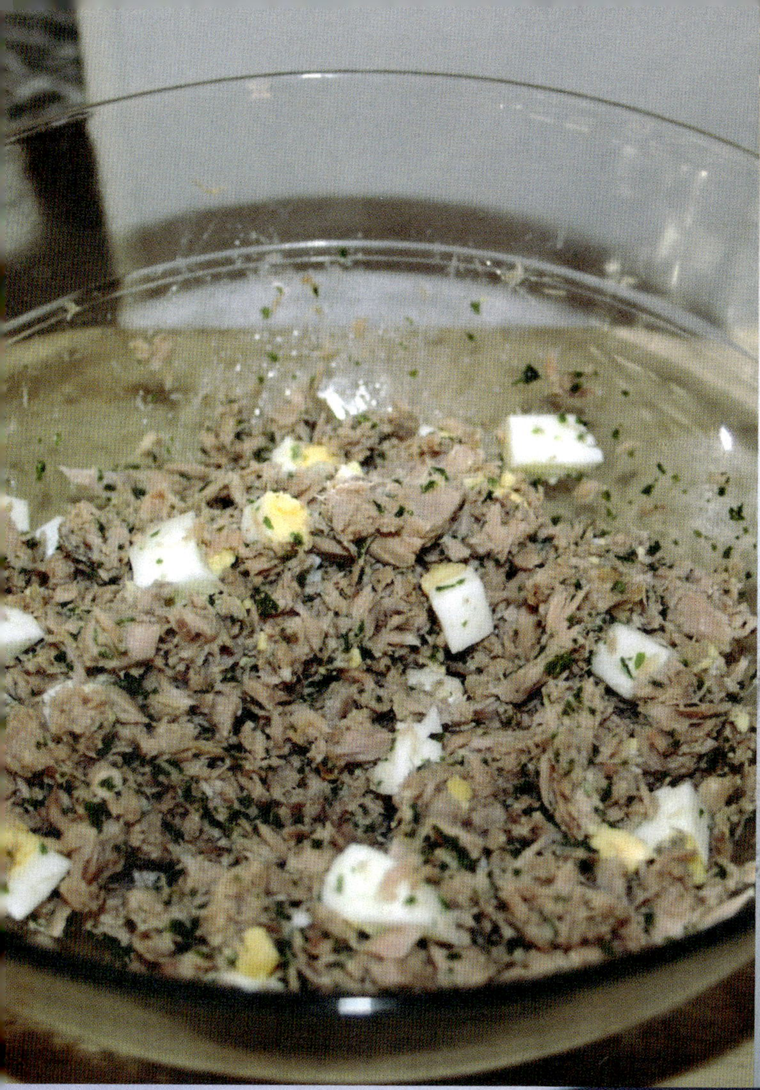
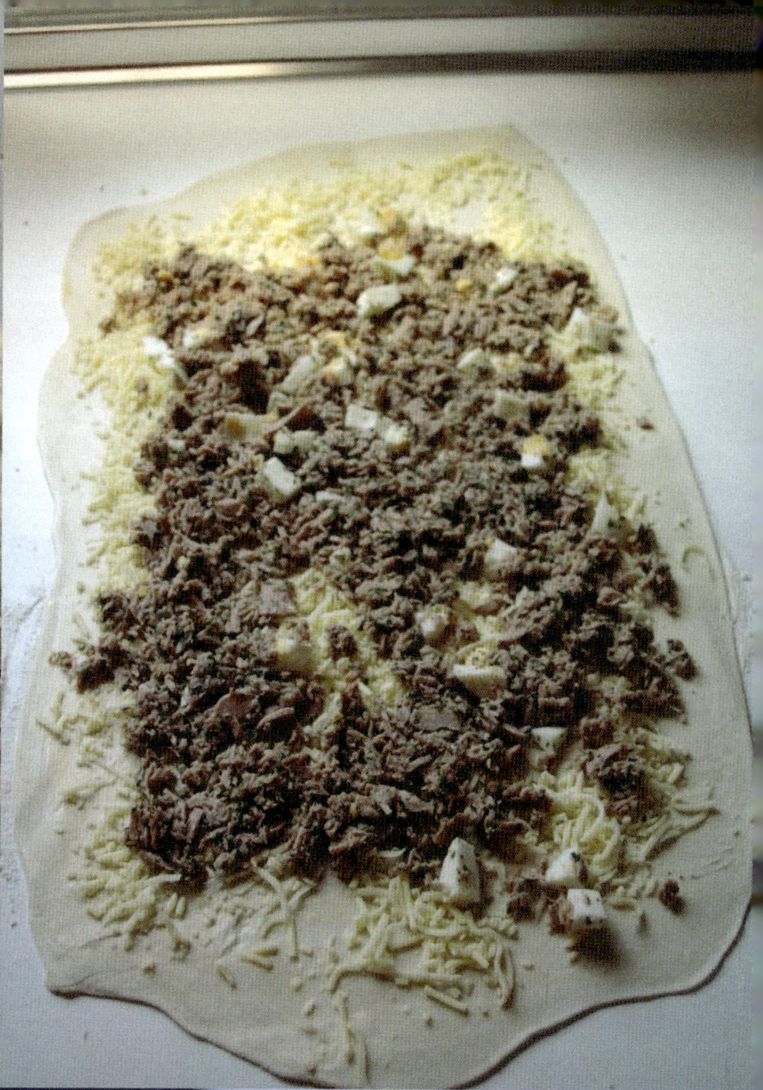
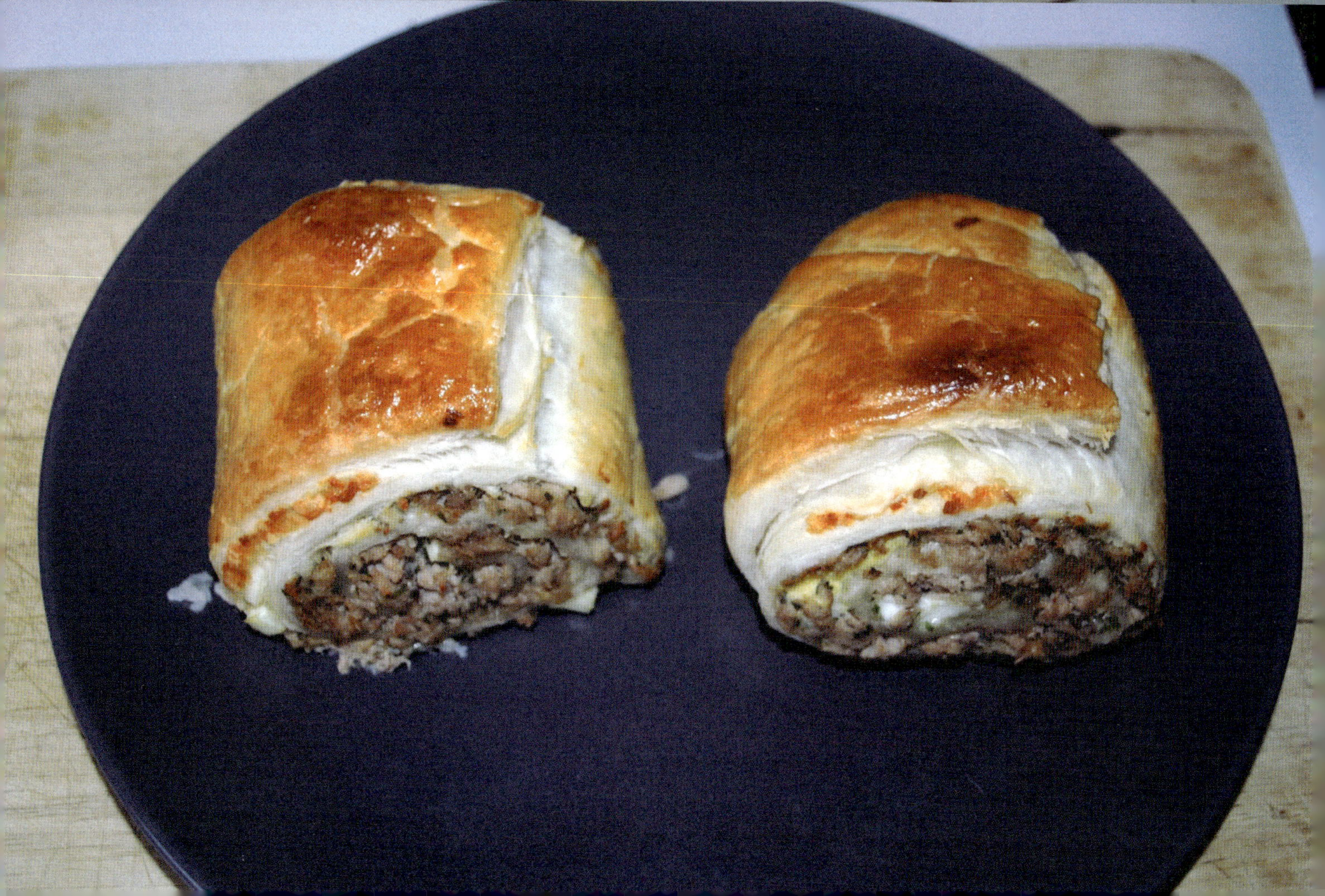

MAMA'S CHILLI AND GARLIC PRAWN SPAGHETTI

SERVES 1

INGREDIENTS

- 80 G PRAWNS
- 3 - 4 GARLIC CLOVES
- 60 G SPAGHETTI
- DRIED CHILLI
- OLIVE OIL

METHOD

1. Chop garlic and fry until soft. Add some ready cooked prawns, break some chillies over and mix all together.

2. Meanwhile boil some spaghetti. Once that is ready, drain and chuck in with the prawns and garlic.

3. Stir everything together, drizzle some olive oil over it and season with salt.

SALMON PATTIES

SERVES 2

INGREDIENTS

- 2 CANS - 102 G SKINLESS AND BONELESS SALMON
- 2 EGGS
- 1 MEDIUM ONION *(CHOPPED)*
- 2 GARLIC CLOVES
- 1/2 TSP DRIED PARSLEY
- CHEDDAR CHEESE
- FLOUR

METHOD

1. Drain salmon, place in a bowl and make sure no bones or skin remain on your piece of salmon.

2. Add two beaten eggs, onion, garlic, cheddar, salt and pepper. Mix together and form into patties. Dust with flour and fry in hot oil.

3. Alternatively heat your oven to 190°C, lay a few patties on an oven tray and bake until golden brown.

RECIPE BY ROSEMARIE MAÑASCO

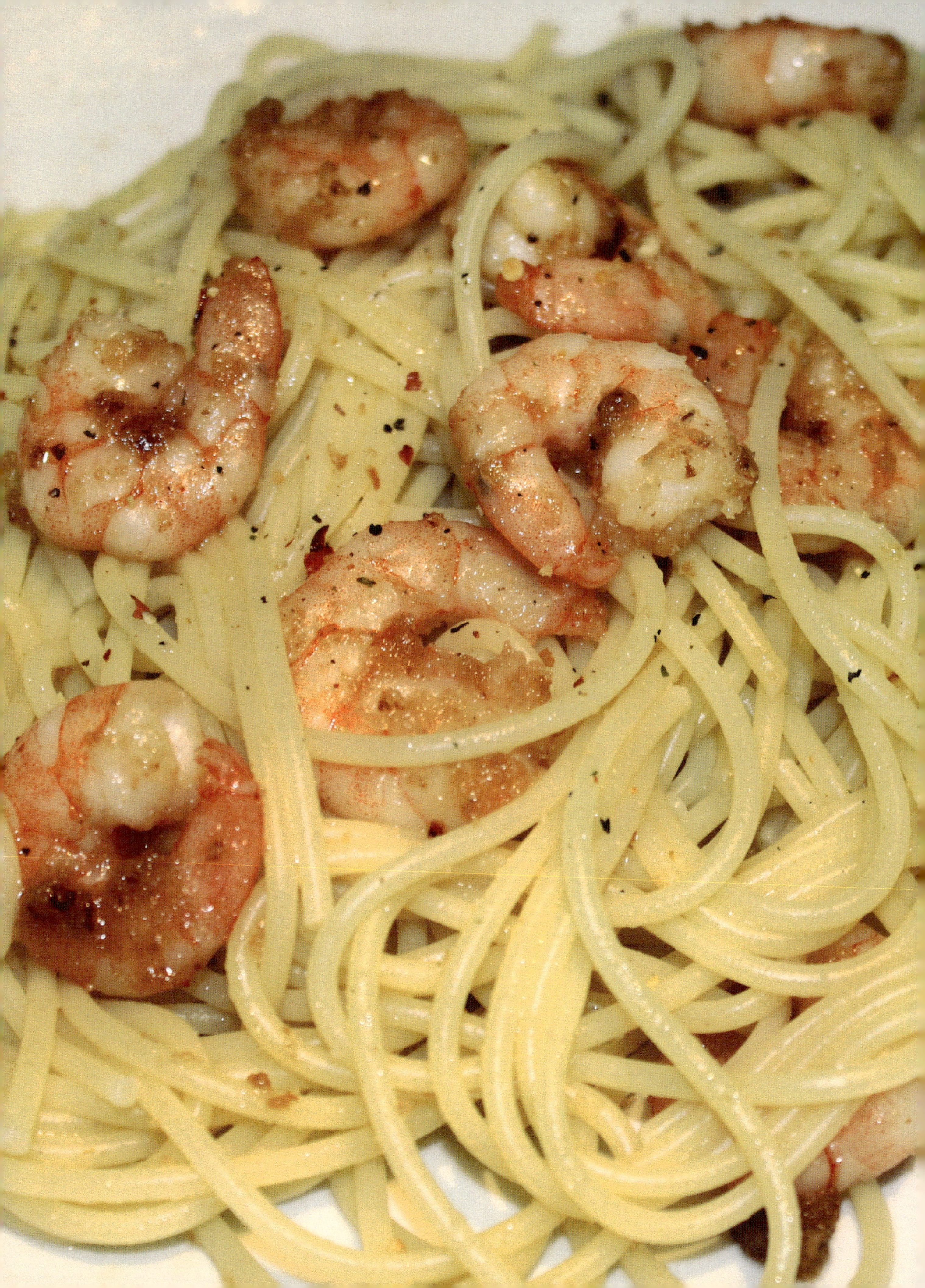

MAMA'S ROAST COD WITH POTATOES & VEGETABLES

SERVES 1

INGREDIENTS

- 2 COD FILLETS
- 2 LARGE POTATOES
- FROZEN VEGETABLES *(CARROTS, PEAS, CAULIFLOWER, BROCCOLI)*
- 2 TBSP BUTTER
- 2 GARLIC CLOVES
- SPINACH LEAVES
- FRESH PARSLEY
- SALT
- PEPPER
- OLIVE OIL

METHOD

Preheat your oven to 200c

1. There are two things you must have before we begin: a large oven dish and a large bowl.

2. In the large bowl, scoop and place two tablespoons of butter and your finely diced garlic. Add in some parsley and a pinch of salt and pepper and mix together into a paste. Leave this to one side for the moment.

3. In your large oven dish place your vegetables, spinach, and diced potatoes. Don't worry about leaving the skin on as this will add flavour, but you must wash the potato thoroughly.

4. Lay your fillets of fish on the side of the vegetables and pour your butter mixture over your fish.

5. Grab your olive oil and lightly drizzle over the potatoes and vegetables and sprinkle a pinch of salt and pepper over.

6. Cover your oven dish with foil and place in the oven for about 20 minutes. Check the fish is cooked and vegetables are soft before serving.

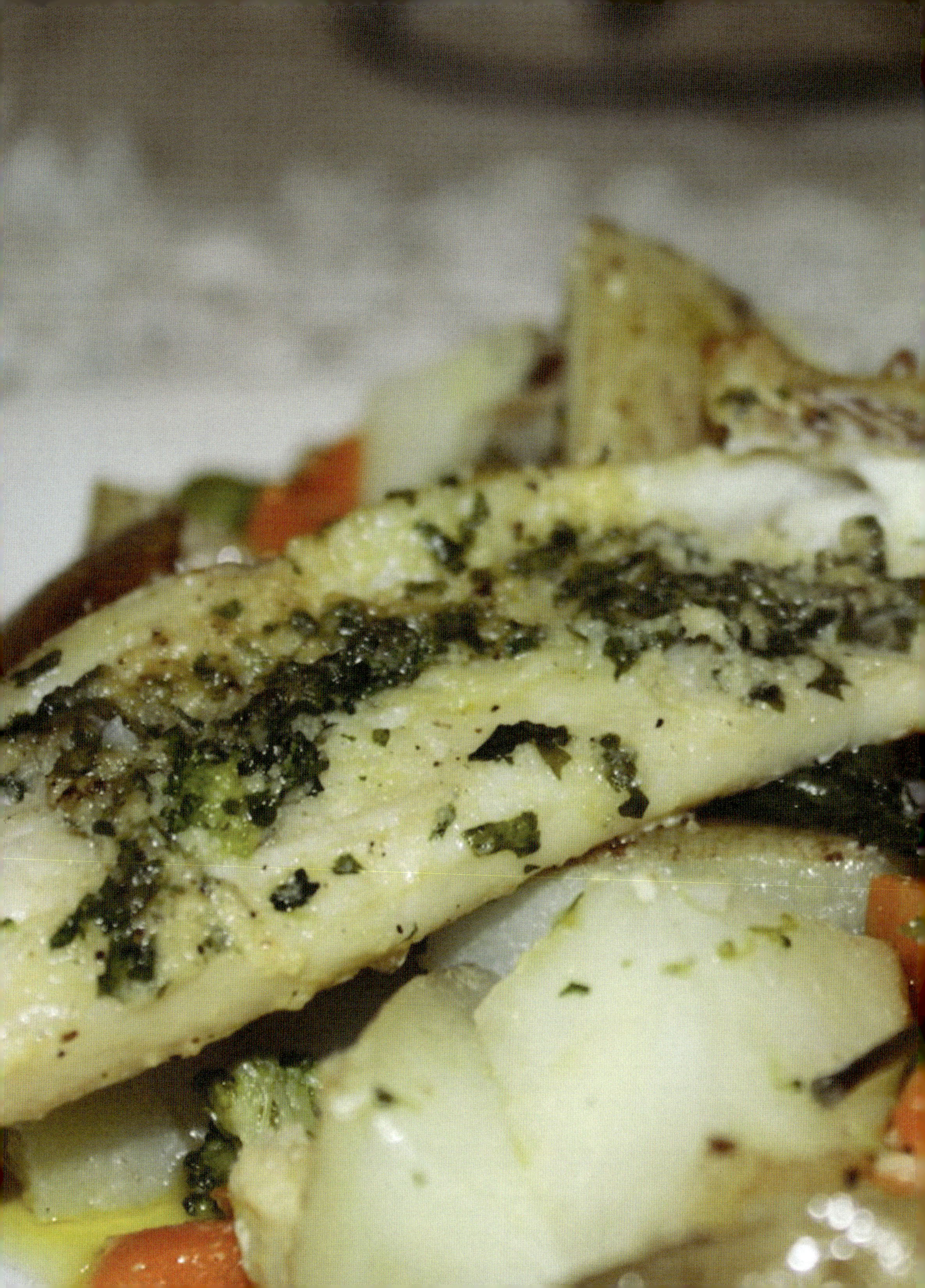

MAMA'S SOPA DE MARISCO
SEAFOOD SOUP

SERVES 3

INGREDIENTS

- 1 MEDIUM MONK FISH
- 225 G CLAMS
- 250 G PRAWNS
- 3 TOMATOES
- 1 GREEN PEPPER
- 1 SMALL ONION
- 2 GARLIC CLOVES
- PIMENTÓN PICANTE (PAPRIKA)
- 1/2 GLASS WHITE WINE
- FRESH MINT
- FIDEUÁ NOODLES
- OLIVE OIL
- WATER

SUGGESTION
The clams should have been soaking in water for several hours prior to cooking, to get rid of any sand.

METHOD

1. Clean and debone fish, cut into small pieces and place to one side. Peel your raw prawns and set aside with your fish.

2. Dice your garlic, onion, pepper and tomatoes, and fry in a large casserole on a low heat with a splash of olive oil, also known as making a *refrito*.

3. Once your vegetables have softened and your onions are translucent, blend together with a hand blender. Now pour in your white wine, mint and paprika.

4. Boil your soaked clams in a smaller separate pan, this will avoid them releasing any sand into your soup.

5. In your main casserole dish, add your fish and cover with water, add a handful of pasta per person and leave to stew. Stir and check regularly. If you see the water is reducing too quickly, just keep topping it up.

6. When your pasta is almost ready, add your cooked clams and prawns and cook for 2 minutes allowing everything to stew together.

7. Your soup is now ready to serve. Season to taste.

MAMA'S CONCHAS EN SALSA DE ALMENDRAS
GRANNY'S GIANT CLAMS IN A NUT SAUCE

SERVES 4

INGREDIENTS

- 3 KG GIANT CLAMS
- 300 G WALNUTS
- 300 G ALMONDS
- PARSLEY
- CHILLI
- CUMIN
- CORIANDER
- 1 GLASS WHITE WINE
- 4 SLICES OF BREAD
- 6 TOMATOES
- 3 GARLIC CLOVES
- 1 LARGE ONION
- OIL
- TIN OF ANCHOVIES IN OIL

Mama's nutty clam sauce is my favourite Christmas and Easter treat. This recipe will leave you cleaning the plate up with slices of bread, but don't just take it from me, try it out yourself!

METHOD

1. Put your clams to boil whilst you make your sauce.

2. Heat up oil and fry the slices of bread until golden brown.

3. Remove the bread and in the pan fry the almonds until golden brown. Place the almonds to one side and fry the garlic, onions and tomatoes on a low heat.

4. Take the almonds, walnuts, parsley, bread, spices and anchovies and blend them together until smooth, then add to the sauce you have made with the tomatoes.

5. When mixed, add the wine, then clams.

This sauce can be used for meat or any other type of seafood. If using for meat leave out the anchovies.

SUGGESTION

I particularly enjoy this sauce with Rolitos. *(Page 72)*

Soak your clams in salt water for a while before cooking so they release any sand inside them.

MAMA'S ROSADA AL LIMÓN
LIGHTLY BATTERED ROSADA WITH LEMON

SERVES 4

INGREDIENTS

- 1 LARGE ROSADA FISH
- LEMON
- OLIVE OIL
- PLAIN FLOUR
- SALT

Found at every chiringuito in Spain the Rosada Frita is part of that Mediterranean fried fish charm. Just drizzle some lemon juice over and a pinch of sea salt and taste the soft splendour that unfurls.

METHOD

1. Cut your fish into chunks and roll them into little ball-like sizes. Dress your fish with a squeeze of lemon.

2. Pour some flour on a plate and cover your fish pieces completely. Meanwhile heat up a pan with plenty of olive oil.

3. Fry until golden and place the fish on a dish on a paper kitchen towel to drain any excess oil.

4. Serve on a dish with slices of lemon.

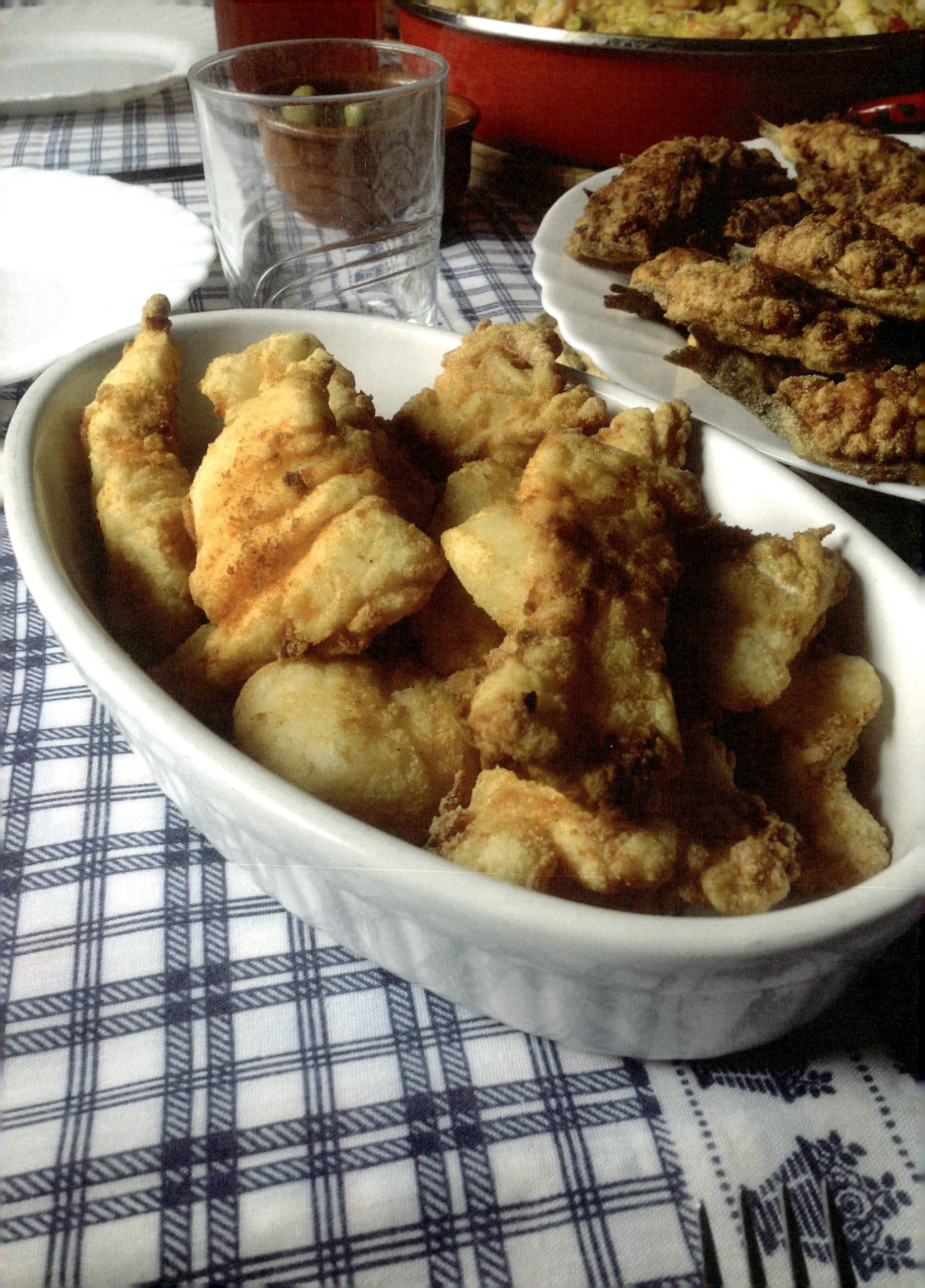

MAMA'S GARLIC STEAMED MUSSELS

SERVES 2

INGREDIENTS

- 1 KG MUSSELS
- 3 GARLIC CLOVES
- PARSLEY
- BUTTER

Mussels are delicious and the fresher they are, the better. The best recipe is the simplest one and I find a bit of butter and garlic goes a long way.

METHOD

This dish doesn't need much as mussels taste beautiful on their own but if you do want that little bit more flavour then why not try this?

1. Chop 3 garlic cloves quite finely along with a bunch of fresh parsley.

2. Simply rinse your mussels in water and place them in a large covered pan and heat on a low – medium heat, with the garlic, parsley and a knob of butter.

3. The mussels will release the water stored in their shells and cook in their own juice.

4. In total this should take about 10 – 15 minutes or once all your mussels have opened. Remember to stir occasionally.

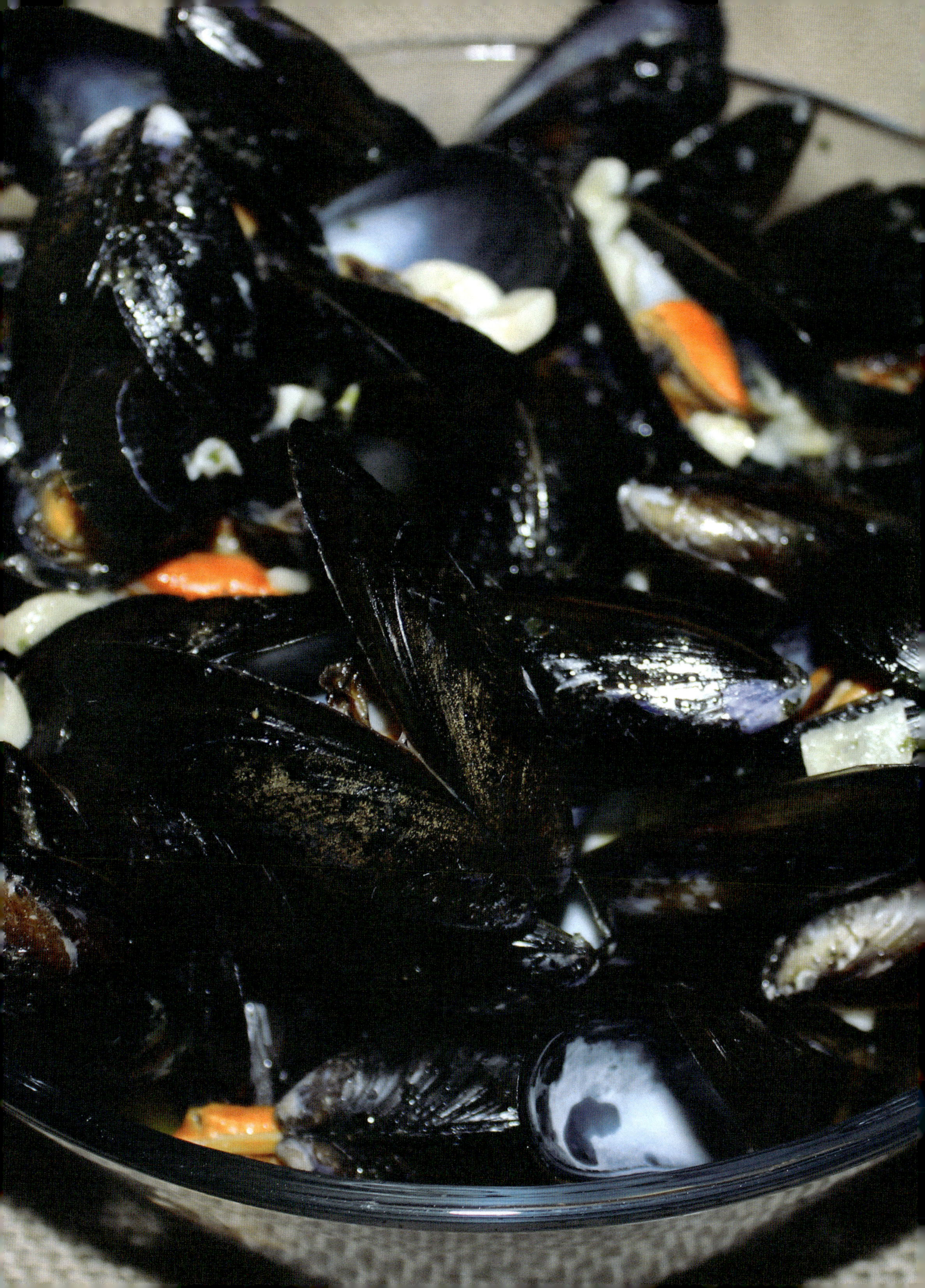

PASTA

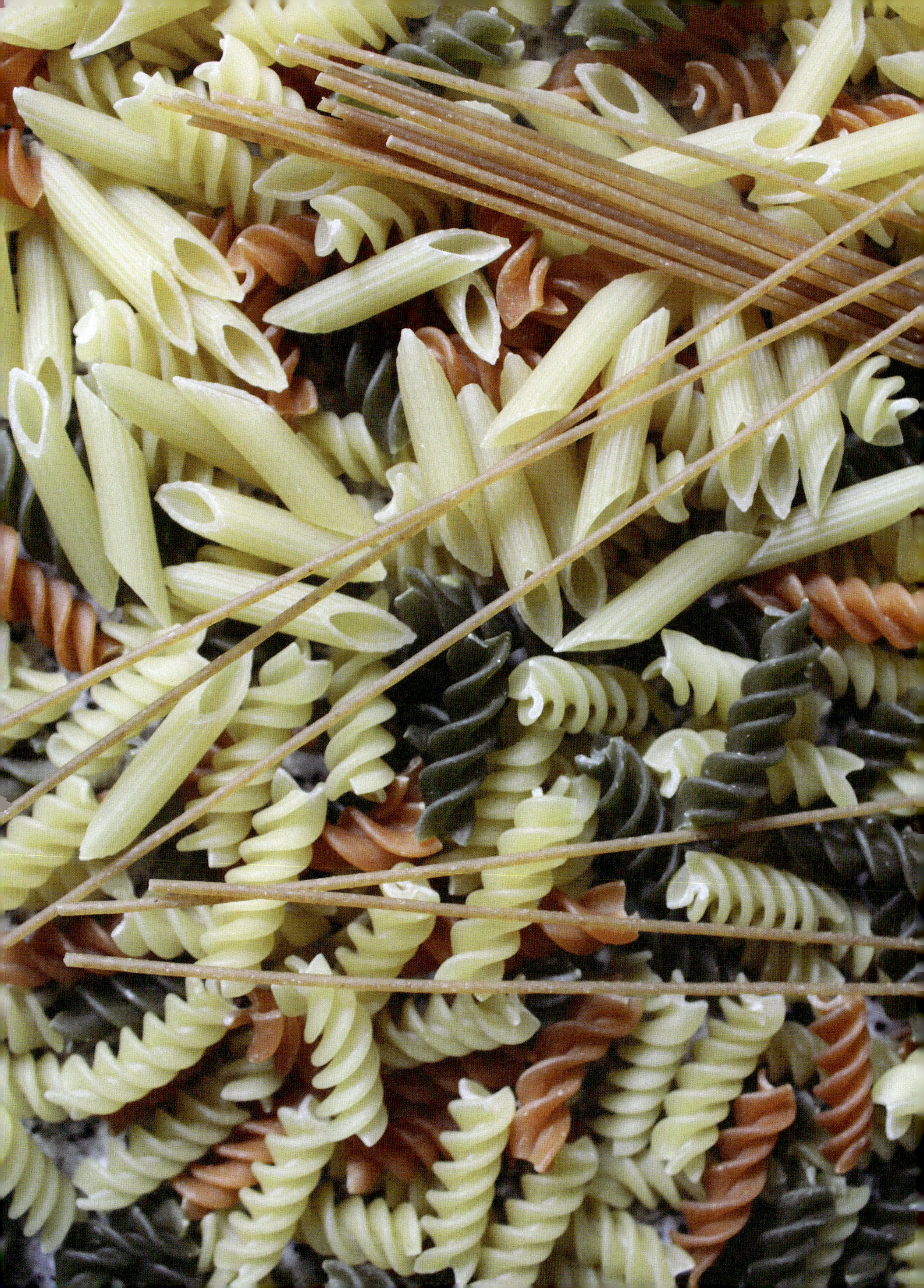

MAMA'S ROSTO

SERVES 2

INGREDIENTS

- MUSHROOMS
  (OPTIONAL)
- STOCK CUBE
- 400 G TINNED TOMATOES
  (CHOPPED OR PASTEURISED)
- 1 SMALL OR 1/2 LARGE ONION
- 1 LARGE OR 2 SMALL GARLIC CLOVES
- 2 LARGE OR 3 SMALL CARROTS
  (PEELED & SLICED)
- OIL
- 1/2 GLASS WHITE WINE
  (DRY)
- 100 G PASTA
  (MACARONI / PENNE)
- 500 G MEAT
  (ANY OPTIONAL) *

* CHICKEN

* BEEF - BRAISING / STEWING STEAK

* PORK - THICK PORK CHOPS

The Rosto recipe has to be without a doubt one of Gibraltar's most well known recipes, passed down through generations. A simple pasta and meat dish with a taste that will leave you craving for more.

METHOD

1. Chop onions and garlic into small pieces and fry. once this is soft and golden add tomatoes and carrots.

2. Dice and mix in the meat with a splash of white wine and stock cube. Cook on low heat and cover until tender.

3. In a separate pan boil the pasta for 9 – 10 minutes until *al dente*, rinse and add in to the tomato and meat.

4. Allow 5 minutes for the flavours to mix together and settle.

If the tomato sauce is a bit sharp add some sugar.

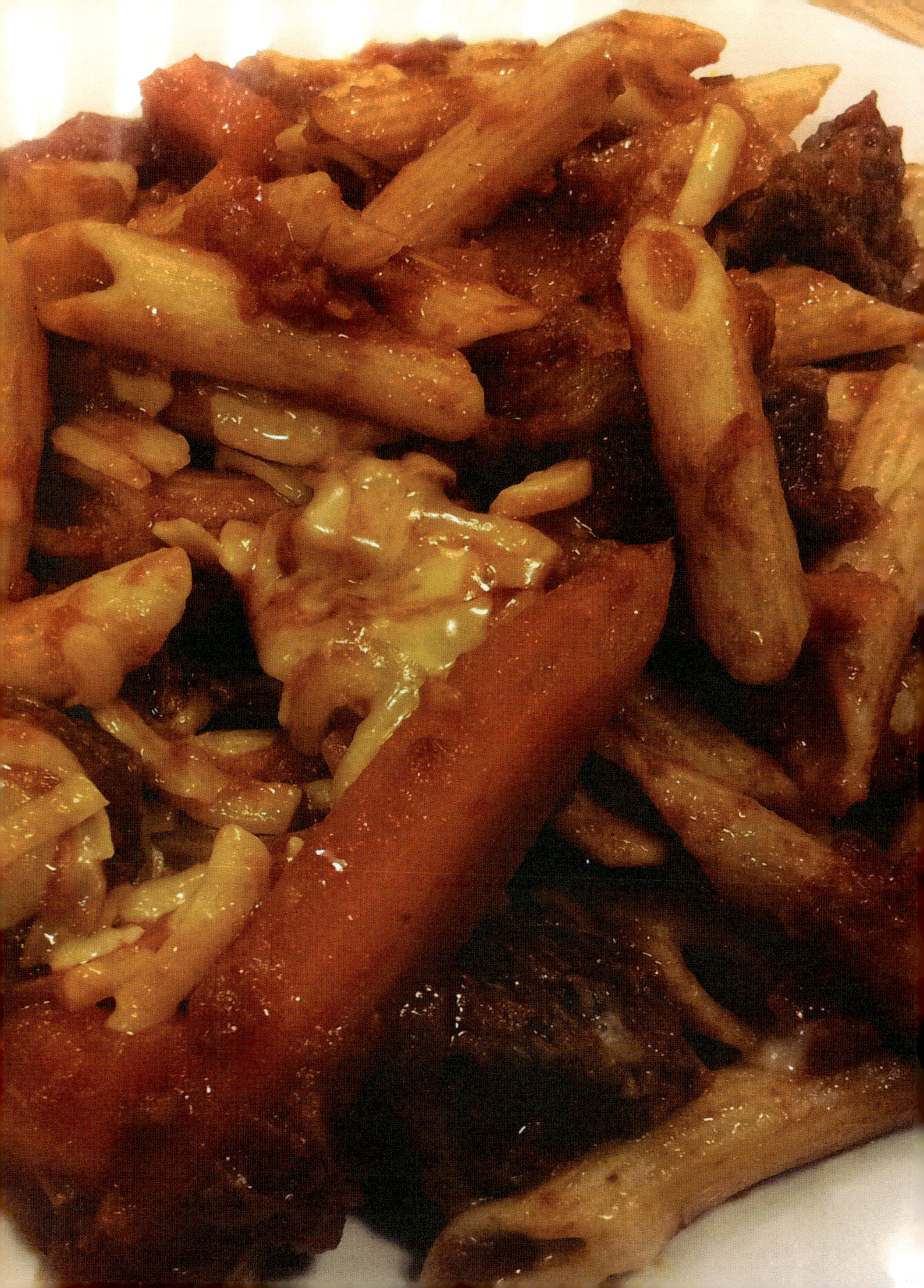

MAMA'S LASAGNE

SERVES 2

INGREDIENTS

- LASAGNE SHEETS

FILLING

- 2 SMALL TINS OR 1 LARGE TIN OF CHOPPED TOMATOES
- 1 SMALL JAR OF SUN-DRIED TOMATOES
- 250 G MINCED BEEF
- 1 SMALL ONION
- 1 GREEN PEPPER *(OPTIONAL)*
- 1 PACKET OF FRESH SPINACH LEAVES
- BEEF STOCK CUBE
- CHICKEN STOCK CUBE
- BASIL
- OREGANO
- 2 GARLIC CLOVES
- 200 G GRATED CHEESE

BÉCHAMEL

- 300 ML WHOLE MILK
- 100 G CHEDDAR CHEESE
- PLAIN FLOUR
- NUTMEG *(OPTIONAL)*

METHOD

Filling

1. Prepare all your ingredients by finely chopping the onions and garlic and setting them to one side. If you are choosing to add the green pepper then finely chop it too and place it to one side.

2. In a large pan add a little bit of oil, about a tablespoon's worth. Add in your meat and cook over a medium heat, season with salt and pepper to taste, a sprinkle of basil and oregano and your crushed beef stock cube. Stir and allow to cook.

3. Stir every now and again to make sure your meat cooks thoroughly, then add in your onion, garlic and your green peppers, stir and allow to cook for 2 minutes. Meanwhile tun kettle on. Once boiled, pour about 100 ml of water in a cup to dissolve your chicken stock cube and add this to your meat.

4. Once the onions and peppers are soft, mix in your chopped tomatoes and about three or four chopped sun-dried tomatoes.

5. Cover your pan and leave on a low heat.

Béchamel:

6. Boil the milk on a medium heat, grate a small amount of nutmeg and once the milk is hot, gently and slowly sift in some flour and whisk the milk so that it thickens. When it begins to thicken add in as much cheese as you would like, depending how cheesy you enjoy your meals. Stir until everything is melted and you end up with a nice thick cheesy sauce.

7. Place to one side away from the heat and prepare your

lasagne dish.

Preparation

8. Preheat your oven to 190°C

9. In a large oven dish spread a little béchamel and lay down some lasagne sheets. Pour some of your filling mixture on top and then some béchamel over and continue to do this, sheets, filling, béchamel, until you have about 3 or 4 layers. On the final layer simply spread your béchamel and cover with the remainder of the grated cheese. Cover your dish in foil and place in the oven for 40 minutes or until the pasta is soft and ready. You can check this by sticking a knife through and feeling whether the pasta is soft or hard.

10. Once ready uncover and leave in the oven for a few extra minutes until the top is golden. Remove from the oven and serve immediately.

MAMA'S MACARONI CHEESE

SERVES 1

INGREDIENTS

- 60 G PENNE PASTA

BÉCHAMEL
- 300 ML WHOLE MILK
- 100 G CHEESE
- PLAIN FLOUR
- NUTMEG

METHOD

1. Boil the pasta with a little bit of salt.

2. Meanwhile prepare the cheese sauce.

3. Boil the milk on a medium heat, grate a small amount of nutmeg and once the milk is hot, gently and slowly sift in some flour and whisk the milk so that it thickens. When it begins to thicken add in as much cheese as you would like, depending how cheesy you enjoy your meals. Stir until everything is melted and you end up with a nice thick cheesy sauce.

4. When that is ready place to one side. Once your pasta is soft drain and rinse with water and pour into an oven dish. Pour the cheese sauce over, covering everything.

5. Grate some cheese over everything and place it in the oven or under the grill until cheese is golden.

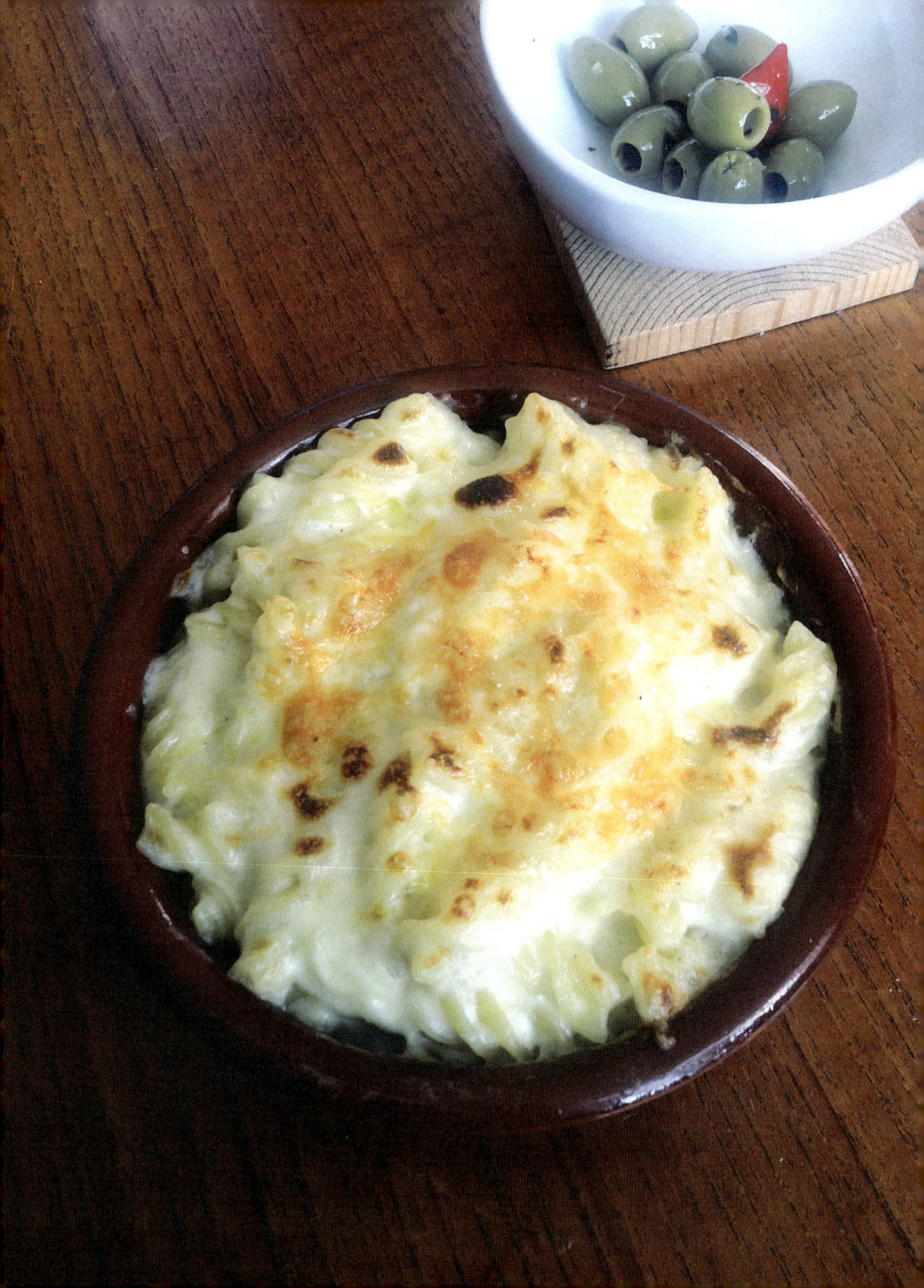

MAMA'S SPAGHETTI BOLOGNESE WITH CHORIZO

SERVES 2

INGREDIENTS

- 100 G CHORIZO
- 100 G SPAGHETTI
- SPINACH LEAVES (HANDFUL)
- 400 G TIN CHOPPED TOMATOES
- 1 SMALL ONION
- 2 GARLIC CLOVES
- 500 G MINCED BEEF
- PLAIN FLOUR
- FRESH BASIL
- DRIED OREGANO
- 50 G GRATED CHEDDAR CHEESE

METHOD

1. Finely chop onion and garlic and fry with a little bit of oil.

2. Once soft, add in the minced meat and season with a bit of salt, pepper and chopped basil.

3. Chop the chorizo into pieces and add in with the meat.

4. Meanwhile, boil some water, chop some spinach and boil some spaghetti pasta in a pan with the spinach.

5. When the meat is ready, add in a little bit of flour and water to thicken with the juices from the meat. Add in your chopped tomatoes and leave on a low heat.

6. When your pasta is ready, drain and serve covered with your sauce and topped with grated cheese.

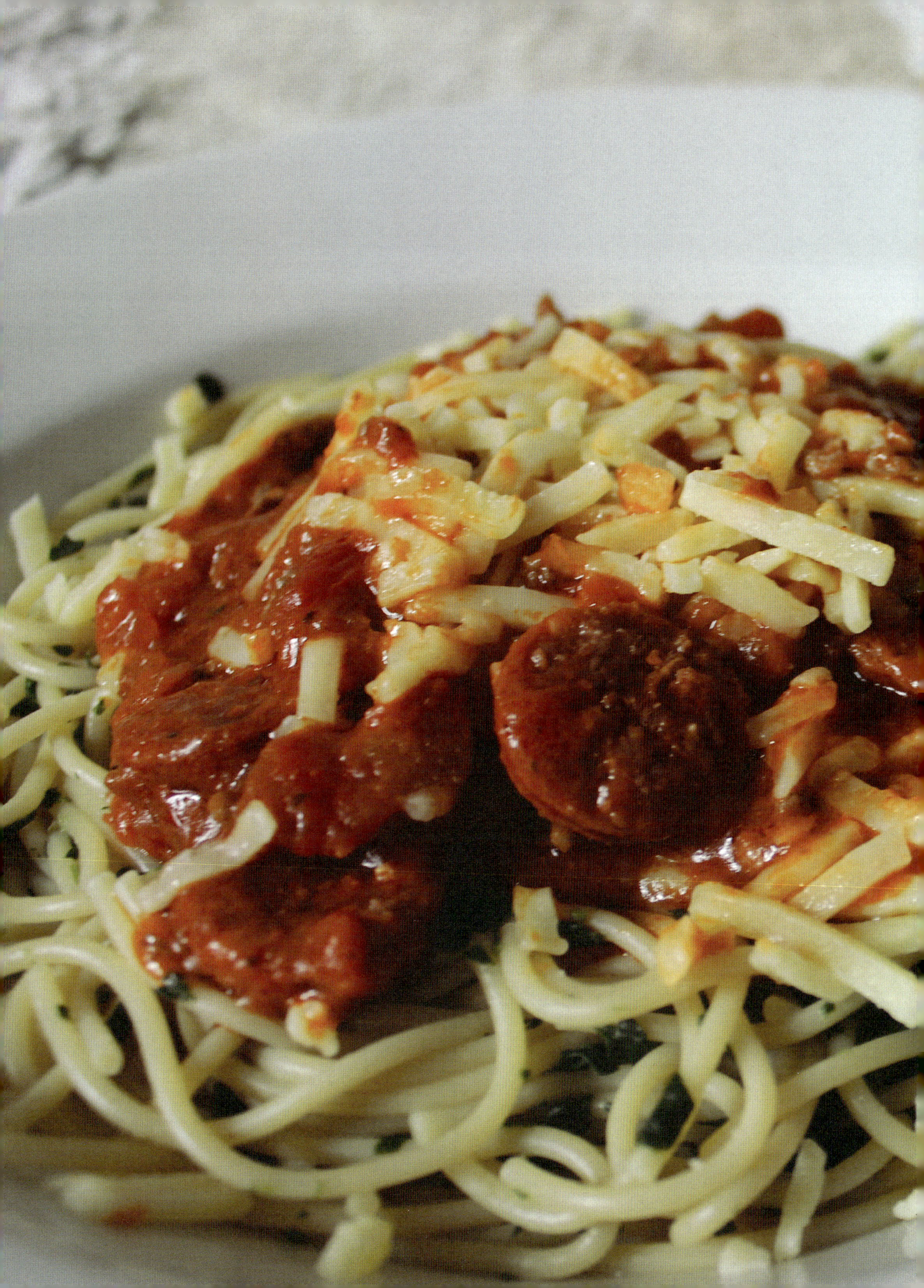

VEGETARIAN

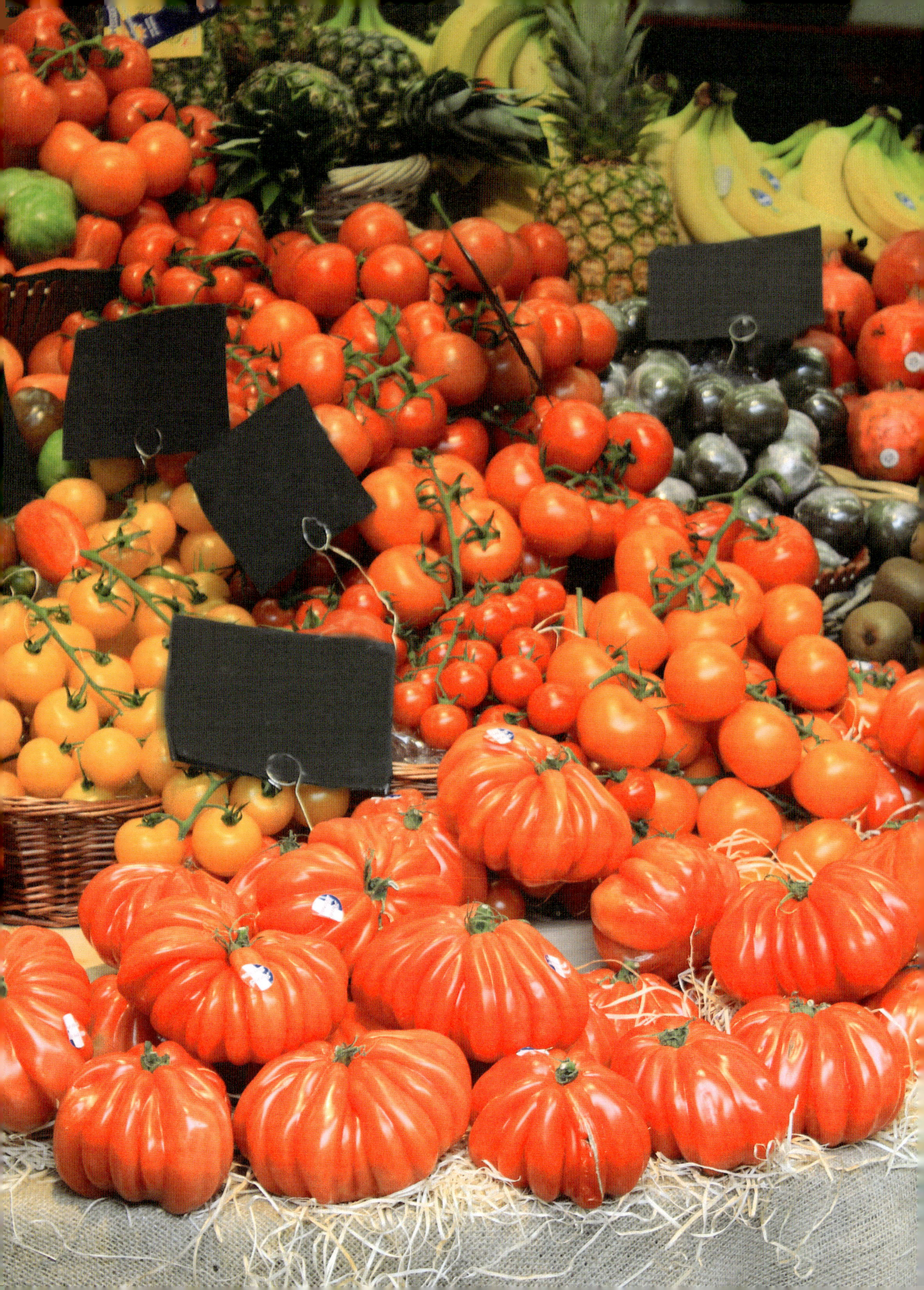

MAMA'S MENESTRA
VEGETABLE STEW

SERVES 6

INGREDIENTS

- 1 KG RUNNER BEANS
- 225 G RED KIDNEY BEANS *(TINNED)*
- 4 LARGE CARROTS
- 1/4 LARGE PUMPKIN
- 1 LARGE AUBERGINE
- 2 COURGETTES
- 1 MEDIUM KOHLRABI
- FRESH BASIL
- 3 GARLIC CLOVES
- OLIVE OIL
- SPAGHETTI PASTA *(2 HANDFULS, BROKEN INTO SMALLER PIECES)*
- SALT
- PEPPER
- WATER
- GRATED CHEDDAR CHEESE

As a little boy, Mama's Menestra always brought a smile to my face and I never failed to lick the plate clean. As a grown up, I can truly say little has changed. The Menestra has always been a classic Mama dish and no matter how many times others have tried to recreate it, there's nothing quite like the original...But it's worth a try.

METHOD

1. Chop all vegetables, crush the garlic and place together in a large casserole dish with a splash of olive oil *(except the red kidney beans)*. Season with salt and basil and boil with plenty of water.

2. Remove the vegetables from the casserole dish and blend together, then pour back into the dish and add the red kidney beans and cook for a further 5 - 8 minutes.

3. Add your pasta and cook until tender; this should take about 10 minutes. Allow to sit for 2 minutes before serving so the flavours mix together.

4. Grate some cheese and sprinkle on top.

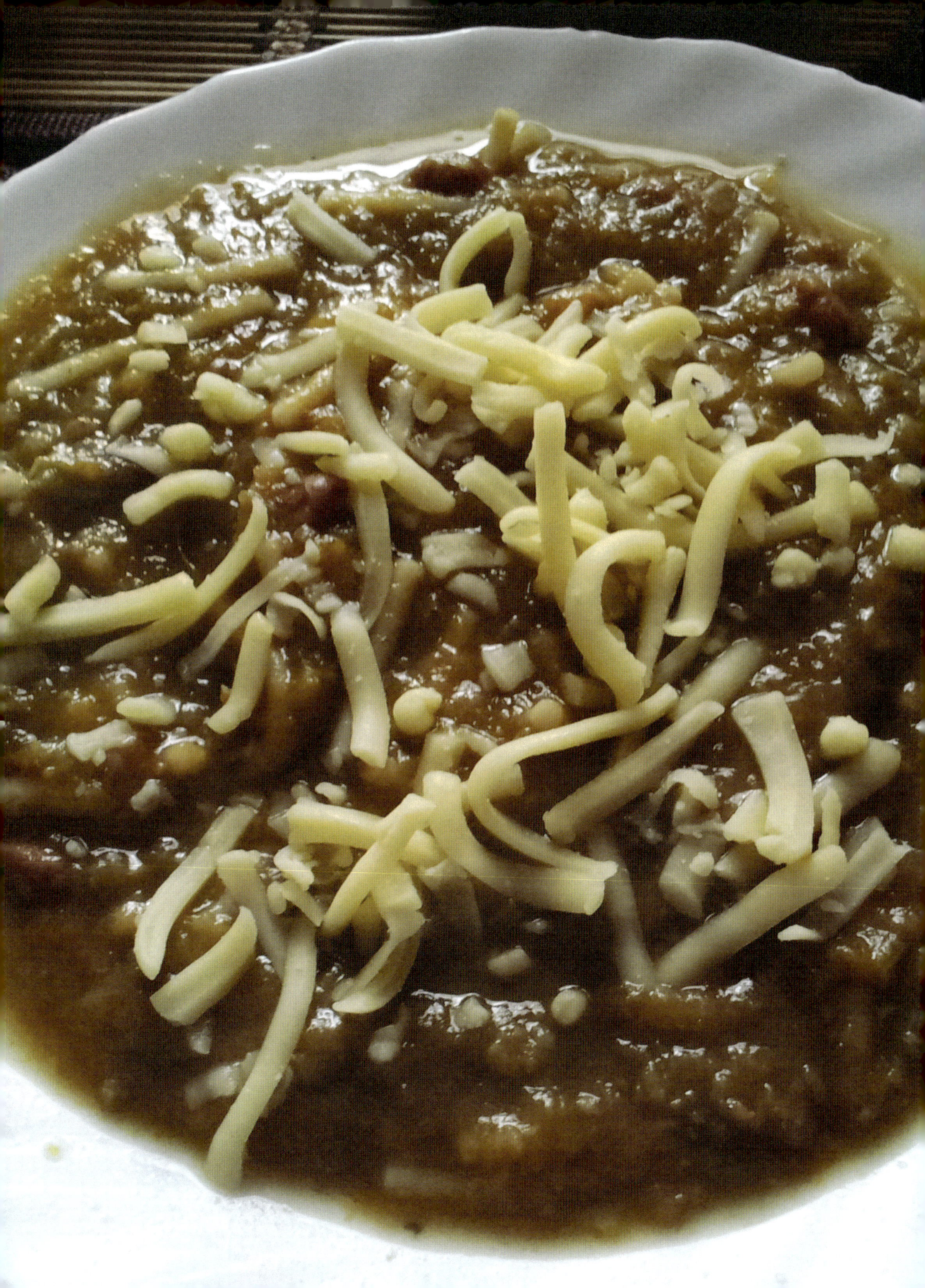

MAMA'S SWEET POTATO TORTILLA WITH RED PEPPERS

SERVES 1

INGREDIENTS

- 1 MEDIUM SWEET POTATO
- 4 EGGS
- 1 RED PEPPER

METHOD

1. Dice your sweet potato into small cubes and fry on a medium heat.

2. Dice your red pepper and fry in a separate pan.

3. beat 4 eggs in a large bowl, season with salt and leave to one side.

4. Once the peppers are soft remove from the heat.

5. When the potato is soft, remove it from the heat, drain the oil from the pan and mix in with the whisked eggs along with the peppers.

6. Stir everything together and pour back into a small – medium sized frying pan with a splash of oil.

7. Leave over a low heat until you see the edges of the mixture cooking. With your wooden spoon gently feel around removing it from the edge of the pan.

8. Using a flat plate flip it over and place it back in the pan. Allow to cook further until you can move the tortilla by shaking the pan.

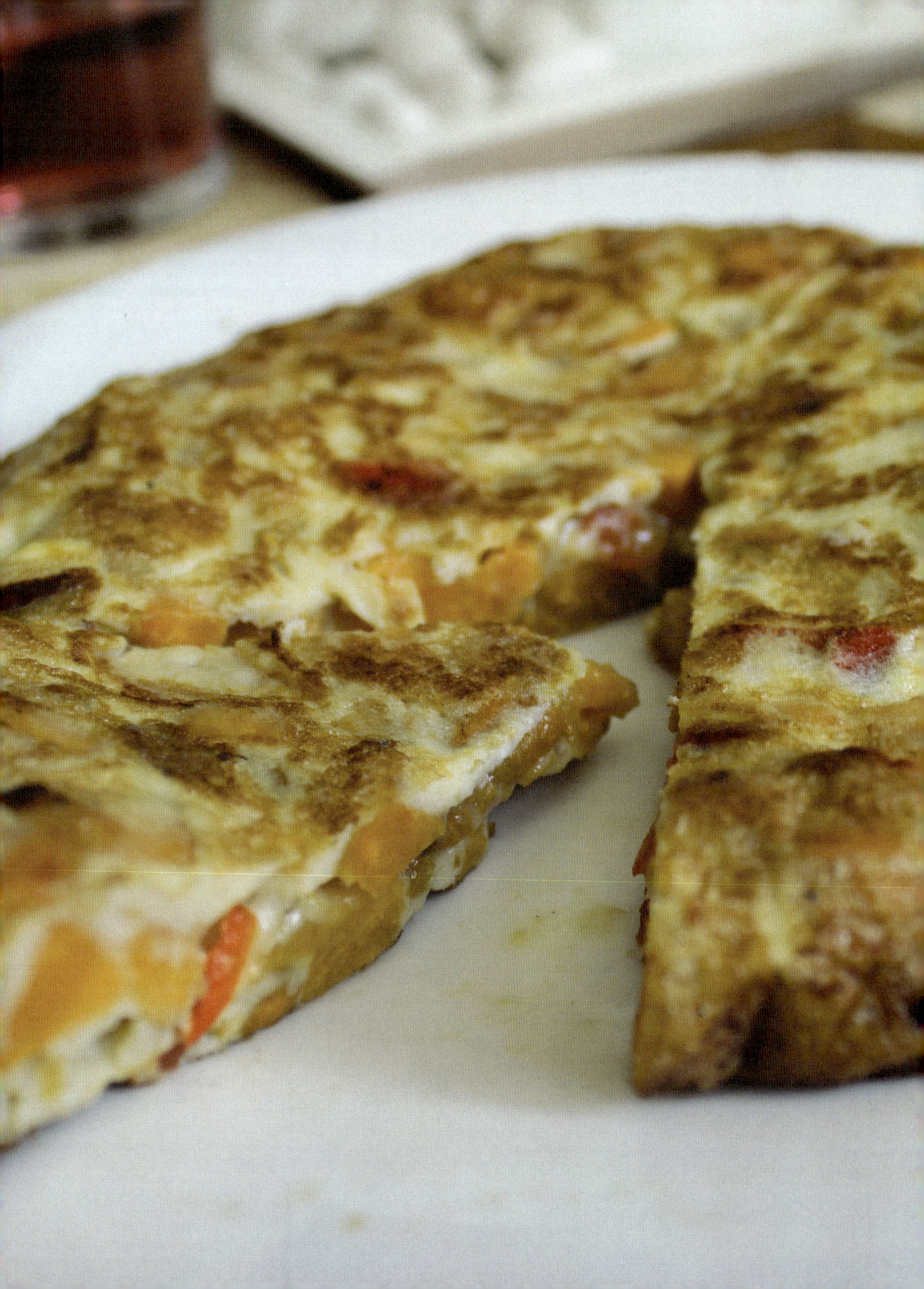

MAMA'S ALCACHOFAS
ARTICHOKE STEW

SERVES 6

INGREDIENTS

- 6 FRESH ARTICHOKES
- 500 G FRESH BROAD BEANS
- 1 KG FRESH PEAS
- 2 SPRING ONIONS
- DRIED MARJORAM
- OIL
- SALT
- PINCH SAFFRON
- 1 POTATO PER PERSON

Alcachofas is equally as delicious as they are messy. Tearing off the artichoke leaves and scooping off the flesh from the leaves with your teeth is worth the wait and cooking time.

METHOD

1. Clean the artichokes by rinsing them thoroughly and chop the onions.

2. Pour enough boiling water in your pan to cover everything and boil together all the vegetables, except the potatoes, with oil, salt and saffron.

3. Once the artichokes are soft dice the potatoes and add to the boiling stew.

4. If necessary add more water but not too much.

5. Simmer until water is reduced and serve.

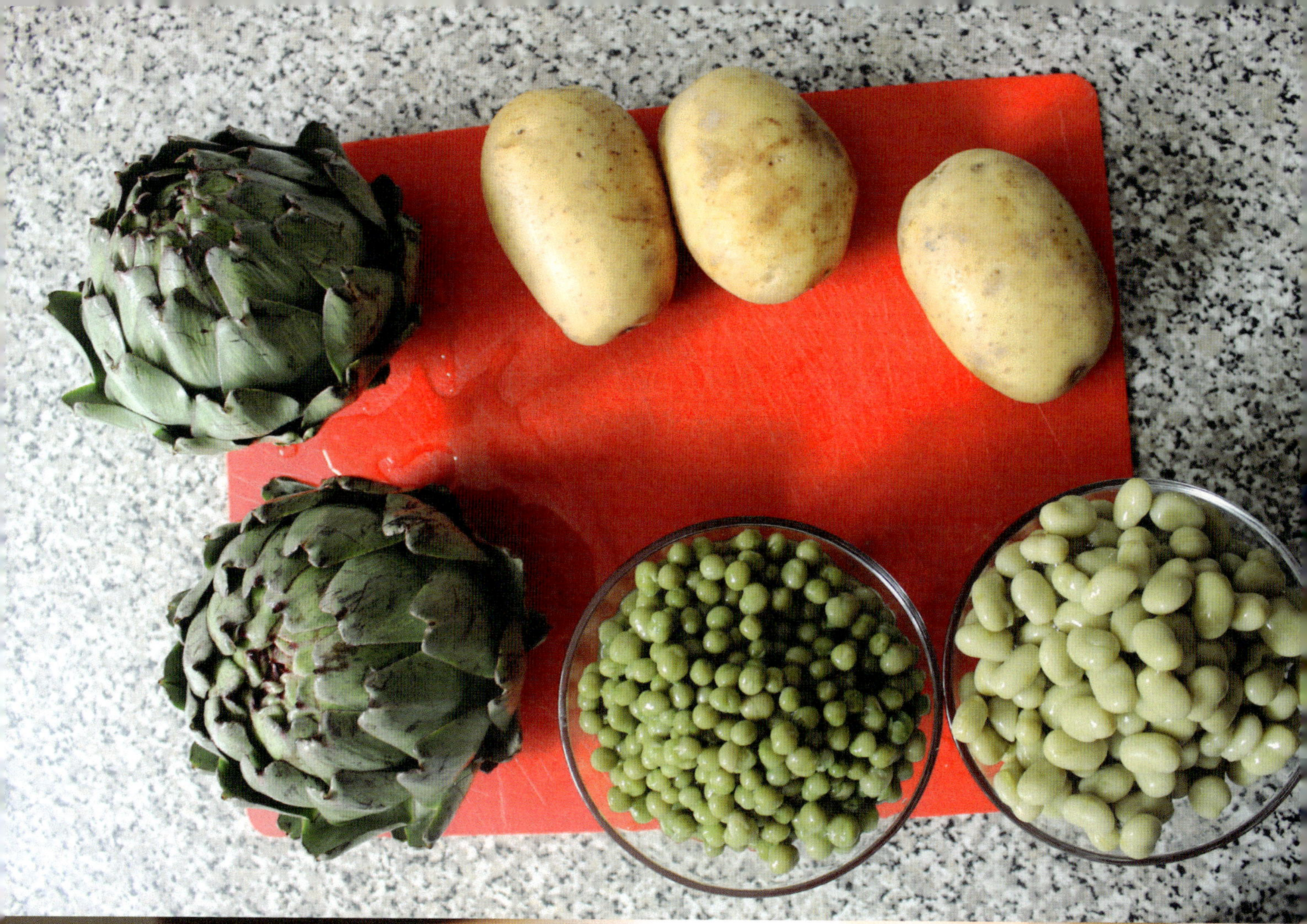

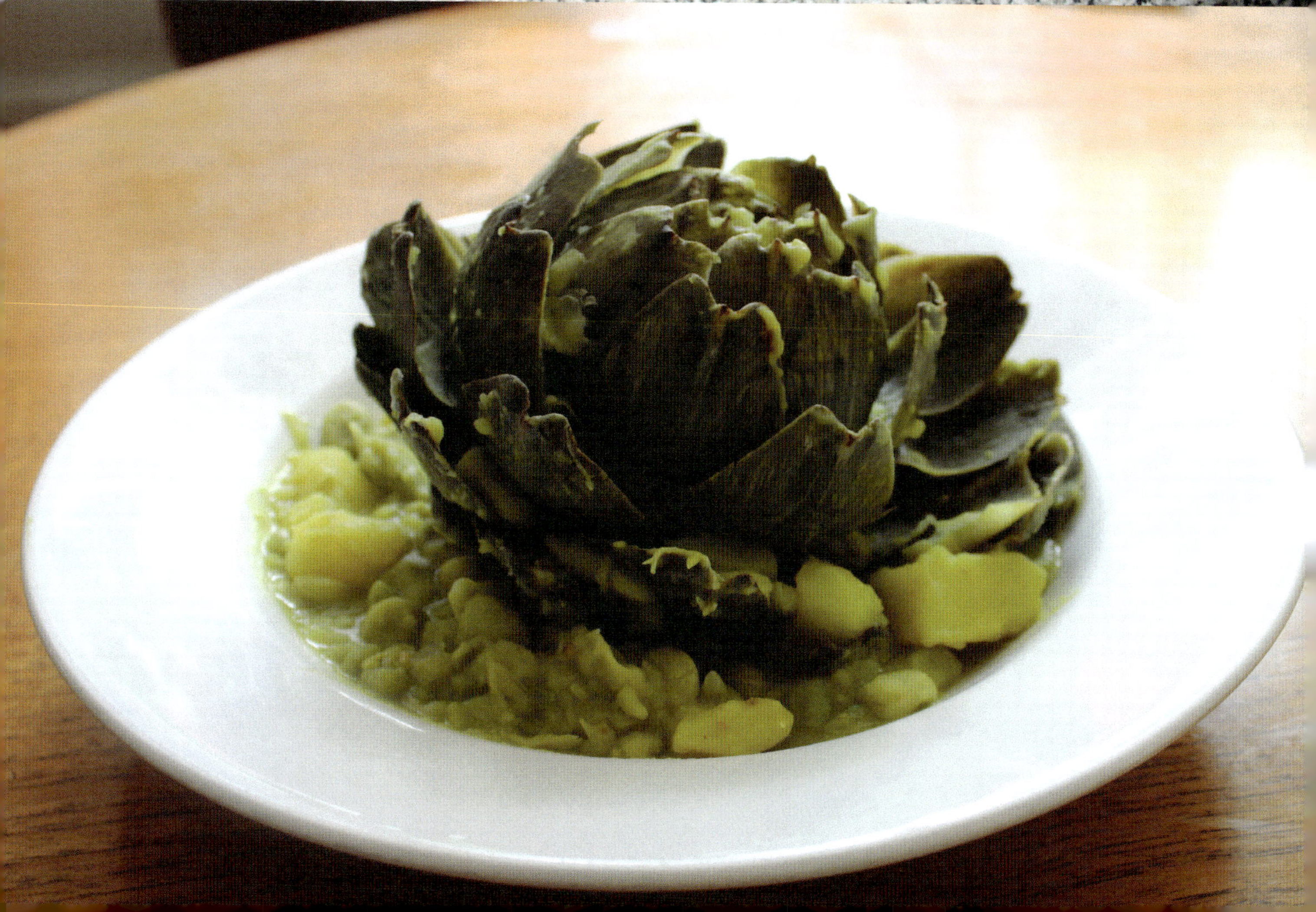

MAMA'S LENTEJAS
LENTIL STEW

SERVES 5

INGREDIENTS

- 250 G LENTILS
- 1 LARGE SLICE PUMPKIN
- 1 GREEN PEPPER
- 1 TOMATO
- 1 ONION
- 2 GARLIC CLOVES
- 1/2 TSP SAFFRON
- 1 BAY LEAF
- SALT
- OIL
- 2 HANDFULS RICE
- 250 G CHORIZO
- 250 G MORCILLA (BLACK PUDDING)

TIP
Soak the lentils in water overnight; this allows them to swell and tenderise

Lentejas is a truly hearty meal. Black pudding, chorizo and vegetables...what more could you want? So much goodness on one plate is almost too much to handle.

METHOD

1. If using dried lentils then soak your lentils overnight.

2. Begin by placing everything whole in a casserole dish with boiling water except for the rice and lentils. Cook over a medium heat until tender.

3. Add the soaked lentils and rice and cook for 15 minutes or until soft.

4. Once this is all cooked, remove the vegetables, leaving the rice and lentils behind and blend the vegetables along with some water until thick.

5. Add your blended vegetables back into the casserole dish with the rice and lentils. Add salt if necessary.

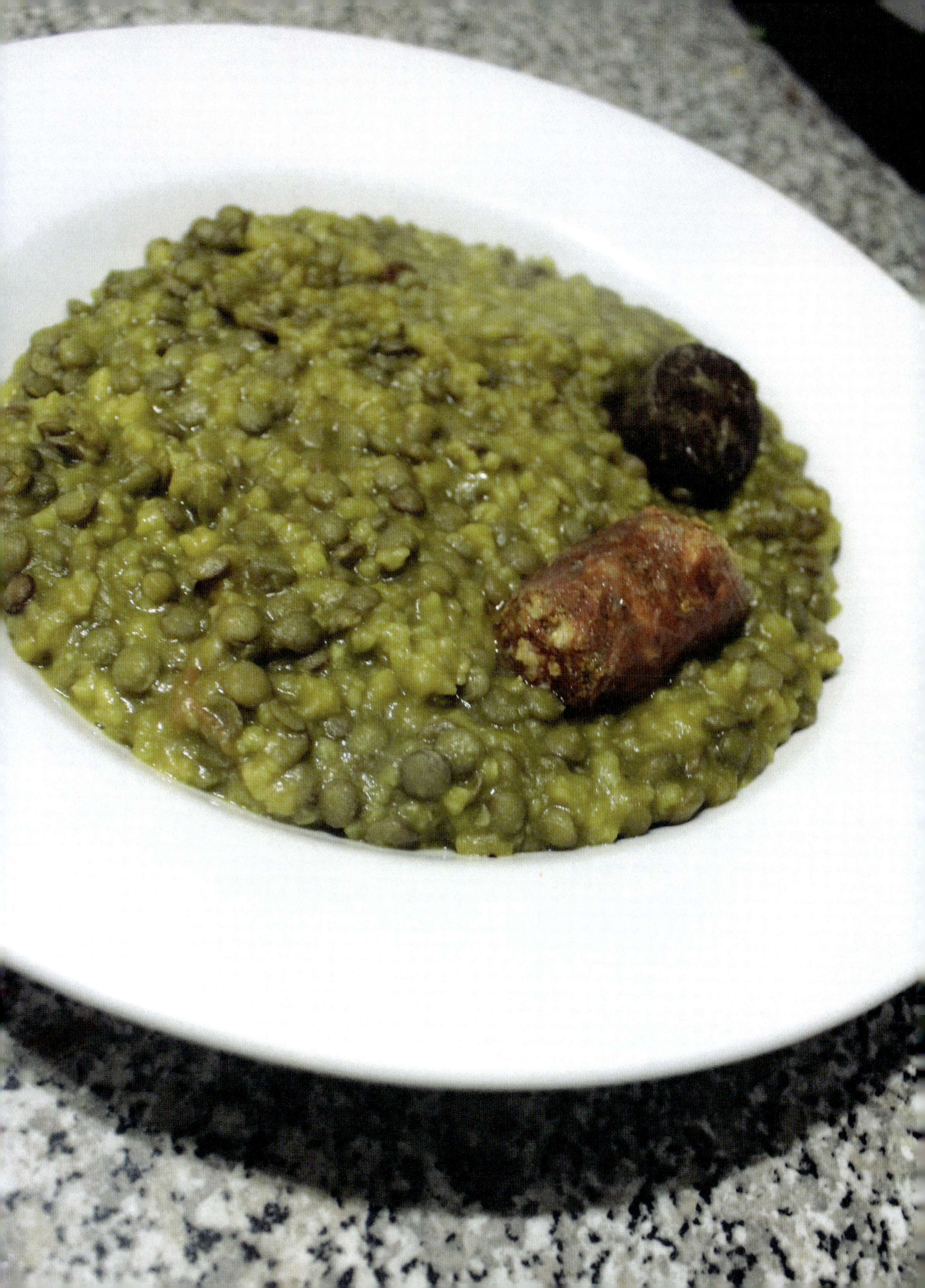

DESSERTS

CAKES AND PUDDINGS

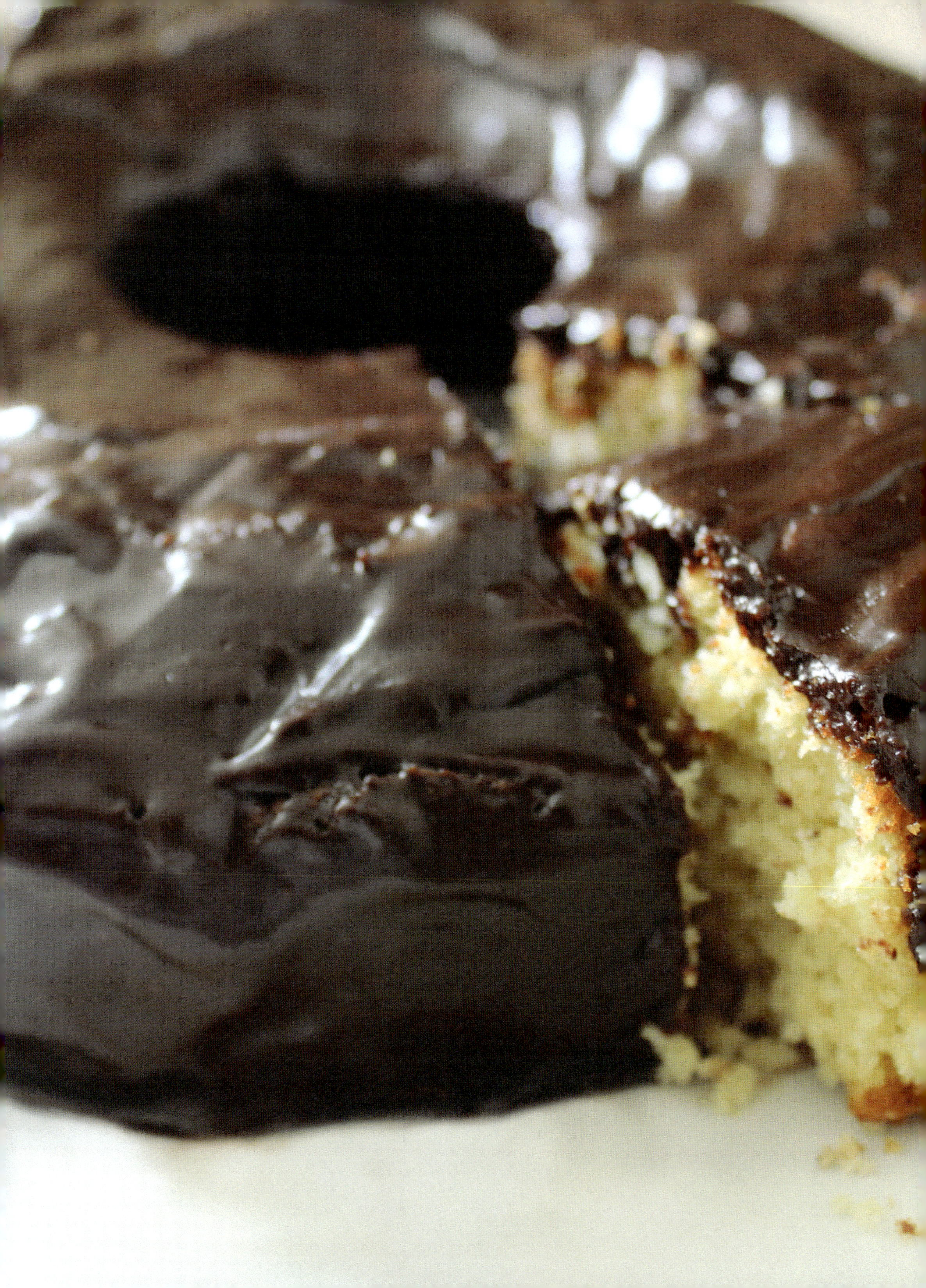

MAMA'S FLUFFY CHOCOLATE CAKE

INGREDIENTS

- 225 G SUGAR
- 225 G MARGARINE
- 4 EGGS
- 225 G SELF RAISING FLOUR
- 2 - 3 TBSP CHOCOLATE POWDER
- 50 ML MILK
- 1 LARGE MILK CHOCOLATE

The name says it all really; the cake is both light and fluffy. Not only does the smell of the cake cause a mouth watering effect, the most enjoyable moment is melting the chocolate to spread over your cake. I dare you to try making it without taking some chocolate for yourself!

METHOD

1. Preheat your oven to 180°C. Mix the sugar and butter in a bowl and beat together into a soft creamy liquid. Grab four eggs and separate the egg whites and yolks. Pour the egg white into a separate bowl and leave to one side. Pour the egg yolks in with the butter and sugar mix.

2. Grab your electric whisk and whisk the egg whites until the white foam peaks and remains pointed. Leave to one side.

3. Grab your bowl with the cake mixture and whisk together with your electric mixer. Once mixed nicely, add in the sieved flour and mix together once again until everything is a beautiful creamy texture.

4. Pour in half the egg white mix and fold over, then pour the rest and fold over once more until everything is blended together.

5. Grab a large ring tin or medium baking tin and place greaseproof paper or foil inside. I tend to rub the inside with butter and sprinkle flour around so that the cake mix doesn't stick to the sides or foil once cooked.

6. Pour in your mixture and place it in the oven for 20 – 30 minutes. After this time, check the cake is baked properly by poking different areas of the cake with a dry knife. If the knife is clean it is ready, otherwise leave a while longer.

Finally the best bit,

7. Grab yourself a pan, pour in a splash of milk, enough to cover the bottom of the pan and place it on a low - medium heat hob. Let the milk heat up then add in your chocolate pieces and stir until all is melted. Save two cubes of chocolate to one side.

8. Do not leave unattended as it will burn and ruin. Once all is melted and creamy remove from the heat and place to one side.

9. Place your cake on a large dish and pour your chocolate over spreading evenly throughout, covering everything.

10. Grate the two cubes you saved earlier over the cake.

ARROZ CON LECHE
RICE PUDDING

SERVES 1

INGREDIENTS

- 105 G SHORT GRAIN RICE
- 1 WIDE SLICE OF LEMON RIND
- 1 STICK OF CINNAMON
- 1 TSP OF GROUND CINNAMON
- 1 PINCH OF SALT
- 500 ML WHOLE MILK
- SUGAR TO TASTE

METHOD

1. Rinse the rice and then put it in a saucepan over a medium heat just barely covered with water.

2. Add the cinnamon stick and lemon rind. Stir continually until all of the water is absorbed.

3. Add milk, about 120 ML at a time, stirring each time until all is absorbed, stirring continuously.

4. When it seems creamy enough, taste to make sure the texture of the rice is correct.

5. When it is to your liking, turn off the heat and add a pinch of salt and a dash of cinnamon, slowly add a few tablespoons of sugar, until it is sweet enough for you.

6. Sprinkle a bit more cinnamon on top to decorate.

RECIPE BY JESSICA BONFANTE

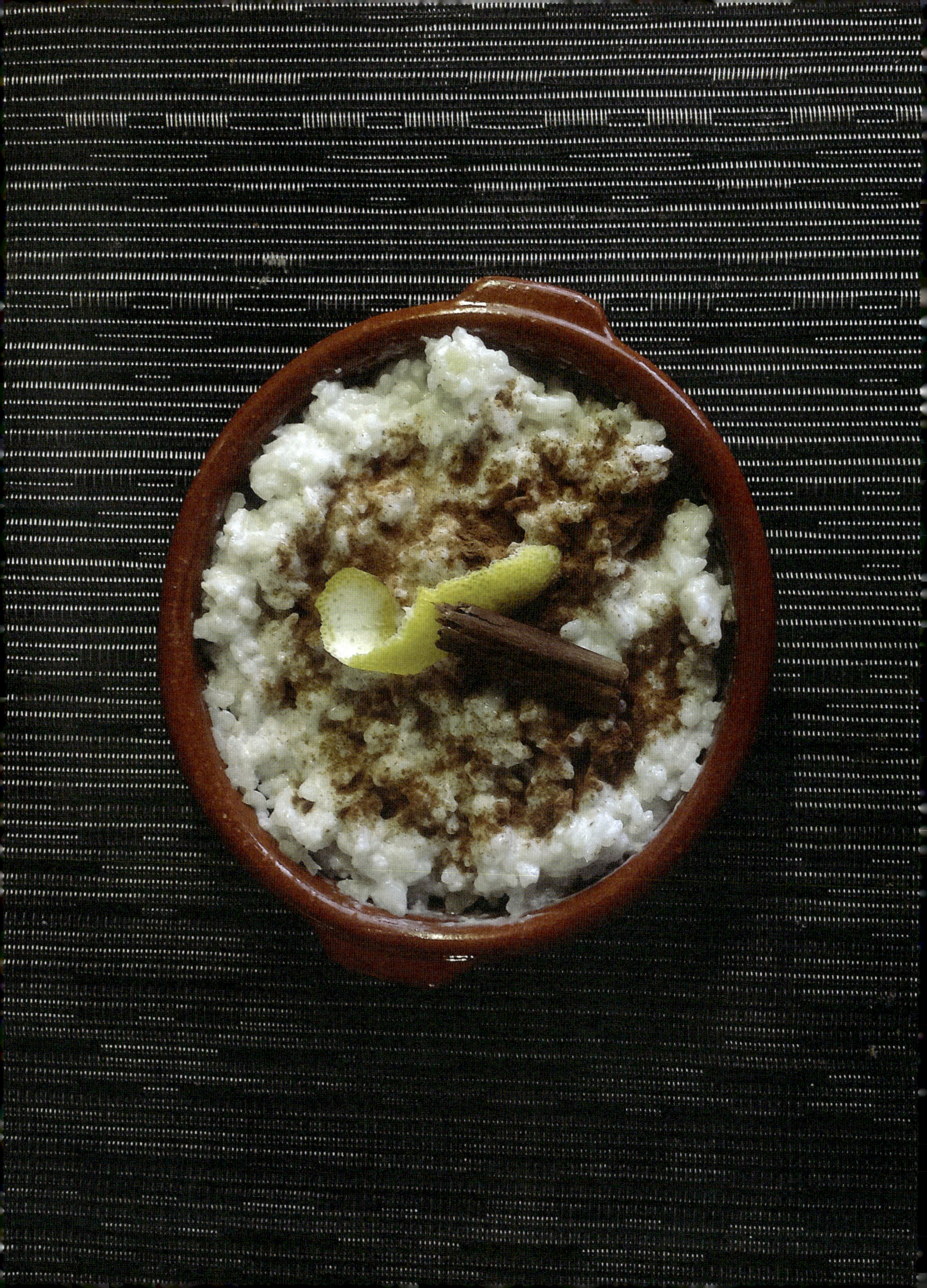

TORRIJAS

SERVES 4

INGREDIENTS

- 4 SLICES OF "SLICED" BREAD, CRUSTS REMOVED
- 200ML WHOLE MILK
- 4 EGGS
- CINNAMON
- OIL
- GOLDEN SYRUP

METHOD

1. Cut the slices of bread in half and place in a bowl with the milk.

2. Beat four eggs in a separate bowl. Dip the bread from the milk bowl into the beaten eggs, allowing it as you drain back into the bowl a little bit as you do so and fry in hot oil.

3. Once all the slices are done, dip them in the syrup and then sprinkle with cinnamon.

RECIPE BY JANET LAGUEA

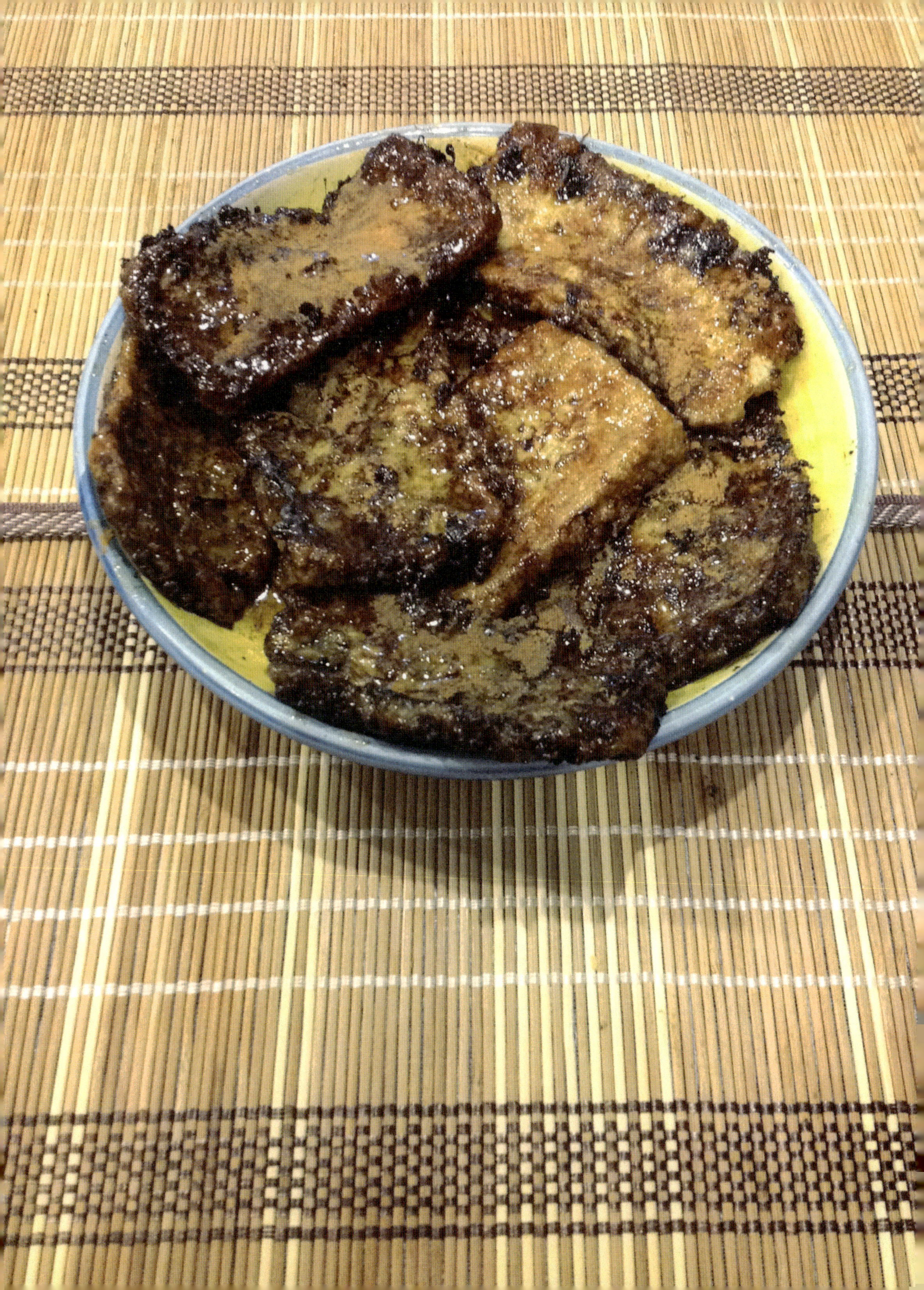

LEMON MERINGUE PIE

INGREDIENTS

- 60 G BUTTER
- 250 G DIGESTIVE BISCUITS (CRUSHED)
- 1 JAR LEMON CURD

MERINGUE

- 4 EGG WHITES
- 50 G CASTER SUGAR

METHOD

1. Melt the butter and combine with the crushed digestive biscuits, stirring until well mixed. Press firmly into the base of the cake tin, and put in the fridge to set.

2. Once set, spread the lemon curd over the biscuit base.

3. To make the meringue, beat the egg whites until stiff. Then gradually beat in the caster sugar. Once ready, carefully spread it over the lemon curd.

4. Use a blow torch to colour the meringue. Alternatively, place under a preheated grill for a few minutes.

RECIPE BY CHARMAIN WOOD

FLAPJACKS

INGREDIENTS

- 225G BUTTER
- 225G SOFT BROWN SUGAR
- 2 TBSP GOLDEN SYRUP
- 350G ROLLED OATS

METHOD

1. In a saucepan place the butter, sugar and syrup over a medium heat. Stir constantly with a wooden spoon.

2. Once the butter is melted and you have a smooth syrup remove from heat and add the oats, making sure that all the oats are well coated.

3. Grease a square tin with butter and add the mixture; press down firmly to make a roughly even layer.

4. Bake at 150°C for about 40 minutes. Leave it to cool for about 10 minutes so that it hardens a bit, then cut into squares.

RECIPE BY CHARMAIN WOOD

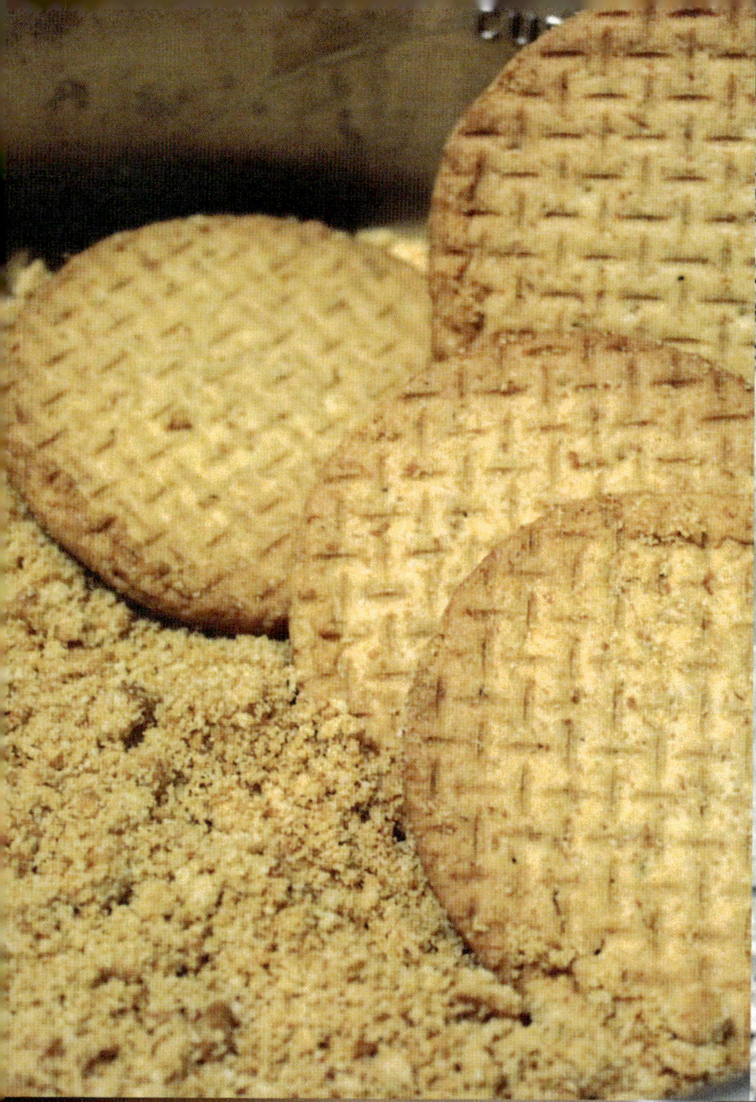
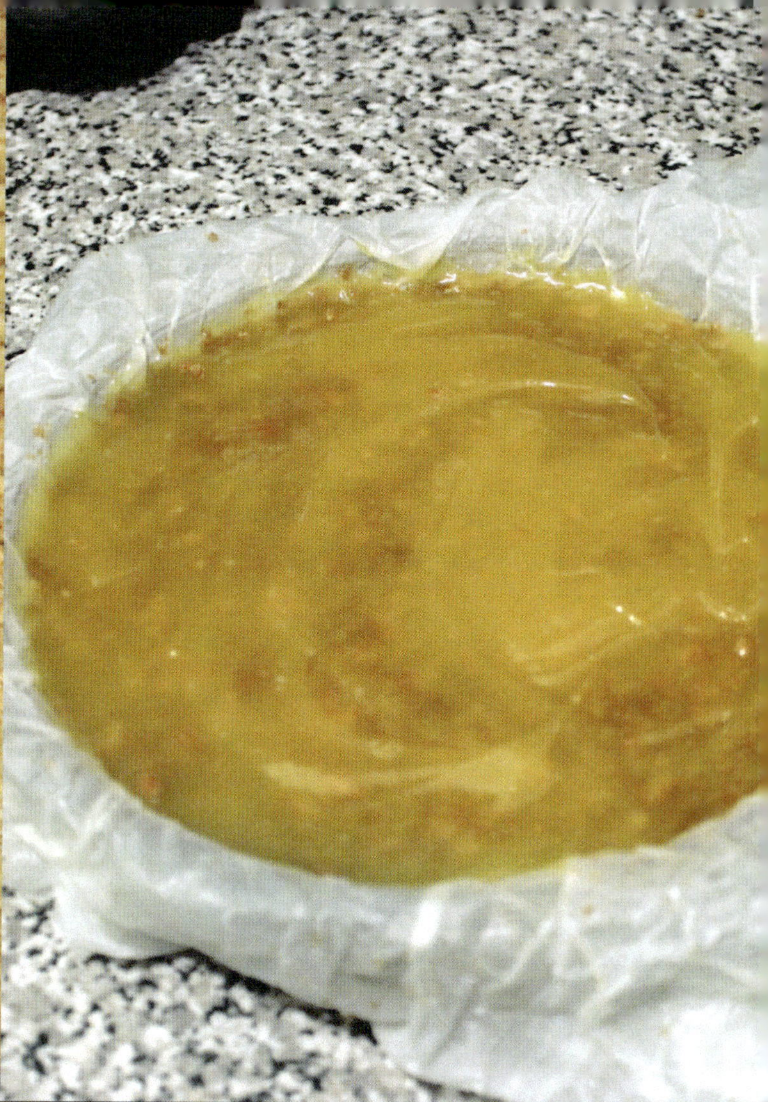
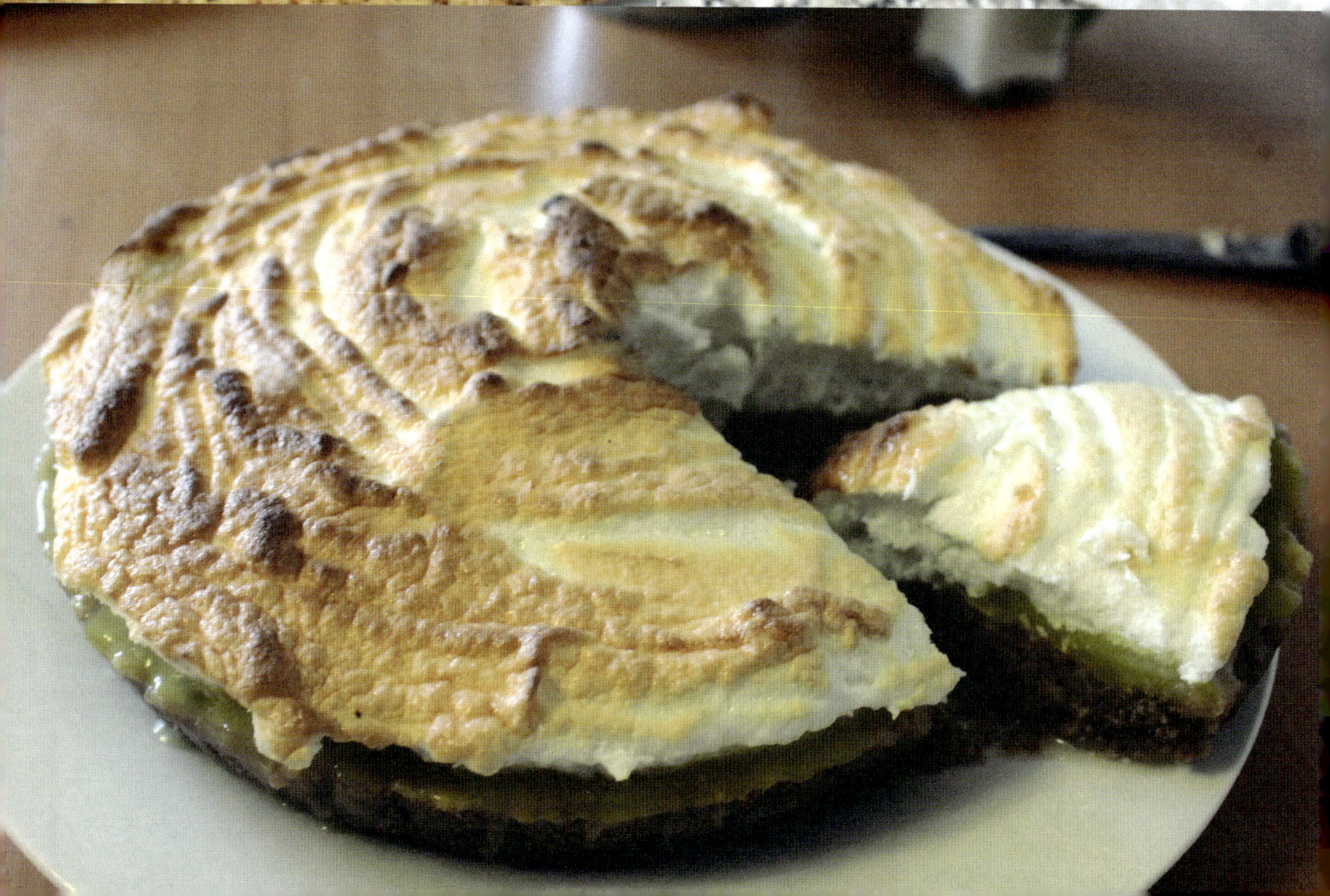

MAMA'S EMPIRE CAKE

INGREDIENTS

- 450 G SELF RAISING FLOUR
- 225 G SUGAR
- 225 G MARGARINE
- PINCH OF SALT
- PINCH OF MIXED SPICE
- 112 G SULTANAS
- 112 G CURRANTS
- 56 G GLAZED CHERRIES
- 2 EGGS
- 150 ML MILK

METHOD

1. Preheat oven to 180°C

Using the rubbing method do the following:

1. Mix flour and butter until they form a breadcrumb texture.
2. Add all the dry ingredients.
3. Beat eggs with the milk and add to the mixture.

2. Once ready pour into a greased baking tin and pop it in the oven for 45 minutes - 1 hour, checking occasionally to avoid it burning.

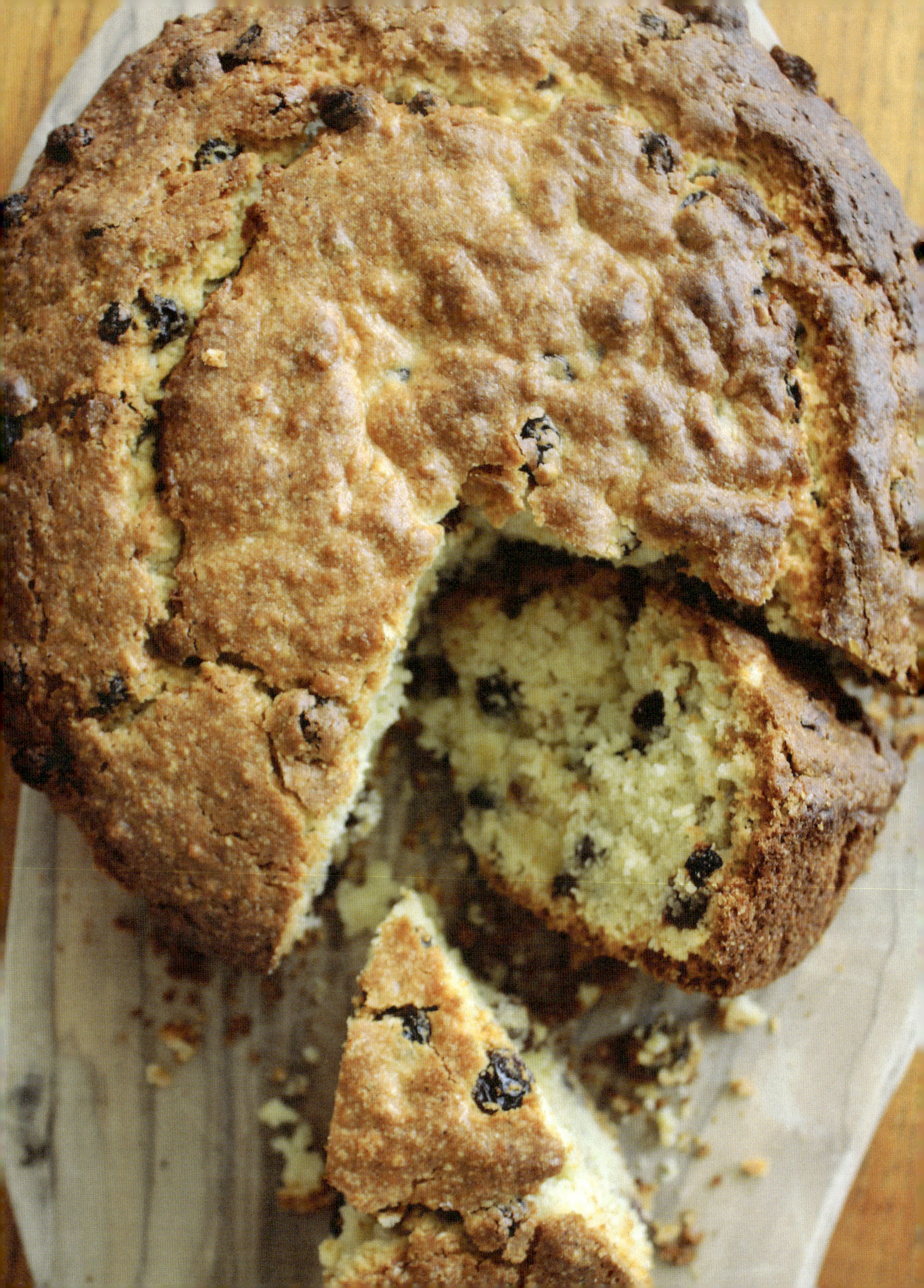

MAMA'S COCONUT CAKE

INGREDIENTS

- 225 G SUGAR
- 225 G MARGARINE
- 1 TBS OLIVE OIL
- 4 EGGS
- 225 G SELF RAISING FLOUR
- 110 G DESICCATED COCONUT
- VANILLA EXTRACT

METHOD

1. Preheat your oven to 180°C.

2. Mix the sugar and butter in a bowl and beat together into a soft creamy liquid. Grab four eggs and separate the egg white and yolks. Pour the egg whites into a separate bowl and leave to one side then pour the egg yolks in with the butter and sugar mix.

3. Add the tablespoon of olive oil and half a teaspoon of vanilla extract.

4. Grab your electric whisk and whisk the egg whites until the white foam peaks and remains pointed and leave to one side.

5. Go back to your cake mix bowl and stir. Now add in your coconut. Once blended nicely, add in the sieved flour and mix together until everything is a wonderfully creamy texture.

6. Pour in half the egg white mix and fold over then pour the rest and fold over once more. Using your electric whisk, mix together the ingredients.

7. Grab your baking tin and place greaseproof or foil paper inside, I tend to rub the inside with butter and sprinkle flour around so that the cake mix doesn't stick to the sides or foil once cooked.

8. Pour in your mixture and place in the oven for 20 – 30 minutes. After this time check the cake is baked through properly by prodding different areas of the cake with a dry knife. If the knife is clean it is ready, otherwise leave a while longer on a reduced heat.

9. You may wish to cover with jam and sprinkle over with more desiccated coconut or if you feel indulgent, a layer of dark chocolate.

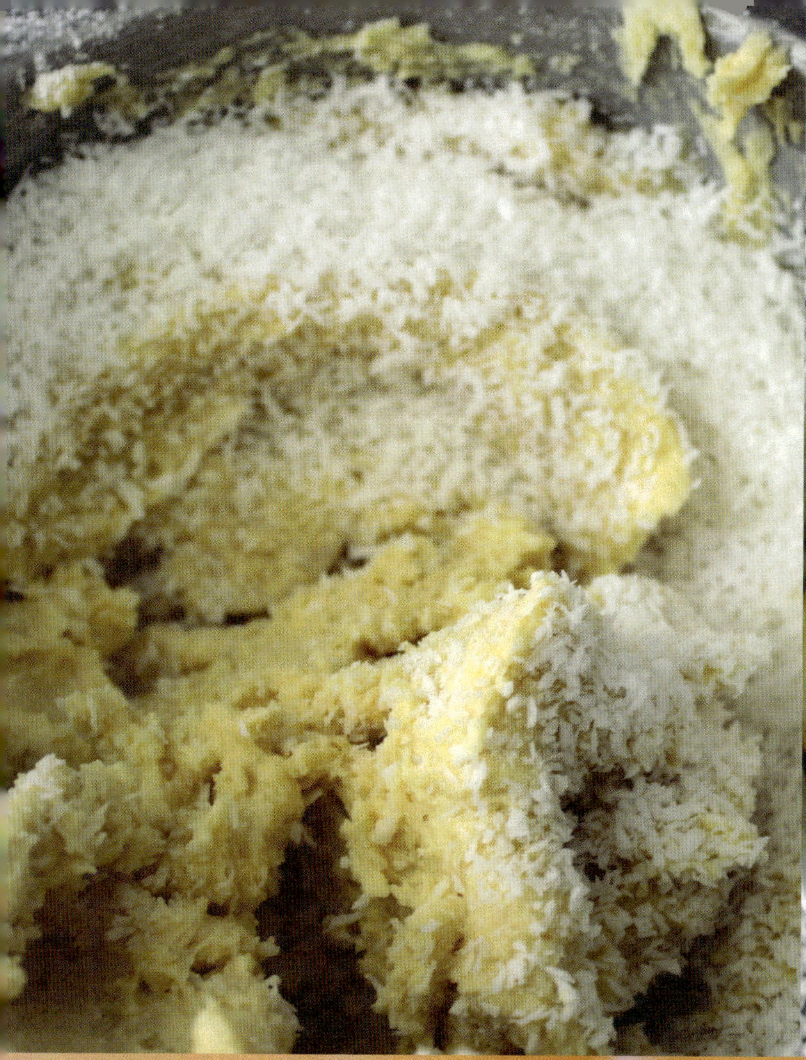

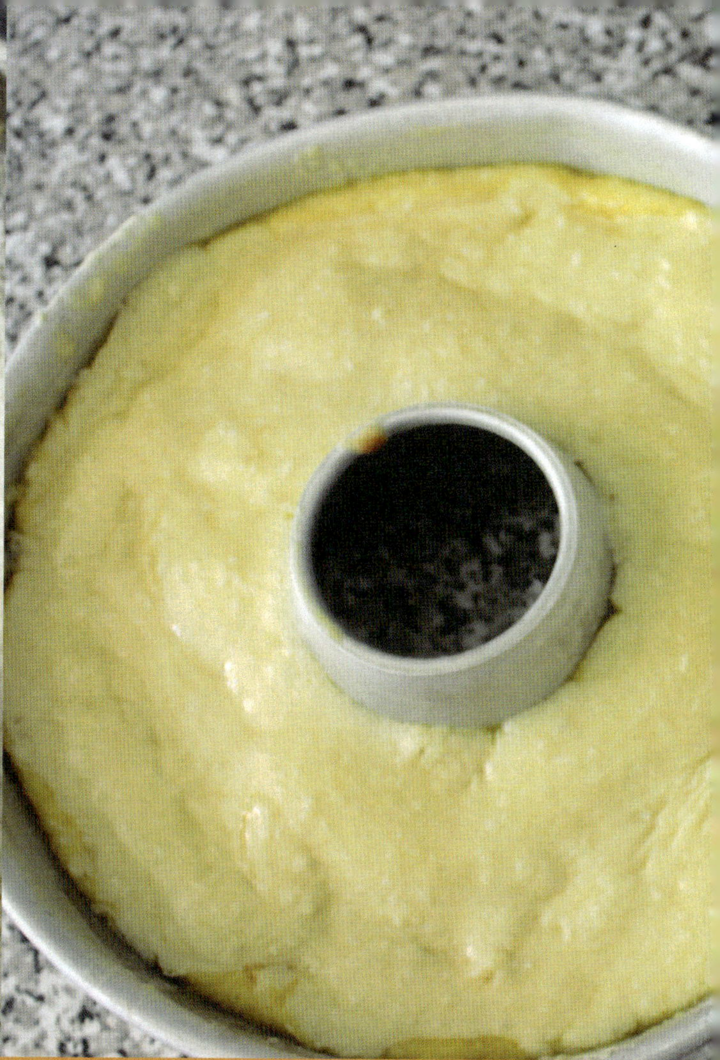

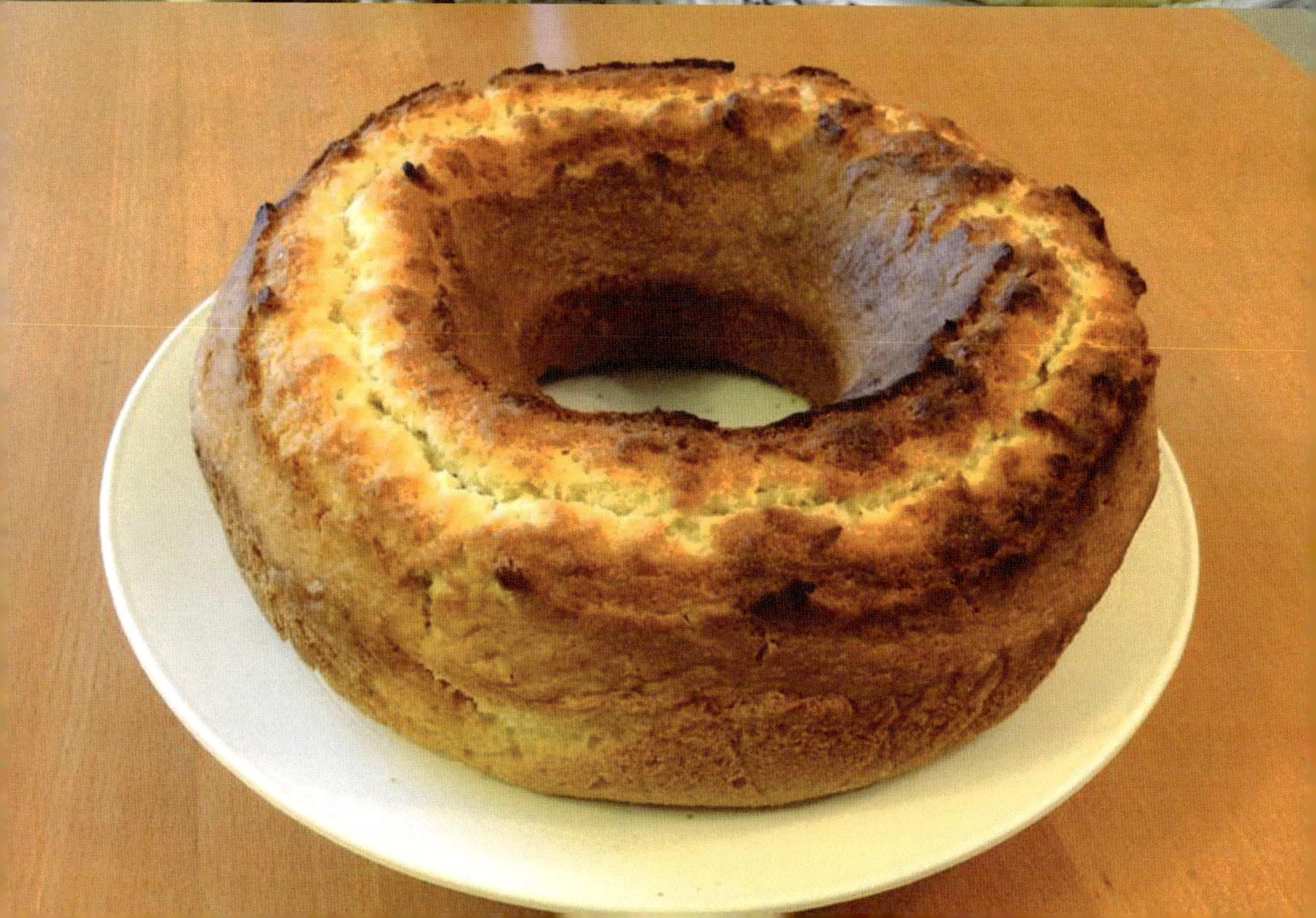

MAMA'S SPINACH, COCONUT MILK, STRAWBERRY AND BANANA SMOOTHIE

INGREDIENTS

- 6 LARGE STRAWBERRIES
- 1 LARGE BANANA
- 200ML COCONUT MILK
- NUTMEG
- FRESH SPINACH LEAVES *(HANDFUL)*
- DESICCATED COCONUT
- WATER

METHOD

1. Peel your banana and place this, your strawberries, spinach leaves, coconut milk and a bit of desiccated coconut in a blender. Add a tiny bit of water as the milk can be quite thick.

2. Blend together, adding a bit of cold water if you see it is too thick.

3. Add a dash of nutmeg and mix.

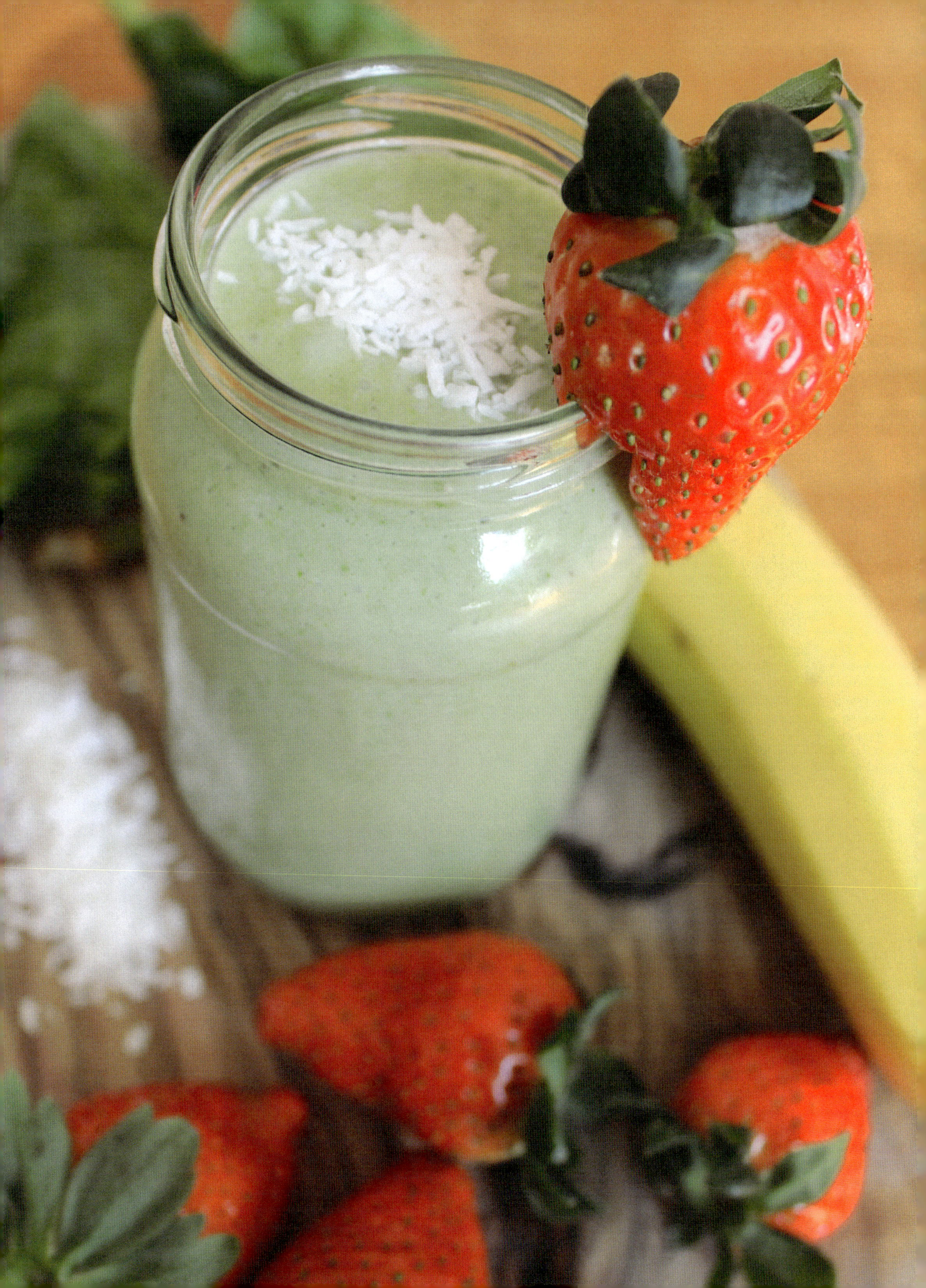

BANANA BREAD

INGREDIENTS

- 175 G UNSALTED BUTTER
- 175G G SUGAR
  (HALF LIGHT MUSCOVADO, HALF GOLDEN CASTER)
- 75 G HAZELNUTS
  (OPTIONAL)
- 2 EGGS
- 175 G SELF RAISING FLOUR
- 2 - 3 VERY RIPE BANANAS
- DROP VANILLA EXTRACT
- A LITTLE DEMERARA SUGAR

METHOD

1. Preheat the oven to 170°C. Line the base and sides of a 20cm x 12cm / 8in x 5in loaf tin with greaseproof paper.

2. Beat the butter and sugars until light and coffee-coloured.

3. Toast the hazelnuts, rub them in a tea towel to remove their skins and finely grind.

4. Slowly add the eggs to the butter and sugar mixture and mix in the toasted ground hazelnuts and self-raising flour.

5. Peel the bananas and chop them into small pieces. Gently fold the vanilla extract and the bananas into the cake mixture, turning gently and taking care not to over mix.

6. Scoop the batter into the prepared loaf tin. Dust with a little demerara sugar and bake for about 1 hour to 1h 10 minutes, covering with foil if the top starts to darken too quickly.

RECIPE BY SARAH-SEAMUS MCCARTHY

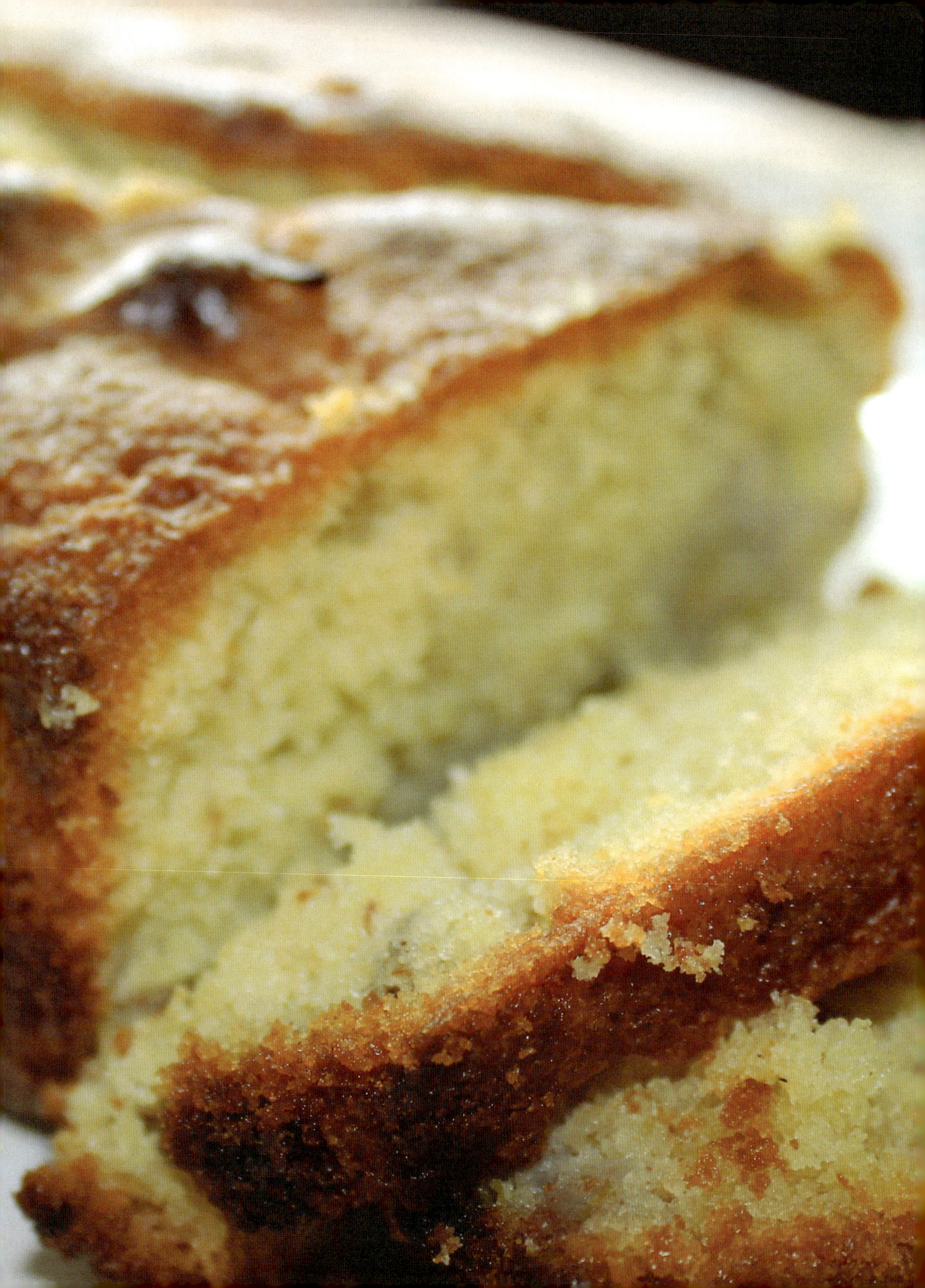

MAMA'S VOLCANO CAKES

INGREDIENTS

- 225 G SELF RAISING FLOUR
- 110 G BUTTER
- 85 G CASTER SUGAR
- 30 G DESICCATED COCONUT
- 55 G GLAZED CHERRIES
- 1 EGG
- 3 TBSP WHOLE MILK
- JAM

These little cakes disappear as quickly as they are made. Small, sweet and fruity they are perfect with a cup of tea or coffee and if you have children then it's a fun one to make as they can help you shape them and pour the jam.

METHOD

1. Mix the flour with butter, and rub together until it resembles a breadcrumb texture. Now add sugar, coconut and cherries and beat the egg with the milk.

2. Place on an oven tray in small heaps and make a thumb size dip in the centre to place jam.

3. Bake in the oven at 200°C and cook for 20 - 25 minutes. When ready, leave to cool and pour a spoonful of jam in the hole.

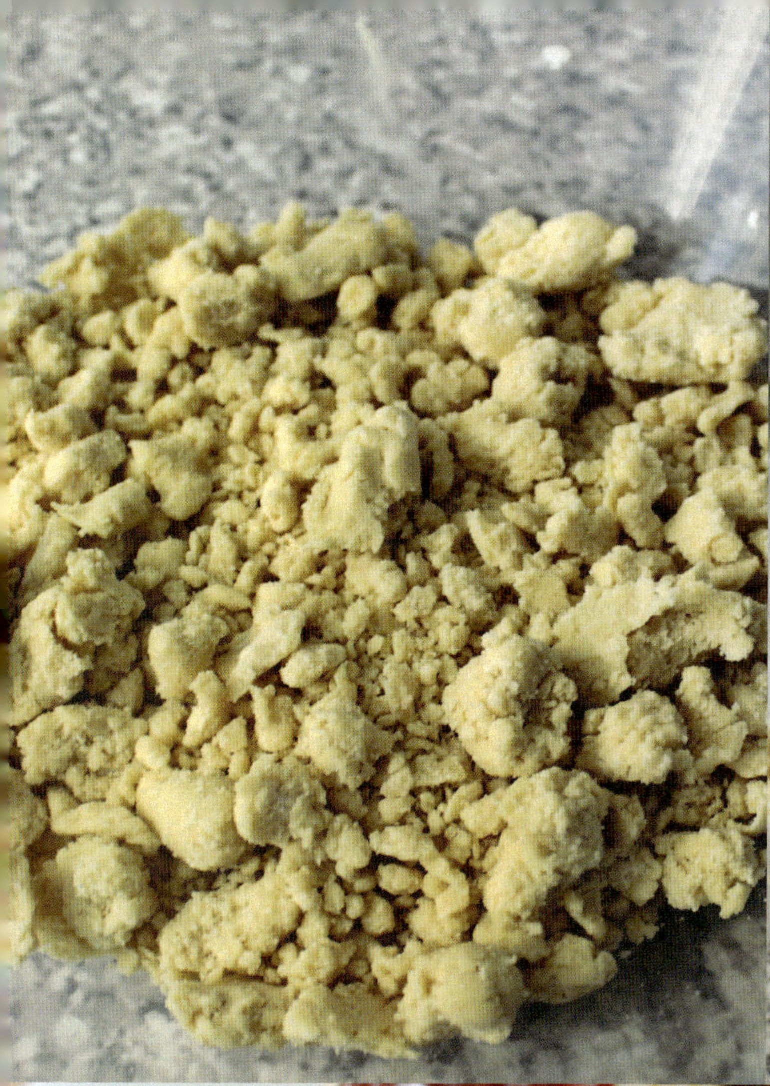
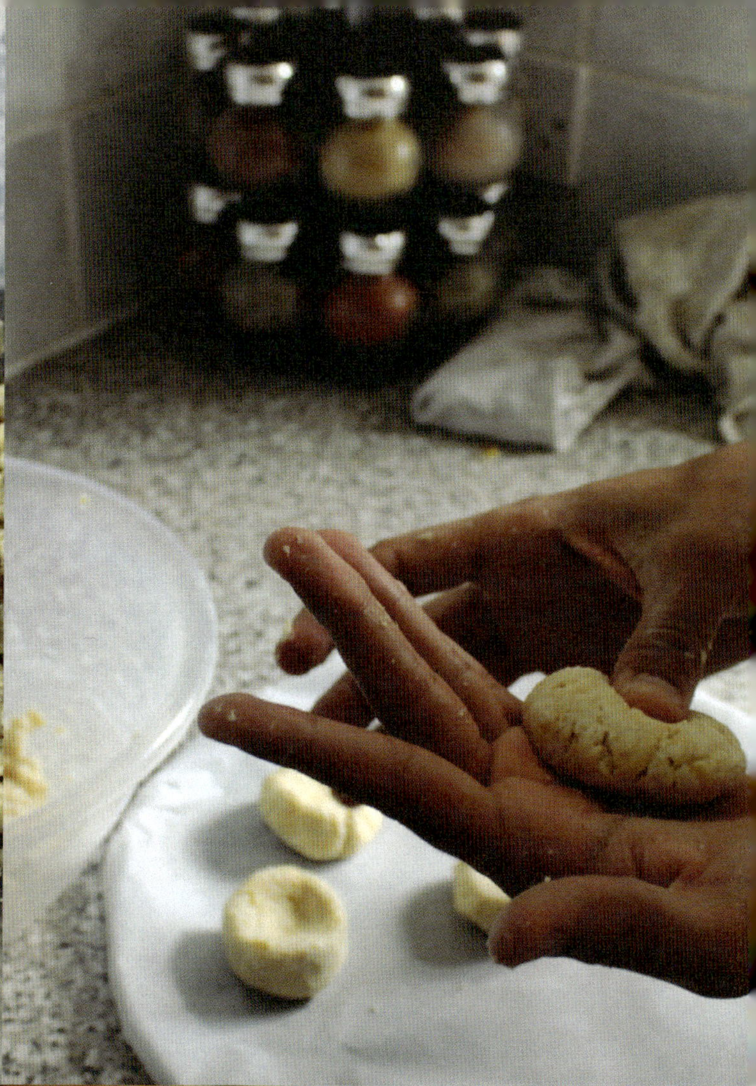
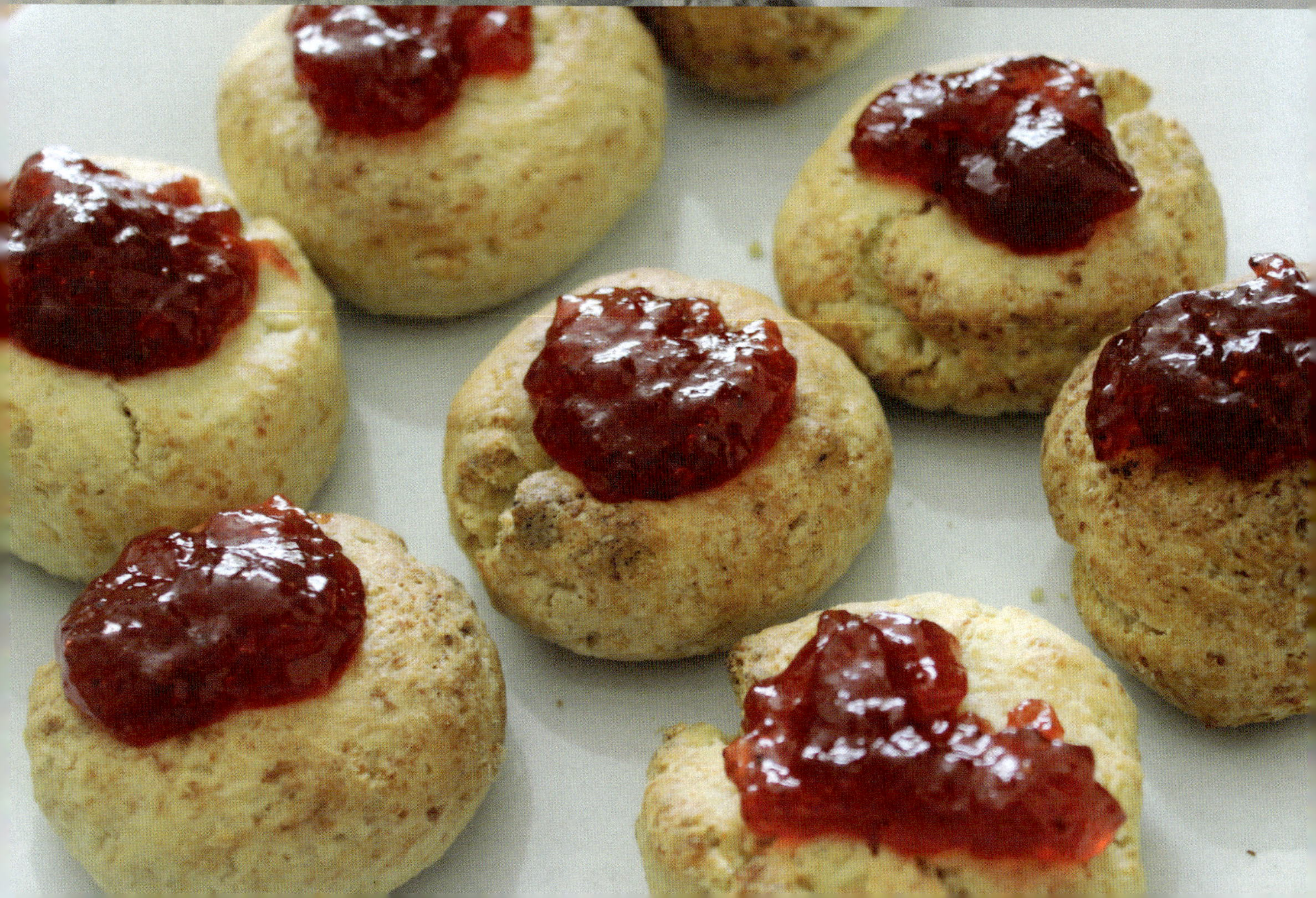

MAMA'S HAZELNUT CHOCOLATE CHEESECAKE

INGREDIENTS

- 1 SMALL PACKET DIGESTIVE BISCUITS
- 55 G MELTED BUTTER
- 200 G CREAM CHEESE
- 150 ML DOUBLE CREAM
- 6 TSP OF SUGAR
- 100 G HAZELNUT CHOCOLATE
- CHOCOLATE *(TO GRATE OVER)*

Christmas is the season for overindulgence and this cheesecake fits in perfectly. If you are as much a fan of hazelnut chocolate as I am, then you must give this a try.

METHOD

1. Mash up the biscuits and mix together with melted butter.
2. Press the mixture down into a tin and leave in the fridge whilst you make the filling.
3. Whip the double cream until thick and mix in the sugar and cream cheese.
4. When you have done so, add the hazelnut chocolate to your cream and cheese mix.
5. Pour over biscuit base and decorate with grated chocolate.
6. Leave in fridge for at least two hours.

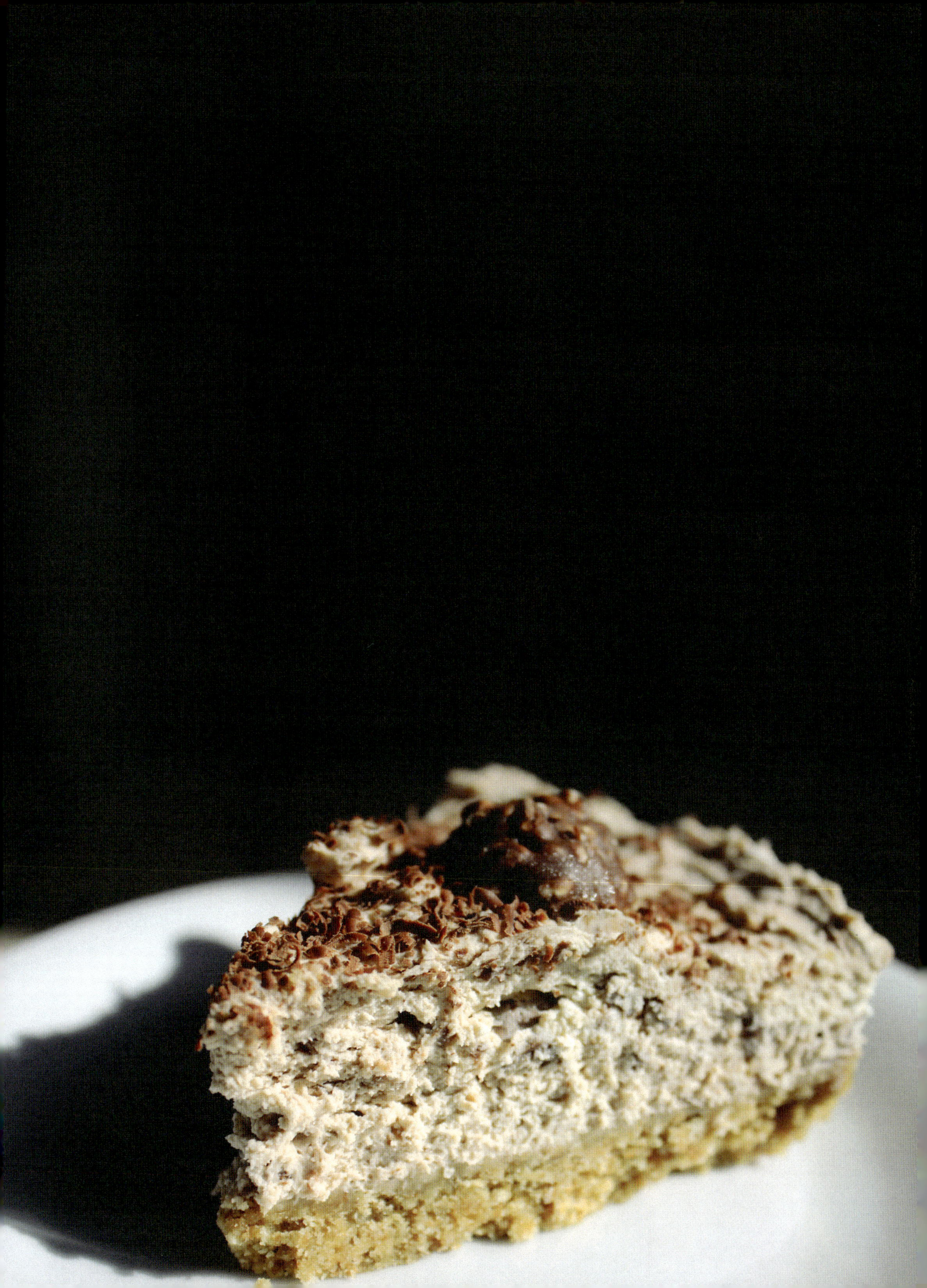

MAMA'S DARK CHOCOLATE COQUITOS

INGREDIENTS

- 250 G COCONUT
- 400 G TIN CONDENSED MILK
- 300 G DARK CHOCOLATE

METHOD

1. Mix the desiccated coconut and condensed milk, slowly pouring in the milk bit by bit, until you get a thick consistency.

2. Roll your mixture into separate balls and place in the fridge overnight.

3. Melt your chocolate - *I used the Bain Marie method*.

4. Roll your coconut balls in the chocolate and lay on a dish. *(it might help to lightly spread your plate with oil to prevent the base sticking)* Place them in the fridge to harden.

You can add nuts to your chocolate before or after rolling for a different taste, or decorate with coconut flakes.

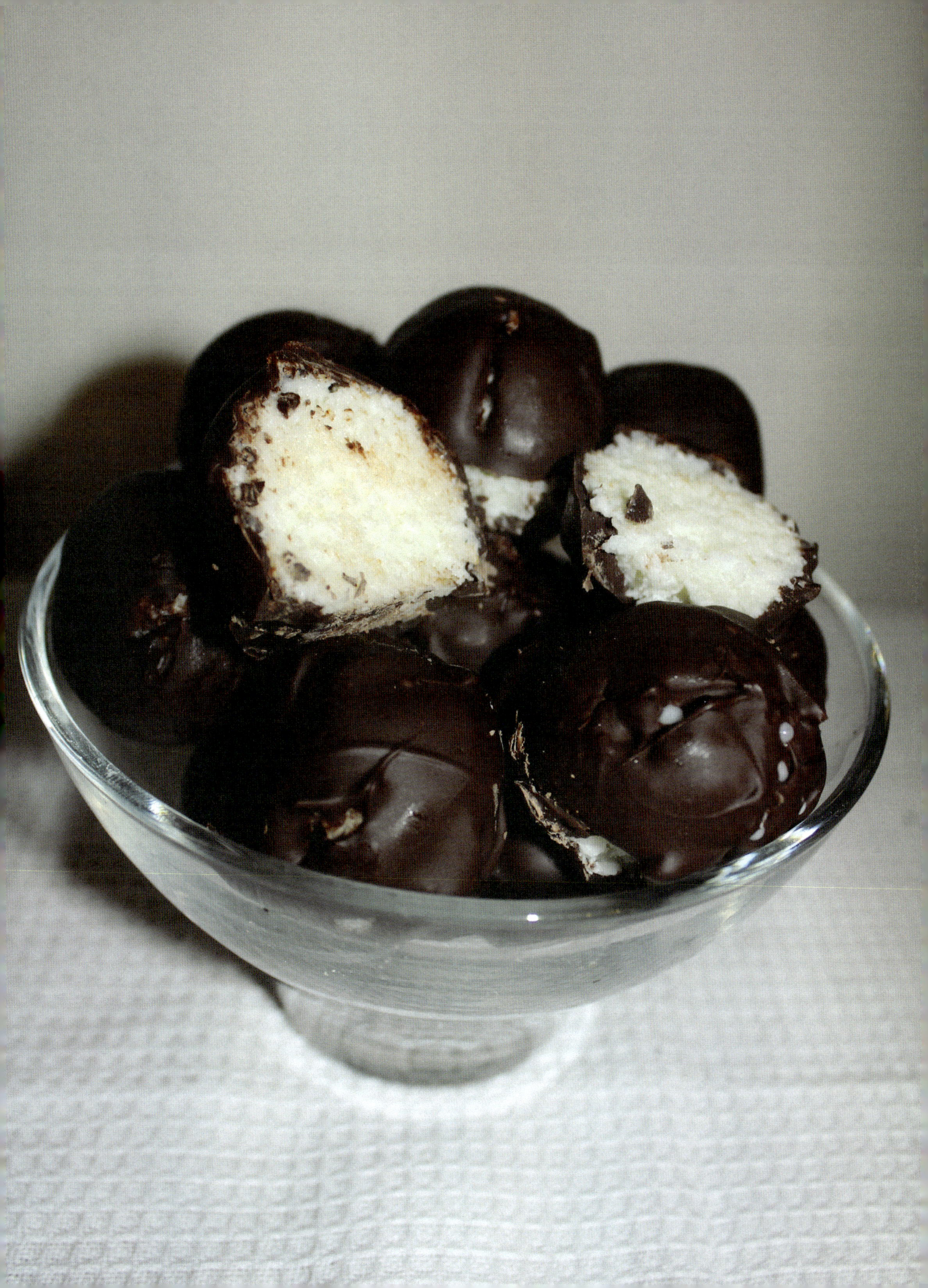

GIBRALTARIAN TREATS

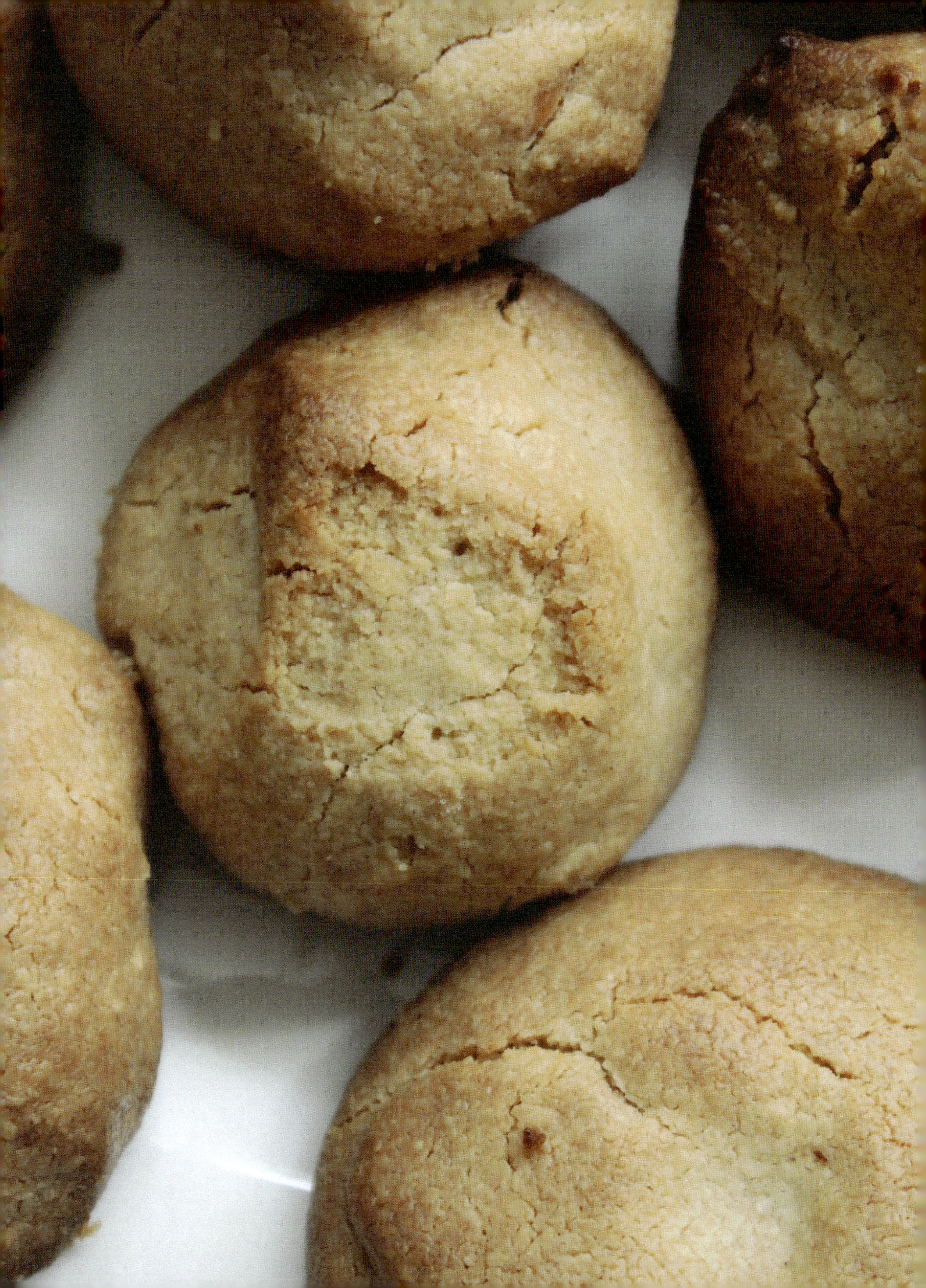

PUDÍN DE PAN
BREAD PUDDING

INGREDIENTS

- 14 SLICES CRUSTLESS BREAD
- 6 EGGS
- 2 PACKETS FLAN CARAMEL
- 410 G EVAPORATED MILK
- WATER
- 600 G SUGAR

METHOD

1. Soak bread in water. After five minutes squeeze water out and mix with milk.

2. Mix caramel with water; measure the water in the evaporated milk tin for quantity and add to mixture. Add beaten eggs and sugar to mixture.

3. Place in an oven-proof dish and bake for 1h 15 minutes at 170°C.

RECIPE BY LILLY ATTARD

MAMA'S BOLLOS DE HORNAZO
SWEET ANISE BREAD

INGREDIENTS

- 700 G SELF RAISING FLOUR
- 225 G BUTTER
- 225 G SUGAR
- 5 EGGS
- ANISEED *(HANDFUL)*
- MILK

METHOD

1. Mix the butter and sugar until its all mixed together well. Add one egg at a time until everything is blended. Add the aniseed and sieved flour and mix together until you are able to slice the dough into a clean half.

2. Divide all of this into several portions and wash with milk or egg and bake in the oven at about 200°C for 20 minutes.

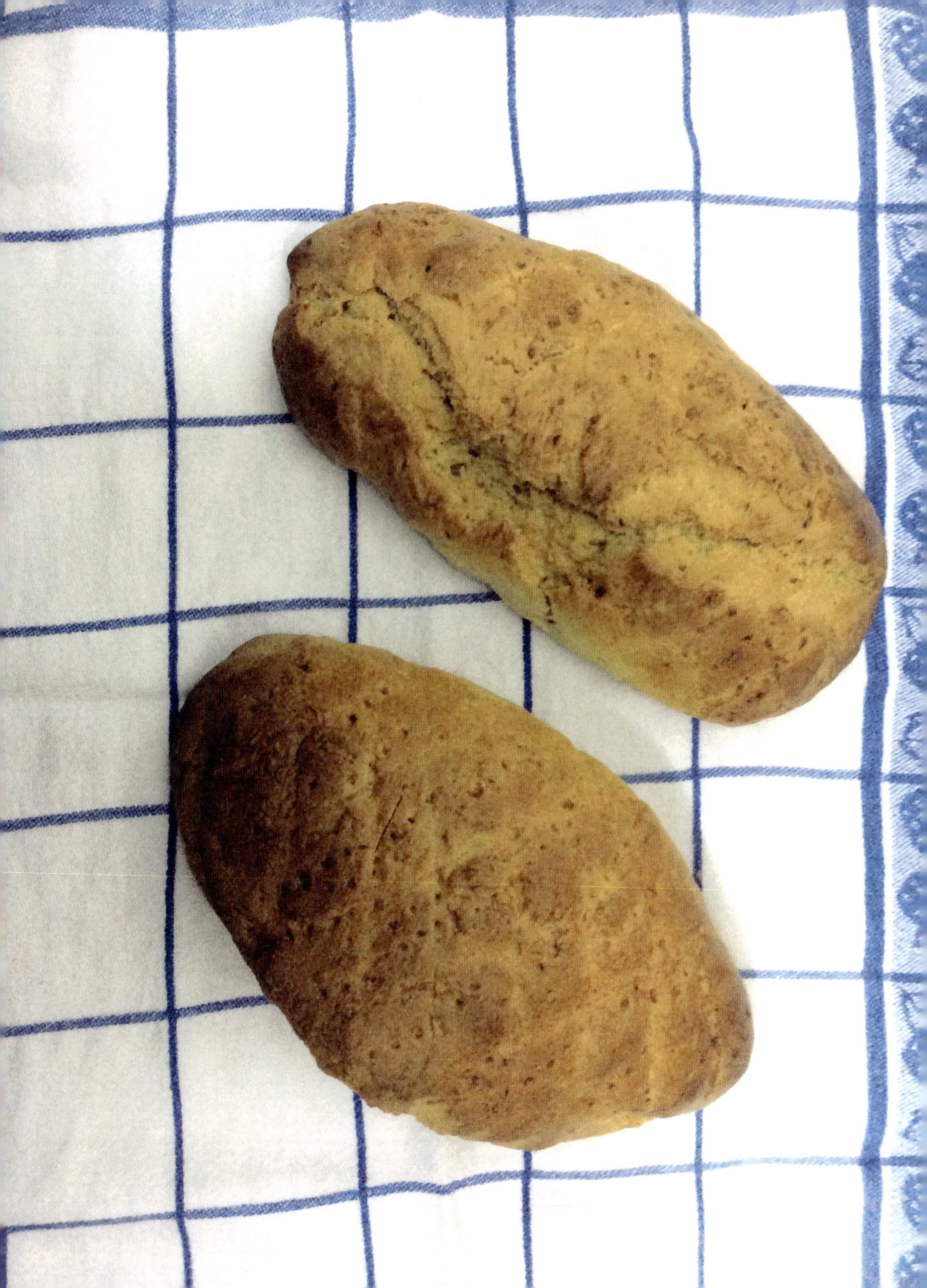

MANTECADOS
PEANUT BUTTER BISCUITS

INGREDIENTS

- 225 G LARD
- 225 G ICING SUGAR
- 340 G JAR PEANUT BUTTER
- 225 G PLAIN FLOUR

METHOD

1. Preheat oven at 180°C for about 20 minutes.

2. Mix and heat the lard with sugar in the microwave to melt, then add the peanut butter and plain flour.

3. Mix together into little balls and flatten the top lightly with your thumb. Place them in the oven and leave to bake for 15 - 20 minutes.

RECIPE BY ROSEMARIE MAÑASCO

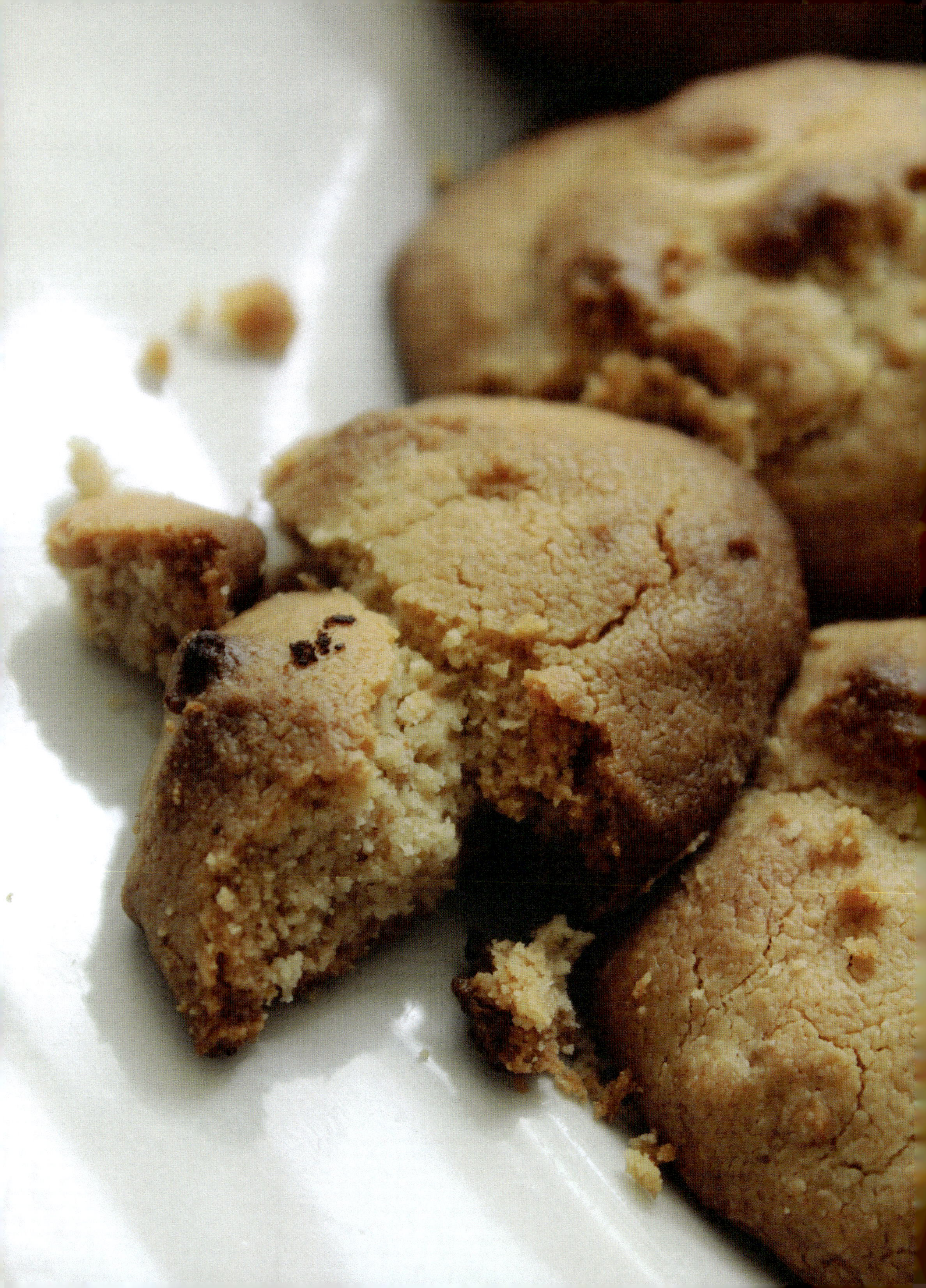

MAMA'S PANISSA

INGREDIENTS

- 225 G CHICKPEA FLOUR
- 285 ML COLD WATER
- SALT
- PEPPER

METHOD

1. Soak the flour in the water and leave for 2 hours. Add salt and pepper, mix well and put in a saucepan, bring to the boil, stirring all the time until it's thick. Once it's cooked divide it between two plates *(soup plates)* and leave to cool.

2. Once the mixture is cold, cut into wide fingers or wedges and fry until golden brown.

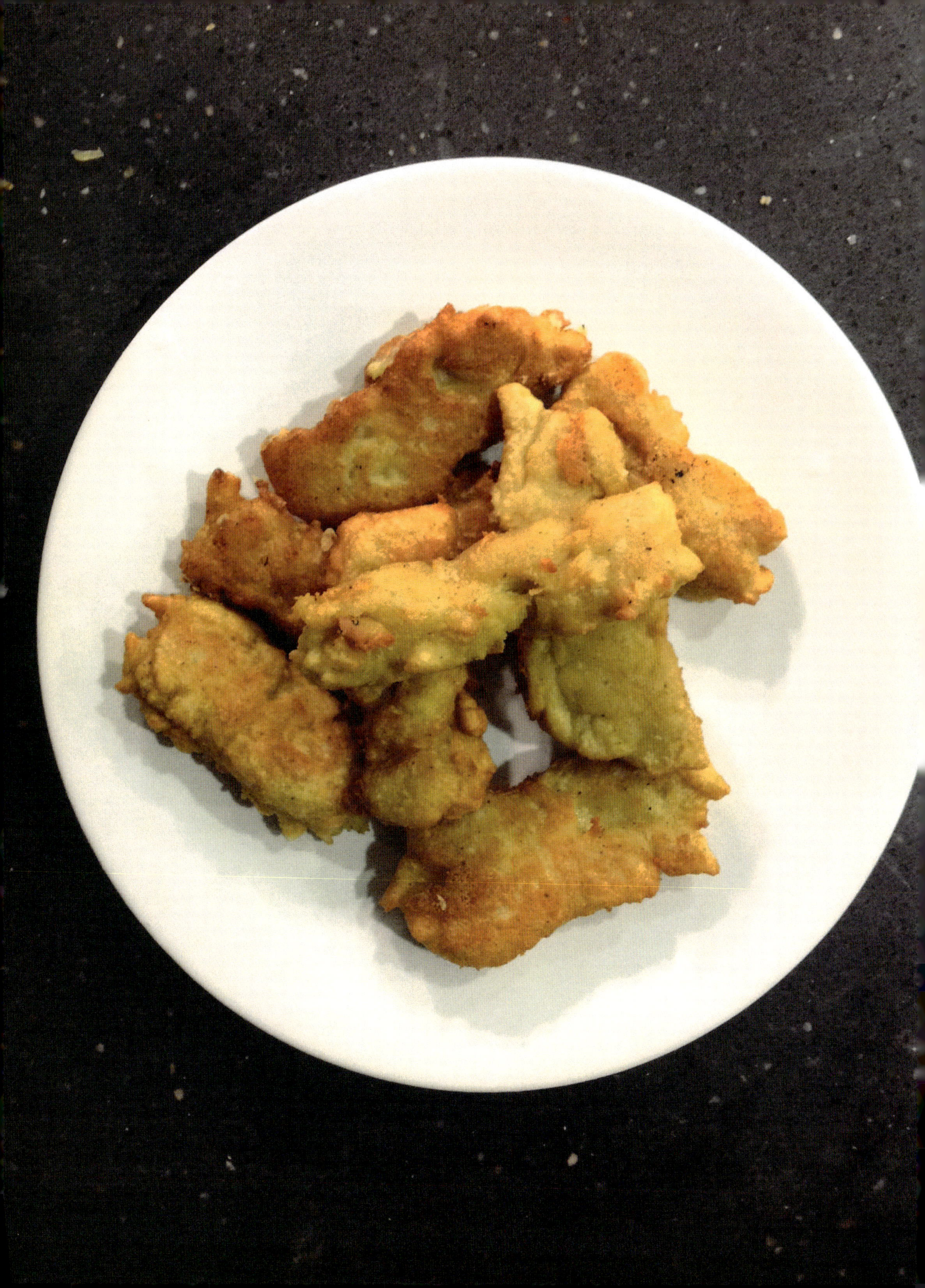

MAMA'S BORRACHUELOS

INGREDIENTS

- 3 ORANGES (JUICED)*
- 680 G SELF RAISING FLOUR
- 280 ML OIL
- 2 TBSP ANISEED
- 200 G SUGAR
- GOLDEN SYRUP
- HUNDREDS & THOUSANDS
- BRANDY*
- WHITE WINE*
- DRY ANISE LIQUEUR*

*THE THREE ITEMS ABOVE AND THE ORANGE JUICE SHOULD MEASURE A TOTAL OF 280 ML BETWEEN THEM

METHOD

1. Heat the oil and once hot, remove from hob and add the aniseed. Allow to cool down, pour in the juice of the oranges, brandy, white wine and dry anise liqueur and leave the mixture to one side.

2. Sieve the flour, place in a large bowl and make a hole in the middle. Add the mixture and sugar and start to fold into the flour until it's ready to knead into a dough.

(When the mixture doesn't stick to the fingers and you cut the dough in half and it doesn't stick, then you know the dough is ready to fry)

3. Make small balls and roll between your hands until it looks like a long finger and knot. Once you have made all of the dough into knots, heat the oil and fry them. Remove them and place them on a paper kitchen towel to remove any excess oil.

4. In a pan heat up some golden syrup until hot and runny, remove from the hob and insert the borrachuelos into the pan 5 - 6 at a time and cover them with the syrup. Place into a large bowl or container and add the hundred and thousands to complete the look.

RECIPE INDEX

STARTERS

Calentita	08
Sweet and Sticky Chorizo	10
Boquerones Rellenos	12
Chicken and Bacon Bites	14
Feta Cheese, Spinach & Tomato Salad	14
Torta de Acelga	16
Pastry-less Torta de Acelga	18
Chicken Revuelto	18
Maruchi's Almejas a la Marinera	19
Mama's Almejas al Ajillo	20
Calabacines Rellenos	22
Mama's Sopa de Verduras	24
Pea Soup with Gammon	26
Caramales Fritos	28
Gambas Pil Pil	30
Battered Dip Prawns	32

MAINS

CHICKEN

Chicken and Chorizo Pinchitos	36
Pollo Al Ajillo	38
Chicken Empanada	40
Arroz con Pollo	42
Pollo en tomate	44
Chicken Fajitas	46
White Wine and Saffron Chicken	48
Creamy Mushroom, Chicken and Pancetta	50

MEAT

Easy BBQ Pulled Pork Parcels	54
Albondigón	56
Pinchitos	58
Cottage Pie	60
Mama's Potaje de Berza	62
Mum's Bacon Croquettes	64
Albóndigas - Meatballs	66
Chorizo, Spinach, Tomatoes & Cheese Stuffed Aubergines	68
Pork, Chorizo and Tart	70
Rolitos	72
Huevos a la Flamenca	74
Pepperoni and Sun-dried Tomato Burgers	76
Mama's Cannelloni Rellenos	78

FISH

Mum's Prawn Stuffed Squid and Rice	82
Pargo al Horno - Oven Baked Bream	84
Mama's Fish à la Meunière	85
Dorada al Sal	86
Mama's Jibia Guisada	88
Calamares Rellenos	90
Tuna Turner	92
Chilli and Garlic Prawn Spaghetti	94
Salmon Patties	94
Roast Cod with Potatoes & Vegetables	96
Sopa de Marisco	98
Mama's Conchas en Salsa Almendra	99
Rosada al Limón	100
Garlic Steamed Mussels	102

PASTA

Mama's Rosto	106
Mama's Lasagne	108
Macaroni Cheese	110
Spaghetti Bolognese with Chorizo	112

VEGETARIAN

Menestra	116
Sweet Potato Tortilla with Red Peppers	118
Alcachofas	120
Lentejas	122

DESSERTS
CAKES AND PUDDINGS

Mama's Fluffy Chocolate Cake	126
Arroz con Leche	128
Torrijas	130
Lemon Meringue Pie	132
Flapjacks	132
Mama's Empire Cake	134
Mama's Coconut Cake	136
Spinach, Coconut Milk, Strawberry and Banana Smoothie	138
Banana Bread	140
Mama's Volcano Cakes	142
Hazelnut Chocolate Cheesecake	144
Dark Chocolate Coquitos	146

GIBRALTARIAN TREATS

Puddín de Pan	150
Bollos de Hornazo	150
Mantecados	152
Panissa	154
Mama's Borrachuelos	156